# FLYING

## TO

# THE LIMIT

# FLYING
# TO
# THE LIMIT

*Testing WWII Single-Engined Fighters*

Peter Caygill

Pen & Sword
**AVIATION**

First published in Great Britain in 2005 and reprinted in this format in 2022 by
Pen & Sword Aviation
an imprint of
Pen & Sword Books Ltd
47 Church Street
Barnsley
South Yorkshire
S70 2AS

ISBN 978 1 39901 439 7

A CIP catalogue record for this book is
available from the British Library

Typeset in Palatino by
Phoenix Typesetting, Auldgirth, Dumfriesshire

Printed and bound in the UK by CPI Group (UK) Ltd, Croydon, CRO 4YY

Pen & Sword Books Ltd incorporates the imprints of Pen & Sword Aviation, Pen &
Sword Maritime, Pen & Sword Military, Wharncliffe Local History, Pen & Sword
Select, Pen & Sword Military Classics and Leo Cooper.

For a complete list of Pen & Sword titles please contact
PEN & SWORD BOOKS LIMITED
47 Church Street, Barnsley, South Yorkshire, S70 2AS, England
E-mail: enquiries@pen-and-sword.co.uk
Website: www.pen-and-sword.co.uk

# Contents

# Introduction

When the aeroplane first went to war in 1914, it did so without any clear duties, other than endowing the ability to see over the nearest hill. Performance was also marginal due to the heavy, under-powered and often temperamental engines of the day. By the end of the First World War, however, it had become one of the dominant weapons and all its various tactical roles had been clearly defined. In the post-war period the pace of military aircraft development came to a virtual standstill and over the next fifteen years performance levels increased at a relatively modest rate. The RAF's biplane fighters finally made it over 200 mph with the Hawker Fury in June 1931, but the standard bomber of the day, the Vickers Virginia, could only just stagger above 100 mph and had even been known to travel backwards when faced with a stiff headwind.

Improvements in metal aircraft structures, in particular the introduction of stressed skin construction, and the development of more powerful engines for air racing and commercial use, gave the prospect of significantly increased capability, however, it was only the worsening political situation in Europe in the mid 1930s that finally released the Governmental shackles that had been inhibiting the progress of military projects in Britain in particular. The sudden prospect of large orders for fighter aircraft spurred the likes of Sydney Camm at Hawker and Reginald Mitchell at Supermarine to formulate advanced ideas which would eventually become the Hurricane and Spitfire. These aircraft and others, notably the Messerschmitt Bf 109, eclipsed everything that had gone before, offering increases in top speed of around 100 mph, greatly improved rates of climb and much heavier armament.

With the coming of the Second World War the impetus was maintained with the development of new engines of up to 2000 hp, all this just a few years after power outputs of a quarter of that amount had been deemed acceptable. Rapid technological advances and the desperate need for large numbers of aircraft put great strain on the various test establishments whose job it was to clear each machine as a weapon of war so that any nineteen-year-old could fly it in reasonable safety. In Britain the Aeroplane and Armament Experimental Establishment (A&AEE), together with the Royal Aircraft Establishment (RAE) and the Air Fighting Development Unit (AFDU) were entrusted with this work. This book looks at some of the more notable single-engined fighter aircraft through the performance and handling trials that were carried out by these units, a task that became more and more complex as the conflict went on and as the boundaries were pushed to the absolute limit, in terms of structures, engines and aerodynamics.

# Acknowledgments

M uch of my research for this book was carried out at the National Archives at Kew and I would like to thank the staff for their help in tracking down all the official reports and documents that form the basis of this work.

During the course of compiling this book I was very fortunate to be contacted by Len Thorne who spent three years with the Air Fighting Development Unit at Duxford, Wittering and, latterly at Tangmere, by which time it had become the Air Fighting Development Squadron, and was part of Central Fighter Establishment. Prior to his involvement with AFDU Len flew a tour on Spitfires in 1941/42 with 41 Squadron at Catterick/Westhampnett and 602 Squadron at Kenley, during which time he flew alongside the likes of Don Finlay, Al Deere, Paddy Finucane and Victor Beamish.

His logbook makes fascinating reading as he flew virtually every mark of Spitfire up to the F.21. In addition, he flew a wide range of single-engined fighters from the P-51 Mustang, P-47 Thunderbolt and Typhoon/Tempest, to lesser known types such as the Bell Airacobra, Blackburn Skua and Fairey Fulmar. During his time at AFDU he was also entrusted with showing off a captured Focke-Wulf Fw 190A at numerous fighter airfields throughout the country, from Exeter in the south-west to Eshott in Northumberland, and in the course of eighty flights he managed to accumulate over 100 hours on type. My special thanks go to Len for answering my numerous queries on the many aircraft he has flown and for his help and hospitality.

Unless otherwise credited, all the photographs in this book were supplied by Philip Jarrett from his extensive archive and my sincere thanks go to him once again.

Finally, I would like to thank Peter Coles and the production staff at Pen and Sword for their help and assistance with this project.

# PART ONE

# British Fighters

CHAPTER ONE

# Hawker Hurricane

On 6 November 1935 the prototype Hawker F.36/34 (soon to be named Hurricane) was taken into the air for the first time by Group Captain P.W.S. 'George' Bulman, Hawker's chief test pilot. The type was to form the backbone of Fighter Command during the Battle of Britain, a conflict in which it destroyed more enemy aircraft than all other forms of defence put together. It was to go on to serve with distinction in many other theatres of war and the last Hurricane (PZ865) was delivered in September 1944.

Unlike the more radical Spitfire, the design of the Hurricane was closely related to its immediate forebears and it was initially known as the 'Fury Monoplane'. It was to have been powered by a steam-cooled Rolls-Royce Goshawk, the favoured engine at the time of its inception, but development problems led to the adoption of the new Rolls-Royce PV.12, which later became the Merlin. Initially a fixed, spatted undercarriage and four guns were included in the design, but these quickly gave way to a fully retractable undercarriage and eight guns. The Hurricane followed Hawker's principles of construction, proved during manufacture of the RAF's classic inter-war biplanes fighters, with a standard cross-braced tubular steel structure, which was fabric-covered aft of the cockpit. The cantilever wing was of two-spar construction and was also fabric-covered.

The Hawker F.36/34 (serial number K5083) was passed to the Aeroplane and Armament Experimental Establishment (A&AEE) at Martlesham Heath in early 1936 for brief preliminary handling trials. Among the pilots to fly the new fighter was Sergeant (later Group Captain) Sammy Wroath, who was to become a distinguished test pilot and was the first Commandant of the Empire Test Pilots' School (ETPS). By the time that K5083 reached Martlesham Heath, it had been modified in several respects and no longer featured the tailplane struts as originally fitted. The sliding canopy had been reinforced with additional frames and the radiator bath had been enlarged to aid cooling. A radio mast had also been fitted and the tail surfaces now had trim tabs.

Initial impressions of the F.36/34 were favourable. Access was easy with the hood fully open and the cockpit was considered to be roomy, comfortable and sufficiently warm, even when flying at an Outside Air Temperature (OAT) of $-50°C$. It was not unduly noisy and the layout of the instruments and controls was good. The vision forwards and above was adequate, but there was a blind spot to the rear, which obscured the tail.

The view immediately downwards was largely blanked out by the wing, but no difficulty was experienced when taking off and landing. At speeds in excess of 150 mph indicated airspeed (IAS) it proved to be impossible to slide the hood to the open position and if already open, air pressure tended to suck it shut. This was obviously unacceptable, as the pilot would have been prevented from baling out.

The undercarriage could be retracted manually in about forty-five seconds without too much exertion and it could be lowered in slightly less than half this time. When in the down position, the wheels could be seen through small windows in the cockpit floor. The only airframe damage caused during the flight trials of K5083 was to the port under-carriage fairing, which struck the ground on landing, resulting also in a fractured pipeline to the brakes.

An assessment of the aircraft's flying qualities showed the ailerons to be light at low speed, but tending to become heavier with increase in speed to the point where they were considered to be rather too heavy for a fighter. A small peculiarity of the lateral control was that at moderate speed when the starboard aileron was raised, the feel suddenly became slightly lighter and control was more effective. The aileron response was rapid under all normal manoeuvres, but tended to deteriorate at speeds close to the stall, with reduced effectiveness. The elevators were light and effective and gave quick response under all conditions of flight from the stall to diving speeds. The rudder loads were light in the glide but a lot heavier with the engine on at high speed, although the response was quick and the control remained effective at all speeds. The elevator trimming gear was easy to operate and had no tendency to slip. The range of control was not quite enough to trim the aircraft for every condition of flight. Also, the operating cables were inclined to stretch, allowing some free movement to the trimming tabs and some fore-and-aft instability.

Dive tests were carried out from trimmed level flight up to a limit of 3150 rpm or 300 mph IAS, whichever occurred first. The aircraft was steady in the dive and small movements of the controls led to the correct response, without any sign of control surface instability or vibration. Compared with the biplane fighters in service at the time, the F.36/34 was not easy to sideslip and could not be held in a sustained sideslip beyond 10 degrees. If the engine was opened up with the undercarriage down and with the tail trimming gear and flaps set for landing, the aircraft could easily be held by elevator control before re-trimming.

The flap control gear was conveniently placed and easy to use, and took about 10–15 seconds to move over the full range. There was a very noticeable nose-down change of trim when the flaps were lowered, but the elevator control was powerful enough to counteract this until the appropriate adjustment was made on the trimmer control. The flaps were very effective and tended to improve aileron control when down. In terms of stability, K5083 was laterally stable but tended to fly left wing low on the climb and right wing low at top speed. Directionally, the aircraft was neutrally stable with the engine on and stable with the engine off.

At an all-up weight of 5672 lb, K5083 achieved a top speed of 315 mph true airspeed (TAS) at its full throttle height of 16,500 ft using 6 lb/sq.in boost. The full test results as regards level speed performance were as follows:

| Height | Sea level | 2000 ft | 5000 ft | 10,000 ft | 16,500 ft |
|---|---|---|---|---|---|
| TAS – mph | 253 | 261.5 | 274 | 295.5 | 315 |
| IAS – mph | 258 | 259 | 258.5 | 257.5 | 237.5 |

| Height | 20,000 ft | 23,000 ft | 26,000 ft | 28,000 ft | 30,000 ft |
|---|---|---|---|---|---|
| TAS – mph | 311 | 306 | 298.5 | 291.5 | 282.5 |
| IAS – mph | 222 | 207.5 | 192.5 | 182 | 170 |

The take-off distance into a 5 mph headwind was measured at 265 yards. The aircraft reached 15,000 ft in 5 minutes 40 seconds and took 8 minutes 24 seconds to reach 20,000 ft. The service ceiling was 34,000 ft. The rates of climb and times to height were recorded as follows:

| Height | Sea level | 2000 ft | 5000 ft | 10,000 ft |
|---|---|---|---|---|
| Rate of climb – ft/min | 2550 | 2650 | 2810 | 2680 |
| Time from start – min | 0 | 0.75 | 1.89 | 3.63 |

| Height | 15,000 ft | 20,000 ft | 25,000 ft | 30,000 ft |
|---|---|---|---|---|
| Rate of climb – ft/min | 2150 | 1620 | 1100 | 570 |
| Time from start – min | 5.7 | 8.4 | 12.08 | 18.1 |

During the period of the trial a number of problems with the engine had to be sorted out. At the time, the Merlin was still in the early stages of its development programme so it was no great surprise when some snags were encountered. K5083 arrived at Martlesham Heath powered by a 990-hp Merlin C (No. 15) driving a Watts two-blade, fixed-pitch propeller, but during early flight tests George Bulman had complained of high oil temperatures. At first the thermostatic bypass valve was suspected, but this was found to be satisfactory and it was then thought that the oil passing through the radiator might be freezing up. Following a further test flight, ground running indicated that a major failure had occurred, which proved to be bearing failure in the super-charger.

A new engine was fitted but then Bulman reported rough running, intermittent cutting of the engine and an oily exhaust – all the result of piston failure. Another Merlin C was fitted (No. 19) but high oil temperature was again experienced, caused by grit in the oil system. Subsequent flight tests were hampered by further rough running and at a 20-hour inspection a number of broken valve springs were discovered. In addition, there were two failures to the automatic boost control. During test flights by service pilots, the aircraft also suffered several engine cuts as a result of the port fuel tank having run dry. With both wing tanks 'on' there was nothing to ensure that they emptied simultaneously, and should either empty before the other, the system was such that the pump was certain to suck in air. It was also considered that the carburettor used on the engine was unsatisfactory for service use. It was far too sensitive to slight mixture adjustments.

After evaluation at A&AEE, K5083 was returned to Hawker and fitted with eight 0.303-in Browning machine-guns, making its first flight in this condition on 17 August 1936. Further handling and performance trials were carried out at Martlesham Heath before the aircraft was handed back to the manufacturer for spin trials.

The first production Hurricane I (L1547) was flown for the first time on 12 October 1937. It differed from the prototype in having a 1030-hp Merlin II (Merlin G) engine, ejector exhausts, a revised hood and redesigned undercarriage fairings. A further modification was carried out in early 1938 with the adoption of a slender ventral fin under the rear fuselage to aid spin recovery. A programme of spin trials was carried out on L1547 at Martlesham Heath, commencing in September 1939 at the following loadings:

| Load for | Weight – lb | CG – in aft of datum |
|---|---|---|
| Typical service load | 6040 | 57.3 |
| Forward CG limit | 5405 | 55.5 |
| Extended aft CG | 6058 | 58.7 |

All spins were entered from a straight stall with the flaps and under-carriage up. The aircraft proved to be easy to spin, especially at the extended aft centre of gravity (CG) loading. The first three turns were irregular but subsequent turns were generally smooth, except at extended aft CG, which was slightly less smooth and had a slightly variable rate of rotation. The first turn of the spin was quick with the nose well down, but after two more turns the aircraft assumed a more normal attitude. For a three-turn spin the height loss was around 1200 ft and took eleven seconds, an eight-turn spin requiring 3200 ft and twenty-three seconds. The recovery was similar in all cases and rota-tion ceased after one to two turns, provided the correct technique was used.

A further 2000 ft could be lost during the recovery and pull out to level flight and it was found that the amount of height loss was very dependent on the movement of the control column. Ideally, the stick had to be moved forwards slowly, after full opposite rudder had been applied, to a position just aft of central. If it was moved further forward, or was moved coarsely, height loss could increase consider-ably. On the other hand, if a pilot was tempted to ease out of the dive too soon, there was a possibility of a flick in the opposite direction, as the aircraft tended to emerge from the spin in a stalled state, which persisted for a considerable portion of the dive with backward pressure on the control column. Quick application of rudder in the dive recovery phase was required to keep the aircraft straight and correct the tendency to flick.

At typical service load, the flaps-down approach needed slight backward pressure on the control column when gliding at a speed of 85 mph IAS. A tail-down landing could be made with ease and full braking could be used on the landing run. There was no tendency to swing. At forward CG limit when gliding with the engine off, the aircraft could not be trimmed longitudinally with the flaps up at speeds lower than 90 mph IAS. With flaps down it could not be trimmed at any speed up to 120 mph IAS, the maximum permitted in this configuration. The normal approach speed with flaps down was between 80–85 mph IAS, with a little back stick to prevent the nose from dropping. After landing, the brakes could be used, but care had to be taken at forward CG as the tail tended to lift on rough surfaces.

Performance tests were carried out on L1547, which was fitted with a two-pitch metal de Havilland propeller. At an all-up weight of 6363 lb and take-off boost of +6¼ lb/sq.in, the take-off run was 280 yards with flaps up and 230 yards with flaps set to 30 degrees (adjusted for zero wind and International Standard Atmosphere (ISA) conditions). The lift-off speed was around 70–75 mph IAS. The maximum level speeds were as follows:

| Height | 10,000 ft | 13,000 ft | 15,000 ft | 16,500 ft |
|---|---|---|---|---|
| TAS – mph | 296 | 305.5 | 312 | 317 |
| IAS – mph | 266 | 262 | 260 | 258.5 |

| Height | 18,000 ft | 20,000 ft | 23,000 ft |
|---|---|---|---|
| TAS – mph | 319.5 | 318 | 312.5 |
| IAS – mph | 254 | 245 | 229 |

Diving trials were performed using L1696 at typical service and extended aft CG loadings. In the event, the CG position did not affect diving characteristics or the recovery, nor did it affect the force required to move the controls. The limiting speed in the dives was 380 mph IAS, although this was exceeded on several occasions, with a maximum of 395 mph IAS being recorded. The aircraft was steady in the dive and it was easy to keep it on a target. It had a tendency to swing to the right above 280 mph IAS, but this could be corrected by left rudder. There was a slight change in longitudinal trim when rudder was applied to induce a 10-degree sideslip. With right rudder the nose tended to go down and with left rudder it went up, but in both cases the change of trim could be easily held with the appropriate movement of the control column. A dive was also made with the radiator flap fully open. This produced increasing tail heaviness as speed was built up, requiring the pilot to push forward on the control column, but at no point did the force become excessive.

Of particular interest in the dives were attempts to open the hood, in view of the difficulty that had been experienced with the prototype. At speeds up to 380 mph IAS the hood could be opened to about halfway by the handgrip provided, but to open it further would have required the pilot to use his elbow. This procedure was not acceptable, however, as there was a danger of the pilot's arm slipping and his forearm being thrown back by the slipstream. With the hood only open to halfway, it would not engage with the locking device, nor was it possible to open the emergency panel as the hood had to be fully open before either of these operations could be completed.

Following their evaluation at A&AEE, L1547 and L1696 were both delivered to Fighter Command. L1547 served with No. 312 Squadron until it caught fire in the air during a patrol on 10 October 1940 and crashed in the River Mersey. Sergeant O. Hanzlicek baled out but was killed. L1696 flew with No. 303 Squadron until it was lost over Kent when shot down during a patrol on 27 September 1940. Its pilot, Flight Lieutenant Ludwik Paszkiewicz, a six-kill 'ace' who had flown with both the Polish and French air forces, was also killed.

The Hurricane entered service with No. 111 Squadron at Northolt in January 1938. By the time that war was declared on 3 September 1939, a total of 497 had been delivered and eighteen squadrons, including four Auxiliary units, had been established. Four Hurricane squadrons were soon on their way to France, Nos 1 and 73 Squadrons accompanying the Advanced Air Striking Force, with Nos 85 and 87 Squadrons providing air cover for the British Expeditionary Force. Shortly before the German invasion was launched on 10 May 1940, No. 1 Squadron pilots got the chance to compare their aircraft with a Bf 109E-3 (*Werke Nummer* 1304 and formerly the property of II/JG 54), which had been captured by the French. Led by CO Squadron Leader P.J.H. 'Bull' Halahan, a section of six Hurricanes flew to Amiens on 2 May 1940 to inspect the Bf 109 and to carry out an assessment of its fighting qualities. The German aircraft was flown by Flying Officer M.H. 'Hilly' Brown and for comparative trials it was matched against a Hurricane flown by Flying Officer Prosser Hanks.

Owing to the lack of oxygen equipment in the Messerschmitt, the trial had to be restricted to a height of 15,000 ft. The comparisons consisted of a take-off and climb to 15,000 ft, a dogfight and line astern formation. Although the Hurricane was fitted with a constant-speed propeller, and full throttle and rpm were used, both the take-off and initial climb of the Bf 109 were better than the British fighter. At 15,000 ft the aircraft separated and approached each other head-on for the dogfight. The Hurricane did a stall turn followed by a quick vertical turn, which brought it down onto the Bf 109 from behind. Brown in the Messerschmitt was unable to prevent the manoeuvre succeeding and found it impossible to shake the Hurricane from his tail until he tried a tactic often used by *Luftwaffe* pilots, a half roll and vertical dive. The 109 drew away at the commencement of the dive and had it been continued, it was felt that it might have got away. During the recovery, however, Brown found that it took all his effort to pull the machine out of the dive as the aircraft had become very heavy, fore-and-aft. He was also of the opinion that had he not used the tail adjusting gear, which was itself heavy to operate, he would not have got out of the dive at all.

In contrast, Hanks was able to pull out of his dive inside the Messerschmitt, but as he did so he had a tendency to black out, which was not experienced by his adversary. In his subsequent report, Squadron Leader Halahan considered that this was due to the rather upright seating position in the Hurricane, which was very different to the semi-reclining position in the Bf 109 where the pilot's feet on the rudder pedals were considerably higher. After the dogfight, the Bf 109 took up position in line astern on the Hurricane, which then carried out a series of climbing and diving turns at high speed. The Hurricane was able to get on the tail of the Bf 109 after four turns and at no time was

Brown able to get his sights on his rival. In climbing turns, although the Bf 109 could climb faster, it could not turn as well, which enabled the Hurricane to get into a firing position. In a climbing turn after a dive, the control forces on the ailerons and elevators of the Bf 109 were so great that Brown was unable to complete the manoeuvre, and in diving turns he was unable to follow the Hurricane for the same reason.

The day after the trial, 'Hilly' Brown flew the Messerschmitt to Boscombe Down with an escort of three Blenheims and one Hudson for it to be evaluated in greater detail (see Chapter 8). The rest of the pilots of No. 1 Squadron returned to their base at Vassincourt much the wiser and not unduly downhearted. Although the Bf 109E was clearly the faster machine by some 30–40 mph in straight and level flight and could out-climb and out-dive the Hurricane, the latter was much more manoeuvrable and could turn inside the Bf 109 without difficulty. After the demonstration of its superior manoeuvrability, there was no doubt in Halahan's mind that provided they were not surprised by Bf 109s and that the odds were no more than two to one, the advantage should be with the Hurricane. Unfortunately for the RAF, the *Luftwaffe* had no intention of dogfighting at medium levels and would continue to employ their dive and zoom tactics to devastating effect.

Although the Hurricane did not have the development potential of the Spitfire, Sydney Camm, Hawker's chief designer, looked at various replacement engines, including the Rolls-Royce Griffon and Bristol Hercules. However, the necessary airframe modifications would have severely disrupted production. The only realistic alternative was the two-speed supercharged Merlin XX. It was first fitted to P3269, which became the first Hurricane II and was flown on its maiden flight by Philip Lucas on 11 June 1940. The first aircraft were delivered in September 1940 with standard eight-gun armament as the Hurricane IIA. These were followed by the Mark IIB in April 1941, which featured twelve 0.303 in machine-guns. Following the trial installation of two 20-mm Oerlikon cannon fitted to L1750 in May 1939, production aircraft with four 20-mm Hispano cannon entered service in June 1941 as the Hurricane IIC.

Handling trials were carried out at Boscombe Down using Hurricane IIA Z2346, with Z3564 (IIB) being used for performance testing. As there had been numerous reports on the Hurricane, and in view of the fact that the aircraft was aerodynamically similar to its predecessor, A&AEE concentrated on the stall characteristics with the Hurricane II. In the clean configuration, the stall occurred at 86 mph IAS. There was a strong tendency for the aircraft to rise to the stall of its own accord and the control column had to be held forward to prevent the nose from rising too sharply. There was very little warning of the stall until a slight lateral rocking occurred at 88 mph IAS, accompanied by a slight snatch of the ailerons. At the stall the port wing went down gently, followed by the nose.

The aircraft was markedly unstable at 1.2 × stall speed, being impossible to trim. When the aircraft was set up in a glide at 1.1 × stall speed, and the nose allowed to rise slowly, it could be kept straight and level with ailerons and rudder fixed, but aileron was needed to check the lateral rock. At 88 mph IAS, rudder had to be used to prevent a swing to the left caused by aileron drag as a result of having to apply aileron to keep the left wing up. When the speed had dropped to 86 mph IAS, either wing was liable to go down sharply, but could be raised by the use of aileron. By using large amounts of rudder and aileron, the control column could be brought right back, but the aircraft tended to pitch violently and either wing could drop, which could only be counteracted by full aileron. There was no tendency for the aircraft to spin unless a big yaw couple was applied.

With the flaps and undercarriage down the aircraft stalled at 68 mph IAS. Once again, there was very little warning and at the stall either wing could fall sharply through about 60 degrees, immediately followed by a drop of the nose. The wing could not be raised by using the aileron until the nose had dropped. Although there was little likelihood of a spin developing, if the control column was brought back a spiral dive was usually the result.

Performance measurements were made using Z3564 at an all-up weight of 7397 lb. During climbing trials using 2850 rpm, the full throttle height was 8300 ft in moderately supercharged (MS) blower and 15,600 ft in fully supercharged (FS) blower. The service ceiling was measured at 35,900 ft. It was noted, however, that increasing the engine rpm to 3000 above 20,000 ft was likely to improve the rate of climb, although it had no effect on the absolute ceiling. The full results were as follows:

| Height | 1000 ft | 5000 ft | 8300 ft | 10,000 ft | 13,000 ft | 15,700 ft |
|---|---|---|---|---|---|---|
| Time from start – min | 0.4 | 1.8 | 3.0 | 3.7 | 5.0 | 6.2 |
| Rate of climb – ft/min | 2710 | 2710 | 2710 | 2610 | 2510 | 2160 |

| Height | 18,000 ft | 20,000 ft | 23,000 ft | 28,000 ft | 30,000 ft | 35,000 ft |
|---|---|---|---|---|---|---|
| Time from start – min | 7.4 | 8.5 | 10.3 | 14.6 | 17.0 | 29.8 |
| Rate of climb – ft/min | 1940 | 1740 | 1440 | 920 | 720 | 200 |

Level speed tests showed full throttle heights of 13,000 ft and 20,800 ft in MS and FS blower respectively, the latter giving a maximum speed of 330 mph TAS.

| Height | 8000 ft | 10,000 ft | 13,000 ft | 15,000 ft | 18,000 ft |
|---|---|---|---|---|---|
| TAS – mph | 288 | 294 | 305 | 303 | 317 |
| IAS – mph | 262 | 259 | 257 | 247 | 247 |

| Height | 20,800 ft | 23,000 ft | 26,000 ft | 28,000 ft | 30,000 ft |
|---|---|---|---|---|---|
| TAS – mph | 330 | 329 | 324 | 318 | 310 |
| IAS – mph | 245 | 236 | 221 | 208 | 195 |

Owing to the Hurricane's lack of development potential, its days as a fighter were soon over. In 1941 it began to be modified as a fighter-bomber with two 250-lb and later two 500-lb bombs mounted under the wings. The first of the so-called Hurribombers were used in Malta in September 1941. By the end of the year the aircraft was also operational from British bases and in North Africa.

In early 1942 handling trials were carried out at Boscombe Down with a Hurricane IIB (BN114) to assess any handling differences between the standard aircraft and the fighter-bomber version. The aircraft was fitted with twelve 0.303-in machine-guns and had an all-up weight of 8416 lb with a full load of two 500-lb bombs. Considering the large increase in weight (nearly 50 per cent more than the proto-type), the handling characteristics were remarkably good and with a symmetrical load the aircraft behaved very like a Hurricane without bombs. With an asymmetric load, however, take-off and landing posed some problems, particularly when a single bomb was carried on the port side.

With two bombs in position under the wings, the take-off was normal, except for a slightly more pronounced swing to the left, but the run was not noticeably longer when compared with that of a fighter Hurricane. The initial climb was a little worse because of the extra load. Stability on the climb was about normal for a Hurricane II, except that the up and down nose couples were rather more pronounced and this tended to affect the climb if the rudder was not held steady. Full rudder bias was not quite sufficient for a full throttle climb at 140 mph IAS, the minimum trimmed speed being 150 mph IAS.

In general flying there was no noticeable difference from the fighter version and in steep turns up to approximately 5 g the aircraft showed no sign of tightening. The stall speeds with flaps and undercarriage up and down were 94 mph IAS and 73 mph IAS respectively. Dives were carried out up to a maximum speed of 397 mph IAS with the engine set to 3000 rpm and +9 lb/sq.in boost, the controls responding normally. There was no tendency to drop a wing and although some vibration was experienced, in general the aircraft was surprisingly smooth for a

Hurricane II. During one dive from 15,000 ft at limiting IAS (390 mph), 10 degrees of yaw was applied in each direction without any adverse reaction. After landing, it was found that the vanes of the tail fuse on each bomb had sheared, leaving them unsafe.

In asymmetric conditions, with a bomb under one wing only, the aircraft did not handle as well, the worst case being when it was flown with a bomb under the port wing. On take-off, if the aircraft left the ground early due to contacting rough ground, the port wing would drop and could not be raised, even with full aileron. The swing on take-off was also much more pronounced and considerable right rudder was needed to keep straight. This had to be maintained during the climb at 140 mph IAS and a small amount of aileron was required to hold up the left wing. In general manoeuvring, rather more aileron was needed to keep the wings level than was the case when carrying a single bomb under the starboard wing, but there was no marked tendency to drop a wing during dives up to 370 mph IAS.

When approaching to land, the aircraft was more unwieldy in this configuration and response to aileron control during recovery from a left turn was slow. At touchdown speed, almost full aileron had to be applied to keep the left wing up. The most dangerous situation when carrying a bomb under the port wing was in the case of a baulked landing. The throttle had to be opened slowly as the change in trim was very marked. At 100 mph IAS almost full aileron and rudder, together with considerable backward pressure on the control column, were necessary to prevent a diving turn to the left. The climb away with full flap selected could not be attempted below 110 mph IAS.

The final variant of the Hurricane II was the IID, which featured two 40-mm anti-tank guns in fairings under the wings. Guns by Rolls-Royce and Vickers were tested, but the former did not find favour following two breech explosions during testing and malfunctions caused by variations in temperature and pressure. The Vickers 'S' type gun passed its ground acceptance trials and despite giving some trouble in the air at first, when ejected cartridges showed a tendency to misfeed, it was accepted for operational use.

Much of the trials work carried out at Boscombe Down was undertaken by Wing Commander 'Dru' Drury, a pre-war test pilot who had specialised in testing aircraft armament. The biggest handling problem with the Hurricane IID was the recoil from its 40-mm guns, combined with the fact that they were positioned well below CG. When fired, the guns caused a severe nose-down change of trim, which was a major problem as the method of attack was to approach the target at very low level. The first unit to fly the Hurricane IID operationally was No. 6 Squadron in June 1942 in North Africa. The unit quickly acquired a formidable reputation in the ground-attack role, its most successful day occurring on 24 October 1942, when it destroyed sixteen German tanks.

With the Hurricane being developed as a multi-role fighter and having to carry a wide range of weaponry, a 'universal' wing that could easily accommodate all the various options was clearly desirable. The new wing was first produced in 1942, incorporating a fixed armament of two 0.303-in Browning machine-guns for sighting purposes. It was capable of mounting two 40 mm Vickers guns, eight 60 lb rocket projectiles (RP), two drop tanks, and smoke curtain equipment or two bombs of up to 500 lb. Designated Mark IV, the new Hurricane was powered by a Merlin 24 or 27 of 1620 hp, driving a three-blade Rotol or de Havilland constant-speed propeller.

The Hurricane was the first RAF fighter to be equipped with RP. The first operational use of this weapon occurred on 2 September 1943 when aircraft of No. 137 Squadron successfully attacked the lock gates of the Hansweert canal in Holland. The first RP trials were conducted at Boscombe Down in February 1942 using Hurricane IIA Z2415 and were continued with Hurricane IV BP173/G in August 1942. When carrying a full load of eight 60-lb RPs and associated mounting rails and blast plates, the take-off weight had gone up to 8480 lb, but handling characteristics showed little change from those of a normal Hurricane II. The aircraft was longitudinally unstable in all except high-speed flight and there was a tendency to tighten up when turning to the left, however, this was considered to be normal behaviour for a Hurricane with CG aft of normal.

In dives up to 350 mph IAS, when trimmed for full throttle level flight, a moderate push force was required to hold the aircraft in the dive, and acceleration was noticeably slower in the dive owing to the drag of the RP installation. Recovery was straightforward and was unlikely to cause any problems for the average service pilot. The top speed was considerably reduced when carrying RP and the best that could be achieved was 267 mph TAS at a full throttle height of 12,000 ft. Much of the drag produced did not come from the rockets themselves, but from the blast plate and rails.

The last Hurricane was the Mark V, of which only two were produced, the prototype (KZ193) being the subject of considerable trials work. Unlike earlier Hurricanes, it was fitted with a four-blade Rotol propeller and a larger radiator. Testing was carried out at A&AEE in late 1943 but it became clear that the Hurricane was beginning to run into longitudinal stability problems, largely as a result of the weapons it was being asked to carry. KZ193 underwent trials at Boscombe Down in November 1943 with two 40-mm Vickers guns. Many handling features were similar to earlier Hurricane aircraft, but a number of differences were noted.

The normal tendency to swing to the left on take-off was slightly more pronounced but if full right rudder trim was used, this could easily be held on the rudder. During the initial climb the aircraft began to pitch and the longitudinal stability characteristics were very poor. The application of yaw at any speed produced a much greater pitching moment than on earlier aircraft, which was particularly noticeable when right rudder was applied, there being a marked change to nose down. There was a corresponding nose-up pitch with left rudder, but this was not quite as noticeable as in the previous case. This interaction between yaw and pitch tended to complicate the directional trim change to be expected when increasing or decreasing power. If the throttle was closed, right rudder was required to keep the nose straight, but this caused a sharp nose-down pitch, which could only be checked with difficulty by applying a heavy pull force on the control column. This adverse feature seriously affected the ease with which man-oeuvres could be made.

The aircraft was stable directionally and laterally, but if it was disturbed longitudinally from a trimmed condition and the control column released, it pitched once nose down before the nose lifted up and a rapid divergence to the stall occurred with comparatively high normal accelerations. This occurred throughout the speed range with the engine on or off, and with flaps and undercarriage up or down. The violence of the divergence decreased to some extent with increasing speed and with the engine on.

A number of dives were made to the limiting speed of 390 mph IAS. Once again, the yaw/pitch combination caused handling problems as any right rudder caused the nose to drop. If the yaw was maintained, it proved to be impossible to bring the nose up by use of the elevator. Aerobatics were not particularly easy as the poor longitudinal stability characteristics caused the aircraft to pitch during a loop, mostly during the upward part. Rolls could be executed reasonably well, except that it was difficult to keep the nose on the horizon.

Problems with longitudinal stability had already been encountered with the Hurricane IV at aft CG but it was considered that the Mark V was as bad, if not worse, due to the fitting of a four-blade propeller. The aircraft was classed as being extremely unpleasant to fly by day and would have been particularly bad for night or instrument flying. The pitching moment that occurred when the rudder was applied seriously interfered with manoeuvring and aerobatics, and was considered dangerous should an inexperienced pilot be flying in cloud, or attempting to sideslip when on the approach to land.

Performance testing showed that the Hurricane V when fitted with two Vickers guns had a top speed of 305 mph TAS at 9200 ft and a maximum rate of climb of 3840 ft/min at 2100 ft. A height of 20,000 ft was reached in seven minutes and the estimated service ceiling

(100 ft/min rate of climb) was 33,000 ft. The adverse handling characteristics experienced with the Mark V prompted a change to a
three-blade propeller, which improved longitudinal stability slightly.
However, as the Hurricane was rapidly becoming obsolescent, no
further development was carried out.

A total of 12,780 Hurricanes were built in the UK with another 1451
being produced by the Canadian Car and Foundry Co. as the Marks X,
XI and XII with Packard Merlins and Hamilton Standard Hydromatic
propellers. Although most Hurricanes had been replaced by more
advanced aircraft by the end of the war, Camm's workhorse was still
giving effective service with No. 20 Squadron in Burma to the last, a full
ten years after its first flight. Very few aircraft flew in such a wide
variety of roles in widely differing theatres, and the Hurricane has gone
down in history as a unique aircraft, which helped to shape the course
of the western world by its heroic deeds in the Battle of Britain.

CHAPTER TWO

# Supermarine Spitfire

Of all the piston-engined fighters of the Second World War, the Spitfire was the subject of the greatest level of development. The later variants had a top speed of approximately 460 mph and a climb rate of 5000 ft/min, which represented performance improvements over the Spitfire I of 28 per cent and 100 per cent respectively. Such advances were largely the result of vastly increased power, the Rolls-Royce Griffon 61 of the Spitfire F.21/24 developing 2050 hp, slightly more than twice the output of the Merlin C type as fitted to the prototype. In addition, there was a four-fold increase in the Spitfire's weight of fire (four 20 mm Hispano cannon in comparison with eight 0.303-in Browning machine-guns) and a doubling of its loaded weight. The prodigious rise in engine power, together with increases in propeller size and blade area to transmit that power, eventually led to handling problems, which the testing regime was able to identify so that modifications could be effected before it became a service problem. In the early days, however, the Spitfire was beyond criticism and the prototype (K5054) was delivered to A&AEE at Martlesham Heath in May 1936 for an initial assessment of its performance capabilities, and for handling trials.

Although the Spitfire had significantly better performance than contemporary biplane fighters, it was found to be extremely easy to fly and had no vices at all. It was stable laterally and if one wing was lowered and the control column released, it would return to a level keel in a reasonable amount of time. The aircraft was also stable directionally under all conditions of flight with the engine on or off. Longitudinally, the Spitfire was neutrally stable with the engine on but stable with the engine off, although it tended to be unstable in the glide with the flaps and undercarriage down. During take-off, there was a slight tendency to swing, but this was not as pronounced as on a Hawker Fury and it could easily be corrected by use of rudder. Landing was also straightforward and if the engine had to be opened up, as in the case of a go-around, the aircraft could easily be held with the stick. A number of aerobatic manoeuvres were flown including loops, half rolls off loops, slow rolls and stall turns and the aircraft was pleasant to handle throughout.

In the air, the ailerons were light to handle in the climb and although they were noticeably heavier with increased speed, they were considered to be not unduly heavy, even during dives up to 380 mph IAS. The ailerons were effective down to stalling speeds and response was rapid at all times. No snatch or vibration was experienced at any time. The rudder was generally heavier than the ailerons, but not excessively so and it was felt that pedal pressures were in line with expectations for a single-seat fighter. The elevator control was also light but, again, tended to become heavier with an increase in speed. A rapid response was obtained for very little control input and on landing the control column did not need to be pulled all the way back to obtain the correct three-point attitude. As it was felt that this particular characteristic could catch out inexperienced pilots, it was recommended that the gearing of the elevator control be adjusted accordingly.

Owing to its very effective elevator control, it was not necessary to pull the control column right back to bring about a stall. When it occurred, the straight stall was normal and there was no snatch. In tight turns of around 3 g at speeds below 140 mph IAS, a distinct juddering was felt by the pilot, but this stopped as soon as back pressure on the stick was released. In a fully developed stalled glide with the flaps and undercarriage up, the aircraft tended to wallow from side to side and some snatch was felt from the elevators, but this was eased when the flaps and landing gear were lowered. Although a wing could be raised when close to the stall, eventually there was a tendency for the aircraft to take over, and although this was rather disconcerting for the pilot, at no time did a spin result. One of the reasons for the Spitfire's controllability at low speeds was that washout had been incorporated into the wing, whereby the angle of incidence at the tip was 2 degrees less than at the root. This allowed aileron control at very low speeds as the wing stalled from root to tip, and the progressive aerodynamic buffet experienced as speed was reduced gave pilots ample warning that a stall was imminent. The stall speed with flaps and undercarriage up was 64 mph IAS, reducing to 58 mph IAS with the flaps and under-carriage down.

In its summary, the A&AEE report concluded that the Spitfire's controls were entirely satisfactory and no modification was required except to the elevator circuits as mentioned above. All the controls were well harmonised and resulted in an excellent compromise between the contrasting requirements of manoeuvrability and a stable gun platform.

Although take-off and landing were easy it was felt that the aircraft had a rather flat glide, even when the undercarriage and flaps were down, which resulted in a prolonged float if the approach speed was a little high. To improve this situation it was recommended that the flaps be modified to move through an angle of 90 degrees instead of the 57 degrees as tested (this modification was applied to the Spitfire I).

In October 1938 a more comprehensive series of tests were carried out to determine the spinning and diving characteristics of Spitfire I K9787. The first spins were carried out from a straight stall. During these it was noticed that there was considerable unevenness, especially when spinning to the right, when the rotational speed showed a pronounced variation during each turn, together with a rising and falling of the nose and large changes of sideslip. After three turns the spin became smoother, except in spins to the right at aft CG, where it remained rough throughout. Some snatching of the rudder and aileron was also noticed during spins to the right, together with much buffeting and vibration, the spin also appearing to be flatter.

To come out of the spin the application of full opposite rudder, together with a forward movement of the control column, brought recovery within 1–2 turns. However, when rotation ceased the aircraft was in a stalled condition and there was a strong tendency to flick into another spin in either direction. Moving the stick forward too soon or too quickly could also result in a delayed recovery and considerable height loss. Spins were also induced from turning flight and although entry was fairly benign off a gentle gliding turn, it was a different matter when entering a spin from a stalled turn. In this case the aircraft carried out a most violent series of evolutions before settling down into a steady spin after 2–3 turns. Violent pitching was experienced, during which the pilot was thrown about the cockpit, and it was felt that the aircraft might turn on its back at any time.

Diving trials showed that the Spitfire was steady in the dive when its Merlin engine was running correctly, but the aircraft showed a tendency for the engine to cut in and out and the resulting intermittent loss of power caused a certain amount of longitudinal pitching. Vibration was also experienced between 350–380 mph IAS and above 400 mph IAS. Slight control movements were made at maximum speed without any sign of control instability. As speed increased, all controls became heavier, especially the ailerons and rudder, the ailerons eventually becoming almost immovable. The aircraft also exhibited tail heaviness in high-speed dives and it had to be held into the dive, a situation that was most marked at normal CG when the force required to maintain the correct dive angle was considerable. Recovery was straightforward, but care had to be taken not to allow excessive accelerations to develop as the control column had a tendency to come back strongly. Another aspect noted in the dive was that the canopy could not be opened at speeds above 300 mph IAS (later aircraft had a small break-out panel incorporated in the hood to equalise the pressure inside and outside the cockpit).

The development process was constant throughout the Spitfire's life and from the seventy-eighth production Mark I the original two-blade wooden propeller was replaced by a three-blade, two-speed de Havilland propeller. With ejector exhausts, the top speed was officially quoted as 367 mph, but increases in all-up weight had reduced the climb performance. By the end of the Battle of Britain, most Spitfires had been fitted with constant-speed propellers. The Spitfire II was virtually identical to the Mark I, apart from having a Merlin XII and Coffman cartridge start. The next major production variant was the Spitfire V, which was powered by a 1440 hp Merlin 45 and was to be the mainstay of Fighter Command from 1941–3. Its problems with the Focke-Wulf Fw 190 (see Chapter 9) led to the hurried introduction of the Spitfire IX in June 1942.

Although it possessed the same basic airframe as its predecessor, the Mark IX introduced the two-speed, two-stage supercharged Merlin 61, which brought about a significant improvement in performance. In April 1942 AB505 (a converted Spitfire V) was tested by the Air Fighting Development Unit (AFDU) at Duxford. These trials included a comparative assessment with a Spitfire V and Typhoon I. On take-off the Spitfire IX was similar to the V but, due to its increased weight, the landing speed was slightly higher. During dives the aircraft felt more stable and showed less tendency to yaw, which was put down to the fact that there was now a radiator under both wings. The elevator control was slightly heavier, but this was considered to be an improvement, as it tended to result in better harmonisation.

The speed of the Spitfire IX was measured at 386 mph TAS in MS gear at 16,300 ft and 409 mph TAS at 28,000 ft in FS gear, figures that were vastly superior to the Spitfire V. Two speed runs were made to compare the Spitfire IX with the Typhoon. At 15,000 ft the Spitfire IX was around 10 mph faster and at 18,000 ft it was 2 mph faster. Comparative climbs were also carried out and the Spitfire IX was superior to the Mark V and the Typhoon at all heights. Under maximum continuous climbing conditions the Spitfire IX was taken up to a height of 39,500 ft at which point its rate of climb was still 700 ft/min. The operational ceiling was considered to be 38,000 ft (the height at which the climb rate fell to 1000 ft/min) and this was achieved 18½ minutes after take-off. The Mark IX proved to be easy to fly at high altitudes, although occasionally the trimming tabs tended to freeze up, which could be a little embarrassing if the aircraft was still trimmed for the climb.

In dogfights there was little to choose between the Spitfire V and IX at 15,000 ft, although the superior speed and climb of the Mark IX allowed it to disengage by climbing away and then attack again in a dive. The Spitfire IX also had the advantage of being fitted with a negative-g carburettor, which allowed its pilot more freedom and lessened the risk of power loss due to fuel starvation. At 30,000 ft the two aircraft were evenly matched in terms of manoeuvrability, but at this height the superiority of the Mark IX with regard to speed and rate of climb was decisive. The pilot of the Spitfire V had great difficulty in maintaining height during steep turns, whereas his counterpart in the Mark IX was able to retain height without difficulty because of the large reserve of power at his disposal. During a simulated dogfight with a Typhoon, the Spitfire IX was found to be more manoeuvrable and superior in the climb, although it tended to lose out in a dive. In a turning competition at 18,000 ft, the Spitfire out-turned the Typhoon and was on its tail after 1½ turns.

Although the Spitfire could out-turn almost any other Second World War fighter, it still lost out to others (notably the Focke-Wulf Fw 190) in the speed with which it could initiate rolling manoeuvres. This problem was addressed by clipping the wings of many Spitfires that were likely to see low-altitude combat and involved the removal of the wing tips, which reduced the span from 36 ft 10 in to 32 ft 6 in. During trials at AFDU in late 1942 using a Spitfire VB, it was found that the rate of roll at all heights up to 25,000 ft had been improved considerably and that the response to aileron movements was much quicker than on the standard machine. Dogfights were carried out in which a standard wing Spitfire was put on the tail of another with clipped wings. In several cases the clipped wing aircraft evaded so rapidly that it was able to reverse the positions in about twenty seconds (by this time problems with excessively heavy lateral control during high-speed dives, a characteristic of early Spitfires, had been improved to an extent by the fitting of metal-covered ailerons).

From the middle of the war, Spitfires began to take on a fighter-bomber role and even elderly Mark VBs were pressed into use with a 500-lb bomb on the fuselage centreline. With a strengthened Type 'C' or 'universal' wing, the Spitfire VC and most Mark IXs were capable of carrying two 250-lb bombs under the wings. AFDU was given the task of devising suitable tactics as Flight Lieutenant Len Thorne recalls:

When they first started to hang bombs on Spitfires, we were given the job of evolving the best way of ensuring accuracy. Obviously, the most effective way was to get enough altitude, point the nose straight at the target in a very steep dive and let the bomb go. However, when we proposed this method of attack to the squadrons, they wouldn't have it as they were concerned that the bombs would hit the aircraft after release. To find out one way or the other, 'Wimpy' Wade [Squadron Leader T.S. Wade DFC, later chief test pilot at Hawker Aircraft] and myself flew two Spitfires, one of which was carrying a bomb, while the other had a camera fitted behind the pilot's seat, pointing sideways. The camera aircraft had a white dot on the end of the wing and the pilot lined up the dot with the bomb on the other aircraft. By such means we got the actual moment of release on film.

'Wimpy' Wade, who was an excellent pilot, did the bomb dropping and I had to remain tucked in tight with whatever he did. We evolved the method that you overflew the target, then looked back behind the trailing edge of the wing and as soon as you could see the target you pulled up into a wing-over to the inverted and then pulled back on the stick until you were heading for the target in a dive at almost exactly 70 degrees. I filmed right through the sequence and it was discovered that the bomb never went anywhere near the aircraft. In the dive you were fairly screaming down at around 480 mph so the first thing you did was to commence your pull out and as a result quickly left the bomb behind. This method was eventually adopted for all high level bombing attacks. I did quite a lot of this type of work over the Holbeach range in the Wash, but I absolutely hated it, in my opinion bombing was a complete misuse of a fighter!

The advent of second-generation piston-engined fighters such as the Hawker Typhoon and Republic P-47 Thunderbolt, and the development of existing types, meant that many service aircraft were now able to exceed the Mach number at which shock waves were produced on the wings during prolonged dives. The effects of compressibility had been known for some time and much work had been carried out in high-speed wind tunnels, but there was little flight data of a sufficiently detailed type to enable the test results obtained on the ground to be checked. From May 1943 an exhaustive series of flight trials were commenced at RAE Farnborough using Spitfire XI EN409 and Mustang I AG393. The pilot throughout the test was Squadron Leader J.R. Tobin AFC.

The trials were carried out from the highest altitude to obtain the greatest possible Mach number while keeping IAS and airframe loads down to the lowest values for flight safety. As the Mustang One used in the trials had an Allison engine that developed maximum power at only 10,000 ft, the flights were made with guns and radio removed to reduce weight but even so dives could only be commenced at 28,000 ft. The Spitfire XI, in contrast, could be dived from 40,000 ft. The dives were started by accelerating to maximum level speed at these heights, before the nose was lowered. At the same time the pilot set the engine controls to a position which would give maximum permissible continuous boost at the end of the dive (MS blower in the case of the Spitfire). The dive angle was usually about 45 degrees, the procedure being to dive steadily until maximum Mach number had been reached (this took about 11,000 ft in all cases) then to continue for a few more seconds before commencing a 2–3 g pull out.

Before beginning the dive the pilot was warned of the possibility of large trim changes in the nose-down direction and of the possible ineffectiveness of the elevator trim tab. He therefore trimmed into the dive at the beginning, but when the nose-down change appeared near maximum Mach, he made no attempt to correct on the trimmer, but held it by stick force alone, always assuming that this was physically possible. In general, the drag coefficient rose very gradually in the region of Mach 0.6–0.7 or more, but this was followed by a rapid increase at higher Mach numbers as the shock-stall commenced over the main wing. The most significant fact to come out of the trial was the difference in the Mach number at which the steep drag rise commenced on each aircraft.

With its low thickness/chord ratio wing (13 per cent at the root and 7 per cent at the tip), the Spitfire was easily superior to the Mustang, despite the fact that the latter had a laminar flow wing with maximum thickness at 40 per cent chord. Although this type of wing had been designed to reduce drag, the Mustang's thickness/chord (t/c) ratio at the root and tip was 16 per cent and 11 per cent respectively and it appeared that at critical Mach numbers, t/c ratio was the dominant factor. The Mustang was dived to a maximum of Mach 0.80, whereas the Spitfire achieved Mach 0.89. Both the Spitfire and the Mustang showed the same tendency, near maximum Mach, to develop a nose-down moment, which had to be countered by applying negative elevator.

The sequence of events involved a push forward on the stick, which was maintained for the first few thousand feet of the dive. The pilot then found it necessary to release this force to maintain the correct angle of dive and finally he had to pull to prevent the dive angle from becoming excessively steep. The pull force reached a maximum upon, or just after, reaching the maximum Mach number. If the pull force was not corrected rapidly, either through unawareness or because the stick load required was too large, the dive steepened and the Mach number increased more rapidly, to the point where the pilot could not exert sufficient force on the elevator to regain control. This had been reported on several types of aircraft, including the P-47 Thunderbolt, which had been tested in terminal velocity dives in the USA. Control would eventually return as the Mach number diminished in the thicker air at lower levels, but this introduced a second danger as the relaxation of the nose-down moment, together with continued use of back stick, could lead to severe accelerations. This was particularly the case if nose-up trim had been applied earlier in the dive to assist in applying the negative elevator angle required near the maximum Mach.

The P-47 Thunderbolt had a relatively thick wing of conventional section (16 per cent and 9 per cent thickness/chord at root and tip) and this produced a steep drag rise at a very low Mach number. Whereas a rough estimate of the pull force required to hold a Spitfire at Mach 0.89 at 30,000 ft was 50–60 lb, a similar calculation showed that a pull of 200 lb, even assuming a pilot was capable of doing this, would still be inadequate to hold a P-47 at 20,000 ft. The maximum Mach achieved in the P-47 was reported as being 0.86, but the aircraft was out of control at this point and remained so until reaching lower altitudes.

With the Merlin engine at the limit of its development potential, the only way for the Spitfire to retain its position at the forefront of fighter technology was for it to utilise another engine of yet greater power. Such an engine already existed in the shape of the 36.7-litre Griffon, which had been developed from the Rolls-Royce 'R' engine of the Supermarine S.6B Schneider racer. Although the Griffon was initially rated at around 1500 hp, thanks to its racing pedigree, the frontal area was only marginally greater than the Merlin and it was a mere 3 in longer. It was 600 lb heavier, however, which necessitated a change from the tubular-type dural engine mounting used on Merlin variants to a girder-type steel longeron. The first Griffon-engined Spitfire was the Mark IV (DP845) which was flown for the first time on 27 November 1941. It was redesignated as the Mark XX in early 1942 to avoid confusion with the PR.IV photo-reconnaissance aircraft. Following a further change of designation, the first Griffon-powered Spitfire appeared as the Mark XII and the third production machine (EN223) was delivered to AFDU for testing in December 1942.

Early examples of the Spitfire XII were based on a standard Mark VC airframe, strengthened to accept a Griffon III two-speed supercharged engine optimised to deliver maximum power at low level. Its role as a low-altitude fighter meant that all Spitfire XIIs had clipped wings. Despite weighing in at 7415 lb fully loaded (approximately 1,000 lb more than a Spitfire V) the Mark XII had a 'normal' Spitfire feel to it, but the increased power was immediately felt on take-off, as engine torque tended to cause a swing to the right which, if not counteracted quickly, could not be held, even with full rudder. This swing to the right was in the opposite direction to that experienced on Merlin-engined Spitfires, as the propeller on the Griffon rotated the other way (i.e. to the left as seen from the cockpit). In the air the handling of EN223 was far superior to a standard Spitfire VB or IX, in particular its lateral control, which was crisp and light thanks to its clipped wings. Longitudinal stability was found to be better than a Spitfire V, particularly in a dive, and the recovery was not as fierce. The rudder was more sensitive to throttle movements and much re-trimming was needed as pedal pressures were too heavy to be held for long periods. Pilots were also quick to notice that the Griffon ran more roughly than the Merlin engines they had been used to.

In terms of performance, the Spitfire XII was considerably faster than a Mark V and also out-performed the Spitfire LF.IX (Merlin 66) by 14 mph at sea level and 8 mph at 10,000 ft. Above 20,000 ft, however, it was slower. In the climb it also lost out to the Spitfire LF.IX and was comparable up to 10,000 ft to the LF.VB powered by the 'cropped blower' M-series Merlin 45, which had been developed to achieve maximum power at low levels. Dive trials showed it to have a slight edge owing to its cleaner design, except at full throttle when there was no advantage either way. Manoeuvrability was as good as earlier Spitfires and it was considered that the XII would be able to out-pace and out-turn an Fw 190 below 20,000 ft. As the Griffon engine was set marginally lower in the airframe than the Merlin, the sighting view downwards for gun aiming was slightly improved. In its summary, AFDU concluded that the Spitfire XII was highly suited to the role of a low-altitude fighter, being capable of speeds of 372 mph at 5700 ft and 397 mph at 18,000 ft.

In the event, only 100 Spitfire XIIs were produced as this variant was quickly supplanted by the Mark XIV, which was powered by a two-speed, two-stage supercharged Griffon 61/65 of 2050 hp. To cater for the increase in power a five-blade constant-speed Rotol propeller was used and the first of several revisions of the tail surfaces were incorporated to maintain directional stability. The airframe used for the Mark XIV was essentially a strengthened and modified Mark VIII, but with the use of the two-stage Griffon with its intercooler, the length had increased to 32 ft 8 in. The loaded weight was now 8500 lb.

Following performance trials with JF319, in which the maximum speed was measured at 446 mph at 25,400 ft, a full tactical trial was carried out by AFDU in early 1944 using RB179. In most respects, the Mark XIV was similar to the Mark IX, except that the need to re-trim following throttle movements (as noted with the Spitfire XII), was quite marked. Pilots also had to be aware of the additional power on take-off as the aircraft tended to swing strongly to the right and drag its right wing. It was recommended that full power only be selected when nearly airborne; prior to that +6 lb/sq.in boost was quite sufficient. The landing run was a little longer and the aircraft tended to sink more rapidly than a Spitfire IX. When stalling from a tight turn, the Mark XIV tended to give less warning, although the characteristic shuddering was still present.

In comparison with the Spitfire IX, the Mark XIV had slightly reduced endurance due to the fact that it consumed about 25 per cent more fuel, but its range was similar as it tended to cruise at a higher speed. At all heights the Mark XIV was 30–35 mph faster in level flight, its best performance occurring below 15,000 ft and between 25,000 and 32,000 ft. It was also slightly superior in the climb and pulled away from the Spitfire IX in a dive. The turning circles of both aircraft were virtually identical, as was the rate of roll. Owing to its short range, it was considered that the Spitfire XIV would tend to be operated with a 90-gallon long-range tank, rather than the more normal 30- or 45-gallon tanks, and in this condition top speed was reduced by about 20 mph. The climbing performance was also affected and with a half full tank, the climb rate was identical to a Spitfire IX when flown clean. If the tank was more than a third full, acceleration in a dive was not affected, but there was a definite worsening of the turning circle with the tank fitted.

The Spitfire XIV was also compared with a Tempest V, the latter proving to be 20 mph faster up to 10,000 ft. There was then little to choose between the two until 22,000 ft when the Mark XIV held the upper hand, being around 30–40 mph faster above this height. The operational ceiling of the Spitfire XIV was 40,000 ft, which was 10,000 ft more than the Tempest. As regards climb rate, the Spitfire XIV possessed a significant advantage, although the Tempest showed a better zoom climb as it held a higher speed throughout the manoeuvre. As speed diminished, however, the Spitfire soon began to catch up and if the climb was prolonged it quickly pulled ahead. Because of its increased weight, the Tempest accelerated quicker in the dive, but it was easily out-turned by the Spitfire. In terms of rate of roll, the Spitfire held the advantage below 300 mph, whereas the Tempest was slightly superior at higher speeds. The Tempest and Spitfire XIV were two very different aircraft and it was clear that the former was best used for combat below 20,000 ft, whereas the latter was greatly superior above that height. A comparison was also made with a Mustang III, which showed that the maximum speeds of the two aircraft were virtually identical. The Spitfire held the advantage when it came to climb rate, turning circle and rate of roll, but it tended to lose out in the dive. One area in which the Spitfire could not compete, however, was radius of action, as even with a 90-gallon long-range tank, it still only had half the range of a Mustang fitted with two 62½-gallon drop tanks.

The opportunity was also taken to compare the Spitfire XIV with captured examples of the Fw 190A and Bf 109G. Up to 20,000 ft the Spitfire was 20 mph faster than the Fw 190, but above this height its advantage rose to 60 mph. In the climb the Spitfire held a significant advantage, but its diving performance was only marginally better. Thanks mainly to its large, well-balanced ailerons, the rate of roll of the

Fw 190 was superior, but in a sustained turn the Spitfire could easily out-turn the German aircraft. Against the Bf 109G, the Spitfire XIV was 40 mph faster at all heights, except around 16,000 ft when this advantage was reduced to only 10 mph. At this height climb rates were the same, but at all other heights the Spitfire was superior. Zoom climbs were similar except when full throttle was used, when the Spitfire pulled away from the Bf 109 quite easily. Dive performance was evenly matched, with the Bf 109 holding an initial advantage until a speed of 380 mph had been reached when this situation was reversed. The Spitfire XIV could easily out-turn the Bf 109 in either direction and it also rolled much more quickly.

The Spitfire XIV was also much liked by A&AEE pilots who had been among the first to assess the new fighter. One of those involved in the testing carried out at Boscombe Down was Group Captain Jamie Rankin DSO DFC, who wrote a short comparative assessment with the Merlin-powered Spitfire VIII in October 1943.

Brief Description – the aircraft flown in these trials was not equipped with the same supercharger gears as the production model. In the aircraft tested the engine gave maximum speed at 7000 ft and 23,000 ft whereas the production Mark XIV will have the maximum speeds at 12,000 ft and 23,000 ft. This difference involved a slight gain in performance at low levels, but a loss of performance between 8–15,000 ft. The boosts used were +18 lb in both the XIV and VIII.

Performance – comparison was made with the Spitfire VIII at all heights. The XIV was found to be approximately 30 mph faster. In the climb the difference was not so marked, but the XIV was definitely ahead of the VIII at all heights, the difference being more marked above 30,000 ft than below. The most noticeable difference between the aircraft arose when using cruising revs and boost, under these conditions the XIV is considerably faster. Probably owing to its increased weight, the diving speeds of the XIV are higher than those of the VIII.

Handling – the XIV handled quite normally in all respects with a Spitfire VIII or IX except in directional stability when changes of throttle setting were used. In this respect it is similar to the Spitfire XII in that frequent adjustment of the rudder trim must be made. It appeared, however, to be less marked than in a Spitfire XII and after flying the aircraft for approximately four hours the pilot becomes rapidly accustomed to this. Aileron and elevator control were normal. The turning circle is also normal and there is no tactical difference between the XIV and VIII. The slight difference in turning circle is in favour of the XIV.

The aircraft handles similarly to the XII on take-off and is naturally not so easy as in a Mark VIII or IX. As in the question of change of rudder trim, however, pilots will rapidly become confident in the aircraft on take-off.

Pilot's View – the view is much superior on the Mark XIV owing to the lower engine cowlings and will be of great advantage in deflection shooting.

Conclusions – the Mark XIV is preferable to the VIII or IX in all respects. Once the initial awkwardness of opposite torque and change of directional trim at speed has been overcome, the aircraft feels exactly as a normal Spitfire with the advantages of improved climb and a considerable gain in level speed.

Another pilot to fly the Spitfire XIV at this time was Wing Commander A.V.R. Johnson DSO DFC, who commented on the aircraft as follows.

Starting – at present starting of the Griffon 65 is by means of Coffman starter and is most complicated. It is recommended that the process be simplified before this aircraft is put into operational use.

Take-off – the take-off is similar to that of the Spitfire XII. Because of propeller torque the aircraft tends to swing to starboard and the starboard wing is inclined to drop until speed is in excess of 30 mph. Immediately this speed is passed, however, no further peculiarities are encountered.

Climb and Level Flight – this aircraft is undoubtedly faster than any Spitfire yet in operational use. It is both faster than the Mark XII at low altitudes and the Mark IX at high altitudes.

General Flying – the ailerons on the aircraft flown were rather heavy but no doubt these could be lightened by experimenting with various sets of ailerons. A great deal of top rudder has to be applied in tight turns, this being due to the additional weight of the aircraft and the position of the CG. Stalling speed is somewhat higher than the Mark IX and the aircraft spins from a tight sustained turn at slightly higher speed than a Mark IX. The aircraft requires constant trimming in diving, climbing and turning flight, and in this respect is very similar to the Mark XII.

Landing – stalling speeds with wheels and flaps down is approximately 10–15 mph higher than the Mark IX and consequently the final approach is made at about 115 mph.

Recommendation – the Mark XIV should be brought to operational service as soon as possible. No difficulty should be encountered by pilots changing from the Mark V to the XIV.

The next Spitfire in number sequence (if not in chronology) was the Mark XVIII, which was the first variant to be specifically designed for the Griffon engine, rather than being a modification of an existing airframe. In appearance it was almost indistinguishable from a low-back Mark XIVE with clipped wings – most of the differences being under the skin, in particular its revised wing structure with solid instead of tubular spar booms. The Spitfire XVIII entered service with No. 60 Squadron at Seletar, Singapore shortly after the end of the war and was also used by Nos 11, 28, 32 and 208 Squadrons in the Middle and Far East.

The final major redesign of the Spitfire resulted in the Mark 21. Although the Spitfire had always been able to out-perform the Bf 109 and Fw 190 during sustained turns, it was not as good in terms of roll response. Supermarine had been looking to improve this aspect of the Spitfire's performance for some time, but it was clear that any increase in roll rate would require a stiffer wing to avoid the possibility of 'aileron-reversal' caused by the wing twisting in the opposite direction to aileron deflection, due to a lack of torsional rigidity. The main struc-tural element of the Spitfire wing was the D-shaped torsion box, formed by the single spar and the heavy-duty leading edge skinning. On the Mark 21 this was augmented by a number of torque-boxes behind the spar that increased stiffness by 47 per cent and upped the theoretical aileron reversal speed from 580 mph to 850 mph. The revised ailerons with piano-type hinges and balance tabs imparted much better lateral control and the top speed went up by 10 mph compared with the Spitfire XIV, mainly due to the use of a larger 11 ft diameter propeller, which required the oleo legs to be extended by 4½ in. On the downside, directional and longitudinal control were by now becoming marginal in certain areas of the flight envelope, largely due to the destabilising effect of the new propeller, which was 7 in greater in diameter than that fitted to the Spitfire XIV.

In late 1944 LA201 was delivered to AFDU at Wittering for a tactical trial and for once the Spitfire came in for a fair amount of criticism. Although the aileron control was rated as the best yet encountered on any mark of Spitfire, the aircraft was found to be unstable in the yawing plane, especially at altitude and at high speed. The rudder was very sensitive to small movements and most pilots had difficulty achieving balanced flight as the aircraft was prone to skidding or slipping. The elevator control was positive and the aircraft was stable in pitch, but constant correction was necessary, especially at low speed, and at high altitude at all speeds. Trimmers were provided for the rudder and elevators, but movement was extremely critical, a factor that was of most relevance when accelerating in a dive, the aircraft being difficult to fly accurately. The combination of instability in yaw, an increased

stalling speed due to higher wing loading and critical trimming qualities, produced unpleasant handling characteristics that compared
unfavourably with other fighters.

The Spitfire F.21's deficiencies were particularly marked when flying
on instruments or at low level. In conditions of bad visibility, it was
considered that the feeling of instability, together with the poor
forward view of the Griffon-engined Spitfire, made flying the aircraft
particularly hazardous. Its sensitivity in pitch meant that it was also
easy for the pilot to over-control, leading to potentially dangerous
height loss when flying at low level. Aerobatics were less easy than on
any other mark of Spitfire, as was formation flying. Despite the fact that
the Spitfire F.21 was 10–12 mph faster than the Spitfire XIV and had
better aileron control at speeds above 300 mph, its handling was otherwise unacceptable as was made clear in the conclusions to the AFDU
report.

> The instability in the yawing plane and the critical trimming
> characteristics of this aircraft make it difficult to fly accurately
> under the easiest conditions and as a sighting platform it is un-
> satisfactory both for air-to-air gunnery and ground attack. Its
> handling qualities compare unfavourably with all earlier marks
> of Spitfire and with other modern fighters and more than nullify
> its advantages in performance and fire power. The Spitfire XIV is
> a better all round fighter than the Spitfire F.21. The handling
> qualities of successive marks of the basic Spitfire design have
> gradually deteriorated until, as exemplified in the Spitfire F.21,
> they prejudice the pilot's ability to exploit the increased
> performance.
>
>   It is recommended that the Spitfire F.21 be withdrawn from
> operations until the instability in the yawing plane has been
> removed and that it be replaced by the Spitfire XIV or Tempest V
> until this can be done. If it is not possible then it must be em-
> phasised that, although the Spitfire F.21 is not a dangerous
> aircraft to fly, pilots must be warned of its handling qualities and
> in its present state it is not likely to prove a satisfactory fighter.
> No further attempts should be made to perpetuate the Spitfire
> family.

It was clear that the only real solution to the Spitfire F.21's handling
deficiencies lay in a redesign of its tail surfaces, but with aircraft already
coming off the production lines at Castle Bromwich and South
Marston, a temporary fix would have to suffice. The modifications
carried out were the removal of the balance function of the rudder trim
tab, together with slightly smaller elevator horn balances and a reduc-

tion in the gearing to the elevator trim tab. Another early production Spitfire F.21 (LA215) was dispatched to AFDU in March 1945 to see if any improvement had been made.

Once airborne, it was apparent that many of the adverse handling characteristics had been eradicated. The 'hunting' which had been experienced as a result of the extreme sensitivity of the elevators was no longer apparent and much less trimming was needed to maintain balanced flight. The rudder control was much improved, although the trimmer was still quite sensitive and care had to be taken to prevent a slip or skid from developing. The reduced gearing to the elevator trim tab had a major impact on controllability and made for smooth and accurate flying. The improvement in handling was most noticeable when flying on instruments and the reduced sensitivity of the elevators in particular made the aircraft acceptable for flying in formation during cloud penetration. In such situations, it was recommended that throttle movements be kept to a minimum to reduce the risk of setting up a strong yawing moment. Low flying was also much more pleasant and low level manoeuvring in bad visibility did not cause any difficulty. In marked contrast to what had been written just three months before, AFDU now considered the Spitfire F.21 to be a satisfactory combat aircraft for the average pilot. Enlarged tail surfaces to restore directional and longitudinal stability were eventually introduced on the F.22 and F.24.

One Spitfire development that may have seen widespread use had it not been for the rapid advance of the jet-powered fighter, was the use of contra-rotating propellers. One of the biggest drawbacks of the piston-engined fighter, as typified by the Spitfire F.21, was the difficulty of harnessing the power of the engine while retaining adequate control. As engine power increased, it was necessary to absorb that power by increasing blade area by having larger diameter propellers and more blades (five on the late mark Spitfires), but this made it increasingly difficult to control the torque reaction and slipstream effects that were produced. Contra-rotating propellers did away with these problems as the two airscrews turned in opposite directions.

The first Spitfire to be modified was AB505, a Mark V that was subsequently converted as a Mark IX and fitted with a Merlin 77 and six-blade Rotol contra-prop. Several Spitfire XIVs were tested with contra-rotating propellers, including the sixth prototype JF321 (Griffon 61) and RB144 (Griffon 85), and a number of Spitfire F.21s were also powered by the Griffon 85 driving either a Rotol or de Havilland six-blade contra-prop. One of these aircraft (LA218) was the subject of a brief test by AFDU carried out in May 1945.

Although the take-off run appeared to be a little longer than a standard Spitfire F.21, the handling was much improved. Provided that the rudder had been correctly trimmed, there was no tendency to swing at all. Once in the air, the pilot was able to climb the aircraft with his feet removed from the rudder controls, without fear of a skid or slip developing. If trimming had been applied incorrectly, however, a swing was likely to develop. Aerobatic manoeuvres were transformed with the contra-prop installation and the pilot could virtually forget about the rudder, irrespective of throttle setting and/or speed. The aircraft's steadiness in the directional sense was particularly useful during simulated ground-attack dives of up to 60 degrees. During these, it was found that the sight could be held on the target with ease and there was not the slightest tendency for the nose to wander. The aircraft did become tail heavy at about 280 mph IAS and a large forward trimming movement was necessary in order to fly 'hands off' especially above 400 mph IAS. Once trimmed, the dive was absolutely straight. The light aileron control of the Spitfire F.21 came to the fore during the breakaway manoeuvre, as it was possible to carry out quite violent evasive action without fear of losing control.

Landing was straightforward, with a very marked braking effect with the propeller in the fully fine position. However, the landing run was considerably longer than on previous aircraft. This was most likely owing to the engine idling a little faster than normal, pilots being reluctant to throttle back fully as this was liable to lead to a complete cut-out. The lack of torque generated was particularly noticeable during a simulated go-around when the throttle was advanced at near stalling speed. The stability was much improved and the possibility of an accident considerably reduced. The significant improvements in controllability of the contra-prop Spitfire F.21 did not come at the expense of performance, which was comparable with that of the standard aircraft. Despite its advantages, contra-prop Spitfires did not enter service with the RAF, although the Seafire FR.47, powered by a Griffon 85 with contra-rotating propellers, did see action with the Fleet Air Arm during the Korean War.

# CHAPTER THREE

# Boulton Paul
# Defiant

T he design concept that led to the Boulton Paul Defiant can be traced back to the Bristol F.2B Fighter of the First World War, which combined the performance of a single-seat fighter with the flexibility of a two-seater, with a rear-facing Lewis gun in addition to a forward-firing Vickers. The idea was perpetuated in the Hawker Demon of the inter-war years and reached its ultimate expression in the Defiant.

Having already developed a pneumatic turret for its Overstrand bomber, Boulton Paul were quick to see the advantages of a hydraulic turret developed in France by de Boysson of the Societé d'Applications des Machines Motrices (SAMM) and acquired licence manufacturing rights in 1937. The rapid advance in aircraft structures and performance in the 1930s had led to a reappraisal of aircraft armament, as it was becoming clear that larger gun batteries would be needed to stand any chance of downing the new monoplane bombers. The combination of four 0.303-in Browning machine-guns in the de Boysson turret (instead of the Darne machine-guns used by the French) seemed to be an ideal solution to the problem of delivering sufficient weight of fire onto a target, and J.D. North, Boulton Paul's chief designer, penned a neat low-wing monoplane to accommodate it. Unlike the Bristol F.2B and Hawker Demon, there was to be no forward-firing armament, as the aircraft was considered to be a 'bomber destroyer', which, it was hoped, would not have to contend with escort fighters. The resultant P.82 Defiant, designed to meet Specification F.9/35 was flown for the first time by Cecil Feather on 11 August 1937 at Wolverhampton Airport. The type was eventually chosen ahead of its main rival, the Hawker Hotspur.

In its construction, the Defiant was more advanced than the Hurricane, which was the culmination of the Hart/Fury design stream. At the same time, it was much simpler to produce than the Spitfire. The front fuselage was built up of four L-section longerons, a number of bulkheads and contained the pilot's cockpit, the floor of which was formed by the upper surface of the wing centre section. The rear fuselage accommodated the turret, which was streamlined fore and aft by fairings made of spruce and three-ply. These were raised or lowered by pneumatic jacks actuated by cams in the turret. Much attention was given to reducing airframe drag, with countersunk rivets being used in the metal skinning to allow a smooth surface finish. The wing was of two-spar construction and consisted of a centre section, two outer panels and detachable wing tips. A semi-elliptical planform was achieved by using a linear taper on the centre section, with a more pronounced taper on the outer sections. Split flaps ran the full length of the wings from the Frise-type ailerons, which (like the elevators and rudder) were fabric-covered. A total of 104 gallons of fuel was accommodated in two self-sealing tanks in the wing centre section. The radiator was mounted ventrally in a similar position to that adopted for the Hurricane.

The turret was hydraulically operated (the pump being electrically driven) and mounted four 0.303-in Brownings in vertical pairs, each gun having 600 rounds in ammunition tanks located under each gun installation. It was able to rotate through 360 degrees and the guns could be depressed to the horizontal, except when facing forwards, when they were restricted to an elevation of 17½ degrees to clear the propeller. The maximum angle the guns could be raised was 72 degrees as the air gunner could not use his sight at higher elevations. Electrical cut-outs were provided to prevent the guns hitting any part of the aircraft.

The prototype Defiant (K8310) was delivered to A&AEE at Martlesham Heath in early December 1937 for an initial assessment. The turret had not yet been fitted, so a metal fairing took its place. Powered by a Rolls-Royce Merlin I, performance testing showed a top speed of 320 mph and the aircraft attained a height of 10,500 ft in 7½ minutes. The handling was acceptable in most respects, the only major complaints being that the ailerons were considered to be too light and the flaps, when fully down, did not produce the desired nose-down attitude on a glide approach. As the cockpit was set further forward than either the Hurricane or Spitfire, access on the ground could be made difficult, particularly if the wing surface was wet. However, the view forwards and downwards was better than on either of the two aforementioned aircraft. The cockpit also proved to be rather draughty with the hood closed.

K8310 was fitted with the four-gun turret in February 1938 and returned to Martlesham Heath for armament trials, with further performance testing taking place the following October. The figures obtained were slightly disappointing as the maximum speed was reduced to 303 mph at 15,000 ft and it took 15.1 minutes to reach 20,000 ft. It had been hoped that the Defiant would have a similar performance to the Hurricane, but its top speed was 17 mph slower and the climb to 20,000 ft took a full 6 minutes longer. It was obvious that more power was needed and the first production aircraft (L6950) was fitted with a Merlin III of 1030 hp and first flown on 30 July 1939. It was delivered to A&AEE (by now at Boscombe Down) on 19 September 1939, together with the second prototype, K8620, for further performance and handling trials.

The provision of a non-slip walkway on the wing root made entry to the cockpit slightly less hazardous, although a spring-loaded step on the fuselage side would have made it easier still. The cockpit was comfortable, with adequate room for a well-built pilot, but in flight a cold draught tended to play on the back of the pilot's neck. It was also rather noisy, but no more so than contemporary fighters. The gun turret was much more difficult to enter, access being obtained either by sliding back the segments of the transparent cupola, or via a hatch in the floor aft of the turret. The latter method could only be used when the guns were facing forward. The turret was perfectly adequate for an air gunner of small stature, but anyone who was taller than average found the accommodation rather cramped when wearing full flying kit.

The control surfaces were operated by a system of cables, pulleys and levers, which produced little friction in the control circuits and only slight play. The elevator trim tab control was located on the pilot's left in the forward upper corner of the cockpit and could be moved over its full range in about three seconds. Rudder trim could be applied by moving a quadrant-mounted lever, which was also on the left-hand side of the cockpit immediately aft of the undercarriage and flap quadrants. The full range of movement could be obtained in about one second. No aileron bias gear was fitted.

The throttle control quadrant was conveniently mounted on the pilot's left and showed no sign of slipping. The propeller pitch could be selected to 'Coarse' or 'Fine' by a control immediately below the panel on the left-hand side. It was within easy reach, but could be easily mistaken for the boost cut-out control, especially when changing pitch after take-off. The radiator shutter control was located on the right of the cockpit, with the fuel cock on the left. Some difficulty was experienced with the fuel cock sticking, which was modified by Boulton Paul. The flap control was mounted in the throttle control box and could be operated with ease to stop the flaps in any position. An indicator on the left-hand side of the panel was marked in degrees and covered the full flap range.

The control for the undercarriage was located next to the throttle box and was easy to operate. The position of the wheels was indicated to the pilot by red and green lights situated in the centre of the panel–red when the undercarriage was up and green when it was down. A warning horn sounded if the throttle was closed beyond the last third of its movement with the wheels still up. There were two methods of operating the undercarriage in an emergency, consisting of two hand pumps, one operating through a hydraulic system separate to the normal system. Pilots faced with such an emergency were then faced with the unenviable task of applying 200 strokes to the pump before the undercarriage was fully down.

The brakes were pneumatically operated via a lever on the control column and performed well. A standard blind flying panel was fitted and the layout of the instruments was good, with no vibration. For night flying, illumination was provided by two lights on movable arms, one on each side of the cockpit. A dimmer switch was provided for each. They could be set to illuminate any particular instrument or the complete blind flying panel and did not cause any unwanted reflections on the windscreen.

In the prototype Defiant no emergency exit was available from the front cockpit. A sliding hood was fitted, but was found to be almost impossible to open at speeds above 210 mph IAS. Knock-out panels were fitted in the sides of the hood, which were sufficiently large to enable a small pilot to climb out of the aircraft should it come to rest inverted on the ground. Later aircraft were fitted with a hood that could be jettisoned. In a bale-out situation, the air gunner had to leave the turret through the trap door in the floor of the fuselage, but this could only be done with the guns in the forward position. It was considered that the chances of the gunner getting out successfully would depend on his size. A tall man might well have difficulty, particularly if the aircraft was not under control at the time. The gunner's exit hatch could be opened from the outside should the aircraft go over onto its back on the ground, but it was thought that it would have been extremely difficult for him to extricate himself without assistance.

For a low-wing single-engine monoplane fighter, the view from the cockpit was better than most other aircraft of the period as the pilot's cockpit was mounted further forward to cater for the turret. Although the view ahead when the tail was on the ground was not good, with the tail up on take-off it was greatly improved, and in flight the view downwards over the leading edge was excellent. No 'direct vision' panel was fitted so there was virtually no forward visibility when flying in rain. Instead, the pilot had to open the hood and peer round the windscreen.

Handling trials were carried out at take-off weights of 7220 lb (forward CG), 7390 lb (normal CG) and 7560 lb (extended aft CG). The aircraft was easy to taxi in winds of up to 30 mph and showed no tendency to lift its tail even with CG at the forward limit. The behaviour of the undercarriage on any surface was excellent and the brakes were smooth and progressive in operation. Prior to take-off the flaps were set at 30 degrees. The tail tended to come up slowly during the take-off run and the swing to the left could easily be held with rudder. As soon as the aircraft was airborne the undercarriage could be raised with little change in trim, the whole operation taking around eleven seconds. It was recommended that the flaps should not to be raised until a speed of 120 mph IAS had been reached, as this caused slight tail heaviness. Once in the clean configuration the aircraft could be accelerated to its best climbing speed of 180 mph IAS. Although there was sufficient elevator trim when climbing at this speed, the rudder trimmer did not have enough authority and some right rudder had to be maintained.

The controls were moderately heavy, the elevator being quick in response and effective at all speeds with the engine on, but becoming heavier in the dive. It was also classed as moderately heavy on the glide but in this condition there was a marked deterioration in response and control was not very effective. The force needed to apply the rudder was similar and once again the response was somewhat worse when gliding, although it remained effective. Full stability tests were not carried out, but the aircraft appeared to be longitudinally stable at maximum level speed at normal CG. The level of stability tended to reduce with decrease in speed, until at low speeds the aircraft was slightly unstable. Directionally, the aircraft was stable at all times.

Night flying did not pose any particular problems, although the poor initial rate of climb whilst gaining speed was a little disconcerting at first, especially when there was no horizon. A fair amount of flame was produced by the exhaust, but this did not seriously affect the forward view. The lookout was satisfactory, particularly forwards out of the glass windscreen. In contrast the Perspex hood was prone to scratches, which affected the pilot's ability to see other aircraft.

During stall tests with the flaps and undercarriage up, the aircraft showed itself to be longitudinally stable when trimmed to fly at 1.2 × stall speed (108 mph IAS). The only warning of the approaching stall was given by the fairly high position of the nose, less effective aileron control and slight tail buffet. The aircraft stalled at 90 mph IAS with the control column almost fully back, but it was not particularly easy to accomplish this as the elevators were not very effective at low speeds, and although the forces involved were not great, the limited amount of elevator travel caused some difficulty. When it did occur, the stall was fairly gentle and generally level, with an occasional tendency to drop either wing quite sharply, but this could be raised by coarse use of rudder. If the wing was allowed to drop, the speed increased and the wing could be raised by aileron. There was no tendency to spin.

With the flaps and undercarriage down the stall occurred at 76 mph IAS, the nose being less high than in the clean configuration. As a result, the control column only needed to be brought back to the three-quarters position. The stall was more marked and a wing, usually the left, was much more likely to drop. If the control column was pulled right back, the aircraft developed a fore-and-aft pitching with variations of speed from 70–85 mph IAS and with considerable tail buffet. Each wing tended to drop alternately, but could be raised by coarse rudder. The aircraft was very difficult to control under these circumstances, but once again there was no sign of a spin developing.

When the flaps were lowered on the approach the aircraft became slightly nose heavy, but this could easily be held. The best speed for the approach was 90 mph IAS. Although the landing was reasonably straightforward, the lack of elevator control at low speed meant that it was rather difficult, but not impossible, to get the tail down into the three-point attitude, even with CG in the forward position. The touchdown speed was about 70 mph IAS. With its wide-track undercarriage the aircraft handled well on the ground; there was no swing after landing, or tendency to nose over at any CG position, although the run was noticeably longer than either the Hurricane or Spitfire.

Both K8620 and L6950 were fitted with a Merlin III with a two-pitch de Havilland propeller of 11 ft 6 in diameter. The take-off run was calculated at 315 yards when corrected for zero wind and International Standard Atmosphere (ISA) conditions, with 560 yards being required to clear 50 ft. The best rate of climb was 1620 ft/min at 10,700 ft, which was attained in 7.1 minutes. The greatest height achieved was 26,000 ft and the estimated service ceiling was 28,100 ft. The full test results were as follows :

| Height | 1000 ft | 3000 ft | 5000 ft | 10,000 ft | 13,000 ft |
|---|---|---|---|---|---|
| Rate of climb – ft/min | 1435 | 1475 | 1515 | 1610 | 1415 |
| Time from start – min | 0.7 | 2.1 | 3.4 | 6.7 | 8.6 |

| Height | 15,000 ft | 18,000 ft | 20,000 ft | 23,000 ft | 26,000 ft |
|---|---|---|---|---|---|
| Rate of climb – ft/min | 1240 | 980 | 805 | 545 | 285 |
| Time from start – min | 10.1 | 12.8 | 15.1 | 19.5 | 27.0 |

With a maximum of 6¼ lb/sq.in boost the highest speed was only 303 mph at 16,600 ft. However, slightly better figures were achieved with an increased boost of 12 lb/sq.in and 100 octane fuel, when a top speed of 312 mph TAS was recorded at full throttle height of 10,000 ft. The maximum speeds at other heights were as follows:

| Height | 1000 ft | 2000 ft | 3000 ft | 5000 ft | 6500 ft |
| --- | --- | --- | --- | --- | --- |
| TAS – mph | 279.5 | 283 | 286.5 | 294 | 299 |
| IAS – mph | 290 | 289.5 | 289 | 288 | 288 |

| Height | 10,000 ft | 13,000 ft | 15,000 ft | 16,500 ft |
| --- | --- | --- | --- | --- |
| TAS – mph | 312 | 308.5 | 305.5 | 303 |
| IAS – mph | 284 | 267.5 | 256 | 248 |

Further performance testing was carried out at Boscombe Down between 22 April and 5 June 1940 using L6954, which was fitted with a constant-speed de Havilland propeller. Despite the fact that the take-off run was slightly longer at 340 yards, the distance to clear 50 ft was reduced to 485 yards. As expected, the change of propeller had little effect on the top speed, although there were slight improvements above and below full throttle height. The major benefit was a substantially better rate of climb, 5000 ft now being reached in five minutes, 10,000 ft in eight minutes and 20,000 ft in twelve minutes.

The Defiant I entered service with No. 264 Squadron at Martlesham Heath in December 1939. However, it was beset by engine and hydraulic problems, which led to a temporary grounding in early 1940 while the snags were rectified by Rolls-Royce and Lockheed. The development of suitable tactics for the Defiant was also causing headaches. Squadron Leader P.A. Hunter, No. 264 Squadron's CO, reported that the Defiant suffered a serious lack of speed, to the extent that overtaking attacks on a single Fairey Battle flying at 180 mph IAS could only be carried out successfully if the Defiant had a height advantage of between 2–3000 ft. He also noted that because of its weight, it was unable to regain height rapidly after a high-speed dive. With full service equipment and fully armed, the Defiant I weighed in at 8350 lb. This reduced the top speed to between 280–90 mph, depending on engine performance and the state of individual airframes, but quite how it was unable to cope with a Battle flying straight and level at such a slow speed was not explained.

Shortly before the Defiant was issued to No. 264 Squadron, tactical trials were carried out by AFDU (then at Northolt) using L6951, L6952 and L6955. The air gunner's vision was found to be severely restricted, being limited to a narrow cone directly in front of him, together with the upper and rear hemispheres of the turret. There was very little room in the turret and the gunner's knees were constantly pressed up against the ammunition boxes. Movement of the turret was effected by a short control lever, with an electrically operated button allowing a high-speed option. The sight was a Mark III reflector, located centrally above and between the two banks of guns.

Practice attacks were made on Blenheims of No. 25 Squadron, also based at Northolt. The easiest form of attack was to overtake the 'bomber' on a parallel course, but against any aircraft faster than a Blenheim it would have to be delivered from a dive in order to have sufficient speed. The most comfortable position for the air gunner, when firing from the bomber's flank, was approximately 100 ft lower than the target at a range of 200–250 yards. Attacks delivered from below were also reasonably successful, although when passing from astern to ahead, the guns could not be used within the vertical 36-degree cone as the sight could not be used. As the Defiant's guns could not be depressed below the horizon, attacks from above necessitated the aircraft being banked so that fire could be delivered. Skidding was not found to be a practical proposition, owing to loss of speed, so attacks had to be delivered from a slight turn.

AFDU considered that the main advantage of the Defiant was its ability to deliver fire onto a bomber from below, where it would not be as protected by armour. To do this, however, the Defiant needed to be able to carry out its approach without being seen, as the Defiant gunner had great difficulty in firing at the target if it began evasive manoeuvres, particularly those involving diving to lower levels. In these circumstances, any burst of fire was likely to be very short and the weight of fire delivered would, in consequence, be limited. It was also recommended that the smallest tactical unit should consist of at least two Defiants and that a section should consist of four aircraft instead of three.

Unfortunately, the Defiant was never to be tested in the role for which it was designed. By the time German bombers began to appear over Britain in substantial numbers, they were able to operate from forward bases and were protected by fighter escort. Comparative trials with a Hurricane had already shown that the Defiant would be no match for single-seat fighters, as it not only lost out in terms of performance, but also in manoeuvrability. The Defiant weighed approximately 1800 lb more than a Hurricane when fully loaded, but its wing area was slightly less at 250 sq.ft. This resulted in a wing loading of 33.27 lb/sq.ft compared with the Hurricane's 25.63 lb/sq.ft. When compared with the Bf 109E, there was en even bigger disparity in weight, the gross weight of the *Emil* being only 5740 lb. The Messerschmitt's much smaller wing of only 174 sq.ft resulted in a similar wing loading to the Defiant, so that the Bf 109's biggest benefits were a speed advantage of 50–60 mph and much better climb and dive performance.

Meanwhile trials were taking place to assess the Defiant's suitability for other roles. Specification F.9/35 had also called for light bomb racks to be fitted under the wings for close-support duties and in early 1940 L6950 was used for dive-bombing trials over the Orfordness ranges. The optimum method of attack was to begin the dive from 5000 ft at an angle of 40–45 degrees, with a pull-out commencing at around 1500 ft. Shallow dive attacks were also tried at angles of 20–25 degrees down to 500 ft. Steep dives at 60 degrees were attempted with speeds reaching 400 mph IAS, but it was found that the height needed to recover was excessive and bombing accuracy was poor. L6968 was used for trials in the Army Co-operation role and although a few aircraft were delivered to No. 2 Squadron, they were quickly withdrawn.

Only two squadrons (141 and 264) were to fly the Defiant as a day fighter, with both units suffering heavy losses during the Battle of Britain. It had always been intended that the Defiant should be capable of fulfilling a night-fighter role and following the severe mauling at the hands of the *Luftwaffe* by day, the Defiant was assigned to night interception. At first crews operated visually, but from September 1941 the first radar-equipped Defiant IAs began to appear with early AI.IV (Airborne Interception) sets with 'arrow-head' aerials on the starboard wing and an 'H'-type aerial on the fuselage side. The cathode-ray tube for the radar was located in the front cockpit on the pilot's left, with the control panel on the right.

To improve performance, Boulton Paul looked at more powerful engines and eventually selected the 1280-hp two-speed supercharged Merlin XX for the Defiant II. The aircraft also featured an increased internal fuel capacity of 159 gallons (two auxiliary tanks being fitted in each outer wing section), a deeper radiator and a lengthened engine cowling. Owing to the changes at the front end, a slightly larger rudder was needed to restore directional control. A Defiant I (N1550) was converted as the Mark II prototype and was flown for the first time on 20 July 1940. This was followed by N1551, which was involved in a ground collision with N1550 before being delivered to A&AEE for brief performance and handling trials. It was flown at a weight of 7690 lb but was not fitted with AI equipment, which would have added another 285 lb. The figures for rate of climb showed a considerable improvement, with 2780 ft/min being recorded at full throttle height of 10,700 ft. The estimated absolute ceiling was now 33,100 ft. The Defiant II could reach 26,000 ft in less than half the time of the Mark I as the following table shows.

| Height | 1000 ft | 3000 ft | 5000 ft | 10,000 ft | 15,000 ft |
|---|---|---|---|---|---|
| Rate of climb – ft/min | 2435 | 2505 | 2580 | 2760 | 2200 |
| Time from start – min | 0.4 | 1.25 | 2.0 | 3.9 | 5.95 |

| Height | 20,000 ft | 23,000 ft | 26,000 ft | 28,000 ft | 30,000 ft |
|---|---|---|---|---|---|
| Rate of climb – ft/min | 1850 | 1610 | 1215 | 950 | 690 |
| Time from start – min | 8.3 | 10.0 | 12.15 | 14.0 | 16.44 |

With its increased fuel capacity the Defiant II had a maximum range of just over 450 miles, which could be attained in MS blower at 10,000 ft with 1900 rpm set. The speed was a relatively sedate 195 mph TAS. The maximum speed was increased only slightly, despite the extra power of the Merlin XX, 313 mph being recorded in FS blower at a full throttle height of 19,400 ft. Other results were as follows:

| Height | 13,000 ft | 15,000 ft | 16,500 ft | 18,000 ft | 20,000 ft | 23,000 ft |
|---|---|---|---|---|---|---|
| TAS – mph | 296 | 301 | 305.5 | 309 | 311 | 305 |
| IAS – mph | 233.5 | 230.5 | 229 | 226 | 220.5 | 204.5 |

Handling tests at Boscombe Down were also carried out using AA370, which was the first purpose-built Mark II. The seven preceding aircraft had all been converted from Mark I airframes. It was flown at a weight of 8510 lb at normal CG loading. During early testing the rudder was found to be unsatisfactory, as it appeared to be over-balanced and caused directional instability. Various steps were taken to cure this trouble and finally a rudder was fitted in which the trim tab acted solely as a trimmer, and not as a balance tab as previously. In addition, the tab was mass-balanced and stringing cord was doped on each side of the straight portion of the trailing edge, immediately above the tab. This rudder performed much better and was adopted for production. The aircraft was also flown with a slightly larger propeller of 11 ft 9 in diameter.

The cockpit was very similar to that of a Defiant I, except that it appeared to be rather less draughty in flight. The heating was adequate but tended to produce an oily smell that was rather unpleasant on long flights. This was not particularly surprising as the heat for the cockpit was drawn via a duct from the oil cooler. The hood was now provided with sliding panels on each side and above. These enabled a clear view to be obtained when flying in rain or if the windscreen had become oiled. In addition, the whole hood could be jettisoned should an emergency exit have to be made. The only major difference in the control layout was the introduction of a lever for the constant-speed propeller. This was situated between the throttle lever and the side of the fuselage. The supercharger gear change knob was now located low down on the left-hand side of the panel in the position previously taken by the control for the two-pitch propeller.

Even though full right rudder trim was used for take-off, a strong swing to the left was experienced, but this could be held with rudder without too much effort. Like the Defiant I, there was insufficient rudder trim to fly 'feet off' in the climb, but the force required to keep the aircraft straight at its optimum climbing speed of 140 mph IAS was only slight. In normal flight the ailerons and elevator were very similar to the Mark I. However, a difference was noted with the rudder, which was heavier than before and directional stability was now neutral. Pilots also had difficulty in achieving trimmed flight. If the aircraft was yawed, it would regain a steady course without oscillation when the rudder was released, but quite often there was a change in direction. At cruising speed, four divisions of right rudder trim were needed to fly straight with 'feet off'.

Dives were carried out with the aircraft trimmed for straight and level flight, i.e. four divisions of right rudder trim and seven divisions of nose-down elevator trim. The forward force required on the control column in the dive increased rapidly above 320 mph IAS and 360 mph IAS was about the maximum speed that a normal pilot could hold. If full nose-down trim was used, the aircraft settled into the dive at about 320 mph IAS. Once again, the push force needed increased rapidly above this speed and became excessive at 380 mph IAS, although the maximum achieved was 395 mph IAS.

Up to 360 mph IAS, directional control was satisfactory; the aircraft wanted to yaw to the right with increase in speed, but this could easily be held with rudder. Above this speed, however, the pilot experienced a rather disconcerting change in the control loads on both the rudder and elevator. Quite suddenly, the forward load on the stick and the load on the left rudder were relieved, as if the control surfaces or the tabs themselves had moved. This change was not persistent, but occurred as a sudden jerk, after which the original trim was regained. This was not explained, although it was thought that it may have been caused by a sudden distortion of the trimmers. In view of the excessive stick forces, combined with this 'snatching' of the rudder and elevator, it was recommended that the limit for diving be reduced from 400 mph IAS to 360 mph IAS.

When trimmed to fly at 1.2 × stall speed and with the flaps and undercarriage down, the Defiant II was just unstable longitudinally, with any disturbances producing slowly increasing oscillations. The stall itself occurred at 80 mph IAS and was marked by a sharp drop of the starboard wing through about 35–40 degrees, although this could be raised by coarse use of the aileron. After about a second in this condition, the aircraft tended to flick violently over to the right with a significant drop in nose attitude, and if back pressure on the control column had not been released, it was thought that a spin might have developed. With the flaps and undercarriage up, the aircraft was longitudinally stable as speed was reduced, but there was an increasing tendency for the port wing to drop. The stall occurred at 92–4 mph IAS. As a large amount of aileron was needed to hold the port wing, this produced considerable aileron drag, with resultant yaw to the left, but in this case there was a tendency to spin.

The Defiant went on to serve with thirteen squadrons in the night-fighter role until mid 1942. By this time aircraft with increased performance were urgently needed and the type was quickly replaced by the twin-engined Bristol Beaufighter and de Havilland Mosquito. Surplus aircraft were used in several other roles, notably Air-Sea Rescue (ASR). The Defiant flew with five ASR squadrons on high-speed search duties until June 1943, before being replaced by converted Spitfire IIs.

In late 1941 Reid and Sigrist at Desford was given a contract to convert 150 Defiant Is as target tugs with the designation TT.III. The turret was removed to be replaced by a small canopy for an observer, but the take-off weight was still 8227 lb and the drag imposed by the target towing equipment reduced the top speed to around 250 mph. A further 140 target tugs were ordered in July 1941 based on the Defiant II, designated TT.I. The Defiant also served as a training aircraft at various Air Gunners' Schools and the Central Gunnery School.

The last Defiant to remain in use was DR944, which was issued to Martin-Baker in December 1944 for ejector seat trials. The observer's position was removed so that an ejector seat could be fitted behind the pilot and a number of ejections were made in 1945 at speeds up to 300 mph using dummies. DR944 was eventually struck off charge on 31 May 1948.

# Blackburn
# Skua / Roc

Although it was to make a name for itself as a dive-bomber, most notably the sinking of the German cruiser *Konigsberg* in Bergen Fjord on 10 April 1940, the Skua was also tasked with fleet air defence and the type was responsible for shooting down a Dornier Do 18 flying-boat off the Norwegian coast on 25 September 1939, the first enemy aircraft to be claimed by the Fleet Air Arm (FAA). The Skua was designed by G.E. Petty to Specification O.27/34. K5178, the first of two prototypes, was flown for the first time on 9 February 1937 by Captain A.M. 'Dasher' Blake. Both aircraft were powered by an 840 hp Bristol Mercury IX engine, but production machines, designated Skua II, featured a Bristol Perseus XII sleeve-valve radial of 890 hp, driving a de Havilland three-blade, two-pitch propeller. The top speed of the Skua II was 225 mph at sea level with an initial rate of climb of 1580 ft/min and a service ceiling of 20,200 ft.

Despite its seemingly modest performance, the Skua represented a radical departure from the fabric-covered biplanes that it replaced. It introduced the all-metal cantilever monoplane to Fleet Air Arm service and also pioneered the use of landing flaps, a retractable undercarriage and a variable-pitch propeller. The two crew members were accommodated under a long canopy, which was protected by two reinforced fuselage frames in case the aircraft came to rest inverted. The fuselage was of flush-riveted Alclad and incorporated two watertight compartments, one under the front cockpit and the other to the rear of the gunner's station. These provided buoyancy in case of ditching. The wings comprised a centre section bolted to the fuselage, with tapered outer panels, detachable tips and fabric-covered ailerons. Wing folding was incorporated, whereby the wings moved back about an inclined hinge and also twisted so that the leading edge was pointing upwards. The tail surfaces were metal cantilever structures with fabric-covered elevators and rudder, and the aircraft was fully stressed for catapult take-offs and arrested landings.

The armament comprised four 0.303 in Browning machine-guns mounted in the wings and a single Mk. IIIE Lewis machine-gun mounted on a Fairey Battle-type pillar for the gunner/observer in the rear cockpit. In the dive-bombing role, a 500-lb semi-armour piercing (SAP) bomb could be carried under the fuselage on a retractable ejector arm or, alternatively, eight 30-lb practice bombs on racks under the wings.

The Skua was first seen in the New Types Park at the RAF Display at Hendon on 26 June 1937. K5178 went to A&AEE at Martlesham Heath for handling trials, which were carried out between 20 October and 8 November 1937. Entry to the cockpit was relatively easy via the wing root and the forward view was adequate, assuming that the seat was raised to its fullest extent. The control column was conveniently positioned, all controls could be moved without any friction or play (although the rudder adjustment was difficult to use), and trimmers were provided for the elevator and rudder. The engine and propeller controls were easy to use, but the controls for the combined flap and dive brake was located too close to the fuselage side, which tended to trap the pilot's hand.

Ground handling at normal and aft loadings was straightforward, but with CG at the forward limit the aircraft became noticeably nose heavy when taxying over rough ground. As a result the brakes had to be handled with care to avoid nosing over. Take-offs were normally made with 30 degrees of flap and the rudder bias was easily able to cope with the swing to the right that was experienced. The aircraft became airborne at around 70 mph IAS, and once the undercarriage was retracted, a rather ponderous acceleration could be made to the best climbing speed of 120 mph IAS.

Flight trials did not involve assessing the Skua throughout its full performance envelope, but at the speeds flown aileron control was found to be generally effective, except near the stall. Aileron control tended to become quite heavy as speed was increased, but the forces involved were not excessive. The rudder and elevator both gave adequate control, but a major problem was discovered during stability tests. Although the aircraft was just stable at speeds higher than 140 mph IAS, below this mark a marked longitudinal instability was experienced, with increased tail heaviness, which had to be counteracted by moving the control column forward to prevent the nose rising excessively. This tendency was very marked when close to the stall at extended aft CG. The work of the test pilots was made more difficult by the fact that the aircraft was also unstable laterally. This meant that normal stick-free stability tests could not be carried out, as the control column had to be held to keep the wings level by use of aileron.

The Skua stalled at about 75 mph IAS with the flaps and under-carriage up and at 69 mph IAS with the flaps and undercarriage down. If the speed was reduced in a glide in the clean configuration, the aircraft tended to self-stall if the pilot did not push the stick forward. There was very little stall warning, with no airframe buffet, but when the stall did occur, a wing would drop, followed by the nose. This tended to occur even if the control column was eased forward, but if the aircraft was mishandled by pulling the stick back, it became quite violent and a falling leaf developed. With the flaps and undercarriage down the aircraft's characteristics were very similar, but it was slightly more mild-mannered. Once the nose had dropped and speed had increased, control could quickly be regained.

When approaching to land, the undercarriage could be lowered in about forty-five seconds without any obvious change in trim. Should the pilot forget to lower the wheels, a warning bell sounded, but un-fortunately this proved to be inaudible and was of no use whatsoever. Owing to the instability at low speeds, nose-down trim had to be applied, which was the opposite of what was normally required. After landing on anything other than a smooth surface, a bucketing motion was liable to set in and at times the aircraft also developed a rolling gait from bumps causing excessive compression of an oleo leg.

After completing its handling assessment, K5178 remained at A&AEE for gunnery trials, before being delivered to Gosport for buoy-ancy tests. It was replaced at Martlesham Heath by the second prototype K5179, which had been flown for the first time on 4 May 1938 at Brough. It featured a nose lengthened by 2 ft 4¾ in which brought CG forward and, together with a tensioning device on the elevator control circuit, was an attempt to overcome the aircraft's habit of self-stalling. K5179 was also fitted with leading edge slats, which were tested locked and unlocked, but the benefits at the stall were only marginal and these were not fitted to production aircraft. In an attempt to improve lateral handling, the wing tips were cranked upwards.

In view of the Skua's longitudinal stability problems, much was expected of the spring tensioning fitted to the elevator control, as this was designed to apply a force to lower the elevators to resist the tendency for the nose to rise of its own accord. To test its qualities K5179 was flown at a take-off weight of 7827 lb at extended aft CG. The effectiveness of the spring depended very much on whether the engine was on or off. With the flaps and undercarriage up, the Skua was still unstable when climbing at low speed, and if the control column was pulled back and released, the nose came up rapidly followed by a sudden stall. A wing tended to drop which, if not corrected immedi-ately, could lead to loss of control. In the glide with the engine off, the spring was more effective as it improved the feel of the elevator control and just about overcame the aircraft's tendency to self-stall, although a little forward stick was still needed. As the engine was opened up, however, the spring gradually became less effective, until it made no difference at all. The aircraft behaved in a similar fashion with the flaps and undercarriage down.

The first production Skua II (L2867) took to the air on 28 August 1938 and was quickly followed by L2868. Both machines were delivered to A&AEE the following month, taking part in performance and armament trials respectively. Subsequent testing showed that the Skua was steady in the dive, without any vibration or instability. It tended to become tail heavy, which required a considerable forward push on the control column to maintain the correct angle of dive, but at reduced throttle settings this force was much reduced. Owing to its steadiness in the dive, pilots had no difficulty holding the aircraft on to a target. Lack of gun heating was commented on during the armament trials, but it was thought that this was would not be too much of a problem, as the Skua was unlikely to have to operate as a fighter at anything other than low to medium levels.

The last Skua to be tested at Martlesham Heath was L2888. Pilots were pleased to discover that the bell warning that the undercarriage had not been lowered had been replaced by a klaxon that could actually be heard. There were still some minor niggles though: the cockpit heating was unsatisfactory; the pilot's seat adjustment was inadequate; and the interconnected throttle and mixture controls were badly positioned. On take-off difficulty was experienced in raising the tail and the aircraft had to be deliberately flown off, otherwise it was likely to remain stubbornly attached to the ground. The rate of climb was poor and, with the power on, the same longitudinal instability as before was experienced, together with some fore-and-aft pitching. Control response and effectiveness were good, except at slow speeds, when there was a marked deterioration, but the rudder and ailerons were very heavy above 230 mph IAS. Despite the spring fitted to the elevator control, the aircraft was still rated as being unstable longitudinally when gliding with the flaps and undercarriage up. At low speeds it was also unstable laterally. Stability tended to become neutral in the same condition with the flaps and undercarriage down. The aircraft was directionally stable at all times.

Such was the desperate need to get the Skua into service, it was accepted with the spring tensioning device to the elevator control and the cranked wing tips as the only major modifications. The first deliveries were to No. 800 Squadron aboard HMS *Ark Royal* in late 1938. By the time that war was declared two more squadrons (801 and 803) were also operational. The Skua's most successful action against the *Konigsberg* was carried out by eleven aircraft from No. 803 Squadron and five from No. 800 Squadron. The attack was launched from Hatston in the Orkneys and achieved complete surprise, with only one aircraft failing to return. Although the Skua's endurance was officially quoted as 4 hours 20 minutes, several aircraft managed to exceed this figure by up to ten minutes. Further dive-bombing attacks against the *Scharnhorst* and the French battleship *Richelieu* at Dakar were failures, as the 500-lb SAP bombs carried were ineffectual against more heavily armoured capital ships. Skuas from *Ark Royal* also provided fighter cover for some of the first Malta convoys and acted as guides for Hurricanes on their way to the island. However, it had never been intended that the Skua should have to fight land-based fighters and its poor performance by comparison led to it being replaced by Fulmars and Sea Hurricanes in early 1941. The remaining aircraft were taken on by No. 806 Squadron at Eastleigh and were used mainly for training and target towing.

The Blackburn Roc was an adaptation of the Skua to meet Specification O.30/35. The most obvious difference was the inclusion of a Boulton Paul power-driven gun turret behind the pilot's cockpit, mounting four 0.303 in Browning machine-guns. To accommodate the turret, the fuselage had to be widened slightly and the wings featured 2 degrees dihedral outboard of the centre section in place of the Skua's upturned wing tips. Provision was also made for a streamlined 70-gallon fuel tank to be carried under the forward fuselage and there were attachment points for a float undercarriage. With Blackburn fully occupied with the Skua and the forthcoming Botha twin-engined reconnaissance bomber, production of the Roc was transferred to Boulton Paul, with the tail units being supplied by General Aircraft at Hanworth. The first Roc (L3057) was flown on 23 December 1938 by Blackburn test pilot Flight Lieutenant H.J. Wilson. This aircraft, together with L3059, was delivered to Martlesham Heath in March 1939 for handling trials, with L3058 being used for testing the turret.

The aircraft was flown at varying weights depending on CG position: 6930 lb (forward CG), 7350 lb (aft CG) and 7815 lb (normal CG). On take-off, very little swing was reported, although the run appeared to be rather long. In the air, the controls were all relatively heavy at high speeds, but at least harmonisation was good. The ailerons were light at low speeds and although they were effective, they were rather slow in response. The rudder was also light at the low end of the speed range, but it was not particularly effective. The elevator was light at low speeds, but was slow in response and ineffective.

Following the tribulations with the Skua, stability was closely monitored on the Roc. It was found to be directionally stable at all speeds, but after this things became a little more complicated. Once again, stability varied greatly throughout the speed range and at different CG positions, varying from neutral at a normal service load in level flight to slightly unstable at aft CG. The behaviour was similar with the flaps and undercarriage up and down. Lateral stability was difficult to assess as pilots were pre-occupied with sorting the aircraft out longitudinally, but it appeared to be just stable with the engine on and neutrally stable in the glide. With the flaps and undercarriage up, the stall speed was 82 mph IAS and with the flaps and undercarriage down, the stall occurred at 76 mph IAS. There was very little warning except for a gradual worsening in elevator effectiveness. When trimmed at 1.2 × stall speed the tendency to self-stall was apparent once again and forward stick was needed to prevent the nose rising too steeply.

All aerobatic manoeuvres could be flown, except aileron turns when diving, as this was prevented by control heaviness with increase in speed. However, when manoeuvring in the horizontal plane care had to be taken in steep turns as high accelerations could lead to tightening. Dives were carried out up to 290 mph IAS, with the flaps up and down, without difficulty and recovery was straightforward. In the approach there was insufficient trim available at speeds lower than 115 mph IAS with forward CG and since the glide was steep and the elevator not particularly effective, a wheel landing was recommended. After touchdown, it was advisable to delay using the brakes for as long as possible to reduce the risk of nosing over. The overall assessment of the Roc was slightly more complimentary than the Skua, as its handling qualities were somewhat better and its stability improved because of its lower all-up weight.

Testing of the Boulton Paul turret showed that movement of the turret in the air produced a slight yaw to the left, which was not dependent on the direction the guns were pointing at the time, and with rudder control heavy at high speed, this could be difficult to overcome. The turret performed reasonably well up to the aircraft's service ceiling, although there was a noticeable drop in the speed of rotation in the colder temperatures at altitude. Problems were also experienced when used in the 'high speed' mode, as electrical fuses tended to blow with monotonous regularity. Continued use of the turret tended to drain the air pressure that was required to operate the fairings, so for a time movement had to cease while pressure built up again. The Roc was also stressed to carry light series bomb carriers under the wings.

In an attempt to improve performance, L3058 was flown with an experimental propeller, which consisted of a normal Skua hub with blades of the type fitted to the Tiger engines of an Armstrong Siddeley Whitley. Although the rate of climb was slightly better, there were no improvements in top speed and the proposal did not go any further. The performance figures for the Roc were very similar to the Skua. The maximum speed was 223 mph at 10,000 ft and the initial climb rate was 1500 ft/min. The service ceiling was 18,000 ft.

It had always been the intention to use the Roc as a seaplane fighter and L3057 and L3059 were sent to the Blackburn factory at Dumbarton in October 1939 to be converted. The wheel wells were covered over and Blackburn Shark floats were mounted on N struts under the centre section with separate front struts. Water rudders at the rear of the floats were connected to the aircraft's braking system and operated pneumatically. By the time the conversion had been completed, the Marine Aircraft Experimental Establishment (MAEE) had conveniently moved from Felixstowe to Helensburgh on the Clyde and tests were commenced in November 1939. The trials were marred by L3059's crash on 3 December as a result of marked directional instability. L3057 was modified to include an enlarged ventral fin in an attempt to improve the aircraft's controllability in this respect. Without the fin, low-level turns were particularly dangerous, but with it in place there was a marked improvement, although the turn and slip indicator still had to be monitored closely as any sideslip could lead to disaster. L3060 was also fitted with floats, but with the withdrawal of British forces from Norway in 1940, the requirement for a floatplane fighter, for the time being at least, came to an end.

The Roc never did operate from aircraft carriers, as had been the original intention, and was only ever used from bases on the mainland. It entered service with No. 806 Squadron at Eastleigh in February 1940 and began flying with No. 801 Squadron at Hatston four months later. Experiences with the Defiant were soon to prove that the concept of a turret-armed fighter was not viable and the Roc was quickly downgraded to second-line duties. One of the largest users of the Roc was No. 2 Anti-Aircraft Co-operation Unit at Gosport, which received sixteen in June 1940, four of which had to suffer the indignity of being used as ground-based machine-gun posts as defence against air attack. The Roc also served with numerous FAA training squadrons and a number were converted as target towing aircraft, the last being withdrawn from use in mid 1943.

CHAPTER FIVE

# Fairey Fulmar

The Fulmar was unusual in that it was developed from a design for a two-seat, single-engine bomber, which was, in effect, a smaller, cleaned up version of the Battle. The Fairey P.4/34 bomber prototype, created by Marcelle Lobelle, was designed to meet a light day-bomber specification and was in direct competition with the Hawker Henley. However, following a change of policy at the Air Ministry, the requirement for a high-performance attack aircraft was dropped, which left the way clear for the type to be adapted to meet Specification O.8/38 for a two-seat fighter for the Fleet Air Arm. The first P.4/34 (K5099) had been taken into the air for the first time by Fairey test pilot Chris Staniland on 13 January 1937, with the second prototype (K7555) following on 19 April 1937. Both aircraft were powered by a Rolls-Royce Merlin II of 1030 hp and attained a top speed of 284 mph.

K7555 was assessed by A&AEE at Martlesham Heath between 24 September and 11 October 1937. The subsequent report, although generally satisfactory, highlighted several areas of concern. The aircraft's stalling characteristics were marginal as a fore-and-aft pitching motion set in, together with some lateral instability. If back stick was maintained with the flaps and undercarriage up, there was also a tendency for the right wing to drop, and if elevator control had not been centralised it was thought that a spin might have developed. The rudder was also criticised for being too heavy at speeds above 80 mph IAS and it was found that the bias gear had to be used to maintain balanced flight. Other criticisms were that the elevator trimmer was too low-geared and that the ground attitude when compared with the stalling angle was too shallow, which caused difficulty on landing as it was possible for the tailwheel to contact the ground first as the aircraft was flared on touchdown. The aircraft was also considered to be excessively stable directionally. Together with the heavy rudder, this meant that flat turns were virtually impossible.

The Fulmar bore a strong resemblance to its clean-lined predecessor, but featured a longer radiator duct under the nose, a non-continuous canopy, folding wings, catapult points, dinghy stowage and eight 0.303

in Browning machine-guns mounted in the wings. Unlike contemporary land-based fighters, it was required to have a two-man crew, with an observer in the rear cockpit to assist with navigation as radio location aids were only just being developed. It was fitted with a 1080 hp Merlin VIII. As much testing had already been carried out on the P.4/34, it was decided that there was little point in ordering a prototype, and the first Fulmar to fly was actually the first production machine (N1854), which was taken into the air on 4 January 1940 by Duncan Menzies.

The forward fuselage comprised a tubular steel framework, with a monocoque rear section with Alclad metal sheet covering. The wing consisted of stub planes with outer wings, all covered in Alclad sheeting. The stub planes were attached to two spars, which passed through the fuselage, and the outer wing sections were built around two girder spars with T-section booms. The tailplane comprised two built-up spars and diaphragm-type ribs of sheet Duralumin, the fin being of similar construction. The elevators and rudder had tubular steel spars and Duralumin ribs. All the  controls were fabric-covered, with the exception of the lower portion of the rudder, which formed the tail end of the fuselage and was covered with Alclad sheeting.

Handling trials were carried out at Boscombe Down in late 1940 using N1854, N1855 and N1858 and deck landing trials took place aboard HMS *Illustrious*. Access to the cockpit was assisted by two handgrips and a non-slip walkway on the wing root, although even this became slippery when wet. The front seat was comfortable, but it was difficult to raise it from its lowest position if the pilot kept his feet on the rudder bar. The seat in the rear cockpit revolved when a spring catch was released, although there was barely enough room for the occupant's knees due to equipment stowed in various locations. The noise level in the front cockpit was high, which resulted in partial deafness after prolonged flights. The observer fared a little better in this respect, but communication between the cockpits, which was by voice pipes, was not particularly effective. Both cockpits were found to be uncomfortably hot at low altitudes and there was no apparent variation in temperature with the heat control on or off. Unlike the Battle, the cockpit floor of the Fulmar ended at the rudder bar, so that there was an open space between the rudder and engine bulkhead, through which warm air was able to enter from over the radiators. A reduction of several degrees was effected by blocking off this space with plywood sheet, but there still appeared to be no difference when the heat was set to on. Ventilation also left something to be desired, as with the hood open, exhaust heat from the manifolds entered the front cockpit, instead of the cold air that was required. The observer could either open his hood or small sliding panels to admit fresh air.

The view from the front cockpit was generally good, except when taxying, but downwards it was obstructed by the wing. No clear vision panel was fitted. The general layout of the controls was similar to the Battle. A throttle box lay conveniently to hand on the port side of the cockpit, which comprised a throttle lever in the centre with the mixture control to the left and propeller control to the right. A friction damper was fitted, which stopped the lever moving from the position it had been set. The elevator and rudder trimmer controls were located under the throttle box. The former was easy to operate, but the rudder trim was just the opposite as it consisted of a small wheel let into the cockpit side, only half of which extended into the cockpit. This was rather annoying, as the aircraft was very sensitive to directional trim, which meant that the trimmer had to be used frequently. The elevator trim indicator had an unfortunate tendency to show different readings at different heights and also altered over time, considering that the trim tab was very powerful, this was considered to be quite a serious fault.

The flap control was located on the floor to the left of the pilot, the indicator being mounted on the left-hand side of the panel. It was easy to use and the flaps could be stopped in any position. Alongside was the undercarriage control, which could not be moved to the retracted position until a 'stirrup' safety lock had been disengaged. An indicator was mounted on the panel, showing a green light for each wheel when the undercarriage was down and a red light for each when the wheels were moving up or down. A horn sounded if the throttle was cut with the undercarriage still up, but this could be deactivated, if required, by a cut-out on the throttle box. The brakes were operated hydraulically by a hand lever on the control column.

The only means by which an emergency exit could be made was by sliding the hood open. The original hood for the front cockpit was found to be far too weak and flight with it in any intermediate position was considered inadvisable above 250 mph IAS. A revised hood was then fitted, but there was no way of locking it in anything other than the fully open position. This was felt to be unsatisfactory, as the hood could not be kept closed on the ground owing to the aircraft's attitude. Should the aircraft come to rest on the ground inverted, it was extremely unlikely that the front and rear canopies could be opened and no break-out panels were fitted.

The Fulmar was flown at several loadings ranging from 8500 lb (forward CG limit) to 9800 lb (extended aft CG). The maximum over-load weight was 10,624 lb. Owing to the wide-track undercarriage, ground handling was straightforward and the aircraft showed no inclination to lift its tail even at forward CG. Taxying in crosswinds of up to 25 mph could be carried out easily. For the shortest take-off run it was normal to set 15 degrees of flap, but at most normal airfields the

Fulmar could take off without flap. It tended to swing to the left but this could easily be held by right rudder. After the tail came up a particular characteristic of the aircraft became apparent, as it was prone to 'crabbing' bodily to the left, although the aircraft was usually airborne before this could cause any major embarrassment. The take-off speed was around 63 mph IAS.

Once airborne, it was recommended that the speed be increased to 100 mph IAS before raising the flaps. By this time 200 ft had been gained, which provided a sufficient safety margin as there was appreciable sink when the flaps were raised, together with a nose-up change of trim. The undercarriage came up in about ten seconds and could be raised as soon as the aircraft was clear of the ground, as there was little trim change, but an immediate effect on forward speed. The best climb speed was 115 mph IAS up to 7000 ft thereafter decreasing by 1 mph per 1000 ft. However, the recommended speed was 125 mph IAS up to 7000 ft as the aircraft was much more comfortable to fly at this speed and the time to 20,000 ft was only one minute longer.

In level flight the elevators and ailerons were light, quick in response and effective. The rudder was light for small movements, but tended to become heavy with large movements, although it was fairly quick in operation and effective. As was to be expected, all the controls became heavier with increase of speed. One particular quirk that was noted was a 'flat spot' in the elevator control when the control column was central. The amount of trim available was just enough to cover both limits of CG.

Stability checks confirmed that the Fulmar was laterally and directionally stable at all speeds, but longitudinally it exhibited some characteristics that were very similar to the Blackburn Skua. Although it was stable with the engine on, in the climb the aircraft was unstable at 125–130 mph IAS, but not to such an extent as to make accurate speed-keeping difficult. If the speed was reduced below 115 mph IAS, however, the nose tended to come rapidly up to the stall unless firmly checked by pushing the control column forward. In the glide with the engine off, the aircraft was unstable with the flaps and undercarriage up and was even more unstable in the landing configuration. In level flight the aircraft was stable but not markedly so, even at full throttle.

The stalling speeds with the flaps and undercarriage up and down were 72 mph IAS and 61 mph IAS respectively (4 mph higher with unsealed gun ports). Very little force was required to bring about the stall, which occurred with the control column only slightly back from the central position. The only warning was a slight fore-and-aft pitching and a loss of elevator effectiveness, the stall being announced by the starboard wing dropping with a pronounced snatch of the ailerons. The wing could not be raised by the aileron and if the control column was moved further back the aircraft dropped sharply to the left, almost in a half roll, but did not spin. The stalling characteristics with the flaps and undercarriage down were very similar. Slow speed turns could be made in either direction down to 76/66 mph IAS depending on configuration, the elevator having to be used with care because of a tendency to tighten up.

The approach was normally carried out at 95 mph IAS. Lowering the flaps produced a nose-down trim change, but this could be trimmed out easily before reducing speed to 85 mph IAS prior to landing. Although the aircraft could be handled reasonably well with the engine off, it was advisable to leave a little engine on to improve the effectiveness of the rudder and elevator. In the case of a baulked landing, opening up to full power caused the aircraft to become tail heavy, although this did not cause any particular problems and it could be re-trimmed before commencing the climb.

Only two landings were possible from HMS *Illustrious*, which was sailing with an over-deck wind speed of 30 kt. Compared with other deck-landing types the Fulmar did not appear to be as stable laterally, the ailerons having to be used continuously on the approach. This was made at 78 mph IAS, although it was thought that this figure could have been lowered with more practice. About one-third throttle was maintained right down to the deck and the landing itself was straightforward. On take-off, despite commencing the run on the centreline, the Fulmar's tendency to crab to the left caused some initial concern, although it was easily airborne before there was any danger of going over the side.

Normal aerobatic manoeuvres could be carried out without difficulty. Loops were best commenced at a minimum speed of 240 mph IAS, but excessive accelerations over the top, caused by too much use of elevator, were to be avoided as the aircraft was liable to flick out in a half roll. When carrying out an intentional half roll off the top of a loop, the entry speed had to be increased to 280 mph IAS. Slow rolls could be made in either direction from an initial speed of 160 mph IAS. Coarse rudder was needed during the last quarter of the roll to prevent the nose from dropping. When inverted, the engine tended to cut out but this could be overcome by 'falling out' of the manoeuvre slightly, as in a barrel roll.

A number of spins were carried out, with entry being made from a gliding turn. If the aircraft was stalled in a gliding turn in either direction, the left wing would drop, followed by a spin with the nose well down and a high rate of rotation. After the first turn the aircraft was reluctant to continue its rotation, unless pro-spin controls were maintained, and as soon as the controls were set for recovery, the spin ceased. Although the recovery began immediately, due to the steep nose-down attitude a good deal of height was lost, and even an incipient spin would result in height loss of 2–3000 ft. Spins to the right were possible, but it was difficult to overcome the aircraft's inclination to spin to the left.

Diving trials involved N1855 at a take-off weight of 9800 lb. A total of six dives were made with three different throttle positions (fully open, one-third open and closed) and dive angles of 30, 50, 60 and 90 degrees. The highest speed recorded was 415 mph IAS in a 90-degree dive from 16,000 ft. The aircraft was trimmed to fly level at full throttle before the dive was entered by half-rolling and pulling through into the vertical. It was extremely steady in the dive and only slight forward pressure was required to maintain the desired angle, together with slight pressure on the rudder. As the limit was approached (435 mph IAS) the ailerons and rudder became very heavy, but the elevator remained reasonably light throughout. An attempt was made to apply a 10-degree yaw in the dive, but this proved to be impossible because of the heaviness of the rudder control. Recovery from the dive was commenced at 5500 ft and was complete by the time that 4000 ft was reached, with a maximum acceleration in the pull-out of 4 g. During this series of dives, minor damage was caused to the starboard side and bottom engine cowlings. The cover for the rear ammunition box was also torn off.

The overall assessment of the Fulmar was that it was easy and pleasant to fly. However, because of its relatively low top speed and modest rate of climb and service ceiling, it could not be compared with land-based fighters of the day. Although it was fairly manoeuvrable at low to medium speeds, it was completely outclassed by the Hurricane due to the heaviness of its ailerons in a dive. The Fulmar's forward-firing armament was adequate for its role, but since there was no rear-mounted gun, the top speed needed to be improved (as a wartime expedient some aircraft were fitted with a Vickers 'K' 0.303-in gas-operated machine-gun in the rear cockpit).

Climbing trials were carried out using N1858 powered by a Merlin VIII driving a Rotol variable-pitch propeller of 11 ft 6 in diameter. The best rate of climb was 1220 ft/min at a full throttle height of 7000 ft which was attained in six minutes. The greatest height reached was 21,600 ft and the absolute ceiling was estimated at 23,700 ft. The full results were as follows:

| Height | 1000 ft | 3000 ft | 5000 ft | 6500 ft | 10,000 ft |
|---|---|---|---|---|---|
| Rate of climb – ft/min | 1120 | 1155 | 1185 | 1210 | 1000 |
| Time from start – min | 0.9 | 2.7 | 4.4 | 5.6 | 8.8 |

| Height | 13,000 ft | 15,000 ft | 16,500 ft | 18,000 ft | 20,000 ft |
|---|---|---|---|---|---|
| Rate of climb – ft/min | 780 | 635 | 530 | 420 | 270 |
| Time from start – min | 12.2 | 14.9 | 17.6 | 20.7 | 26.6 |

Take-off and level-speed trials were also performed by N1858. The take-off run was 320 yards when converted to zero wind and ISA conditions, with 510 yards being needed to clear 50 ft. The top speed was 246.5 mph TAS at a full throttle height of 9000 ft. The full results were as follows:

| Height | 1000 ft | 3000 ft | 5000 ft | 6500 ft | 10,000 ft |
|---|---|---|---|---|---|
| TAS – mph | 216.5 | 224 | 231.5 | 237 | 245 |
| IAS – mph | 214 | 215.5 | 216 | 216.5 | 212 |

| Height | 13,000 ft | 15,000 ft | 16,500 ft | 18,000 ft | 20,000 ft |
|---|---|---|---|---|---|
| TAS – mph | 240 | 236 | 232.5 | 227.5 | 220 |
| IAS – mph | 198 | 188 | 181 | 172 | 160.5 |

Further speed trials were undertaken by N1854, which was flown at a take-off weight of 10,620 lb using 100 octane fuel and with the engine boosted to +9 lb/sq.in instead of the more normal +4 lb/sq.in. Its low-level performance was improved and at 1000 ft a top speed of 250 mph TAS was recorded. The maximum speed was 255.5 mph TAS at a full throttle height of 2400 ft but above this height performance was gradually reduced so that parity with N1858 was reached at 10,000 ft.

The Fulmar I entered service with No. 808 Squadron at Worthy Down in June 1940 and a total of 250 were to be produced. Subsequent aircraft were designated Fulmar II and were powered by a Merlin XXX of 1300 hp. Other changes included a revised Rotol propeller, a tropicalised radiator and oil cooler, and a fully mass-balanced rudder. The prototype Fulmar II was N4021, a converted Mark I, which was flown for the first time on 20 January 1941.

During early testing of the Fulmar II, the rudder, which was not then fully mass-balanced, was suspected of being responsible for an aircraft breaking up in a dive. The mass-balance was therefore increased and diving trials were carried out at Boscombe Down using N4079 in order to assess its suitability. The range of the elevator and rudder trimmers was also checked, since early flights had suggested that these might not be adequate. The aircraft was dived to 415 mph IAS at both forward and extended aft CG (although the maximum permissible diving speed was 435 mph IAS, it was thought that this speed would not be achieved in service due to excessive height loss). In the dive, rudder was applied in both directions. The aircraft behaved normally with no vibration or control surface instability and it was also found to have sufficient elevator and rudder trim for all conditions of flight. As a result of the trial, the fully mass-balanced rudder was cleared for use on production aircraft.

Fuel consumption trials were carried out with N4021, which showed a maximum still air range of approximately 950 miles from a total fuel capacity of 155 gallons. This was obtained with a weak mixture at 5000 ft using 1600 rpm and 2 lb/sq.in boost. The speed was 142 mph IAS, which was a little lower than the best speed for comfortable control. This was achieved at 150 mph IAS with 1650 rpm and 1.2 lb/sq.in, but the range was slightly reduced at 925 miles. The maximum endurance was 6.18 hours. Further consumption trials were made with X8641, fitted with a jettisonable 60-gallon overload fuel tank under the fuselage near the wing trailing edge. The maximum still air range was found to be 1100 miles at 5000 ft and 140 mph IAS (1750 rpm, 0 lb/sq.in boost) with an endurance of 7 hours.

Further Fulmar trials involved N1859 for radiator suitability, cockpit heating and CO contamination tests, X8756 for Identification Friend or Foe (IFF) tests and N4079 for flame damping investigations with triple ejector fishtail exhausts (with and without anti-glow paint). X8757 was also used for brief handling tests with a small bomb container fitted under the fuselage loaded with three 65-lb bombs. A bomb release was made at 243 mph IAS at a height of 50 ft in a shallow dive without any alteration to basic handling.

Two Fulmar IIs (N4016 and N4079) were also used for Rocket Assisted Take-Off Gear (RATOG) trials at RAE Farnborough from May to July 1941 and again in July 1942. It was hoped that the aircraft could be airborne within 300 ft at a take-off weight of 9800 lb. The rocket used was a standard 3 in type. The rocket carrier was fitted to the standard catapult spools and was designed to take up to six rockets on each side, which were arranged to fire slightly downwards with respect to the aircraft's axis. A plate was fitted between the aircraft and the rockets to minimise the effects of a possible burst rocket. After take-off, the carrier could be jettisoned by a device incorporated in the rear spool, the carrier then rotating through 30 degrees about the front spools before falling away. Modifications to the aircraft were few, comprising the various electrical connections, together with a firing control unit and switchbox.

The take-off was begun in the normal way and when a speed of about 20 knots had been reached, the pilot pressed the firing button mounted on top of the throttle lever. The rockets then fired at pre-determined intervals so long as the firing button was kept depressed. During tests with N4079 at a take-off weight of 10,580 lb, take-off runs were achieved well within the limit set and with a 5-knot headwind the aircraft was airborne in only 55 ft. Acceleration levels were in the order of 2 g. The behaviour of the aircraft on a rocket assisted take-off was normal in every way and it was considered that a pilot of average experience would have little difficulty. The trials also showed that rocket blast on aircraft parked directly behind was negligible and RATOG was also feasible on the wooden decks of auxiliary carriers, assuming that the decks had been hosed down beforehand.

The Fulmar provided a much-needed boost to the FAA's capability in the early years of the Second World War. It was not superseded until 1943, when it was replaced by the Seafire. It was first in action against the *Regia Aeronautica* in the Mediterranean during the protection of convoys heading for Malta, destroying ten Italian bombers between September and October 1940. Fulmars were also involved in providing cover for the Taranto operation in November 1940, during which they shot down six defending fighters, and fought in the defence of Crete in March 1941. By this time, Fulmars were serving far and wide, providing cover for Russian convoys as well as air defence over Ceylon, which was threatened with invasion by the Japanese. In addition to continued duty in Malta, Fulmars were also active in North Africa defending the Suez Canal zone and later were involved in Operation *Torch*, the Allied invasion of Algeria and Morocco in November 1942. The Fulmar remained in first-line service in small numbers until the end of the war, its heavy armament and excellent endurance being put to good use as a night-fighter protecting Arctic convoys.

# CHAPTER SIX

# Hawker
# Tornado/Typhoon

A s the Hurricane was the culmination of a design theme extending back to the 1920s, Hawker's next fighter, designed to meet Specification F.18/37, had to be much more radical. Although the centre and front fuselage featured the familiar tubular construction with detachable panels for maintenance purposes, the rear fuselage aft of the cockpit was of stressed skin construction and was attached to the forward section at four points. The wings consisted of two built-up box spars and ribs, the whole covered with flush-riveted Alclad sheet. The wing exhibited a modest crank with 1 degree of anhedral on the inner section, changing to 5½ degrees dihedral on the outer section. A wide-track, inward-retracting undercarriage was located at the point of wing crank, the outer wings being designed to house a total of twelve 0.303 in Browning machine-guns, although this armament fit was soon dropped in favour of four 20-mm Hispano cannon. Two versions were proposed, the Tornado with a Rolls-Royce Vulture 24-cylinder 'X' layout engine and the Typhoon, powered by a 24-cylinder Napier Sabre sleeve-valve engine. Both units had the potential of producing around 2000 hp. As each engine was still a long way from being fully developed, two very similar prototypes were ordered as insurance against one being a failure.

Development problems with the Napier Sabre engine meant that the Tornado was the first to take to the air, when Philip Lucas flew the prototype (P5219) on 6 October 1939. Early flight testing went well until the aircraft was flown at speeds approaching its design maximum of 400 mph, when excessive drag was experienced at the exit of the radiator, which was mounted under the centre section. This problem was eventually solved by moving the radiator under the nose, a position also adopted for the Typhoon. The latter joined its stablemate in the air on 24 February 1940, but the first aircraft (P5212) was very nearly lost on 9 May when a failure occurred in the rear fuselage monocoque where it joined the cockpit section. Rather than bale out, Philip Lucas elected to stay with his stricken aircraft and carried out a successful landing, for which he was subsequently awarded the George Medal.

The second Tornado (P5224) was flown on 5 December 1940 and, together with P5219, was fitted with a Vulture V of 1980 hp early the following year in place of the original 1760 hp Vulture II. P5224 was eventually delivered to A&AEE in late 1941 for performance and handling trials. This was some time after a similar assessment had been carried out on the Typhoon, as the Vulture engine had also hit serious development problems. Flying was carried out at an all-up weight of 10,690 lb at a CG 11.6 in forward of datum (the design limits were 12.6 in to 9.6 in forward of datum).

The recommended flap setting on take-off was 30 degrees, with the tail trim set slightly forward of central (slightly nose heavy) and with rudder bias halfway to the full left position. Even so, there was a strong tendency to swing to the right, which became very pronounced as full throttle was reached, but this could easily be held by applying left rudder. For take-off, the tail could be easily raised with only a small throttle opening. Retraction of the undercarriage produced noticeable tail heaviness, which could be held before re-trimming, but there was no trim change when the flaps were raised. Sufficient rudder bias was available to trim the aircraft 'feet off' in the climb.

The handling characteristics were virtually identical to the Typhoon, although the Tornado appeared to have greater longitudinal stability. All normal aerobatics could be performed without difficulty and dives were made up to 450 mph IAS. The aircraft was very pleasant to fly in MS gear, but a rather disconcerting vibration was felt in FS gear, which was at its worst at maximum power. The source of this vibration could not be determined, but it was less apparent when flying with a weak fuel mixture. If the throttle was opened very slowly, the engine would run smoothly for about thirty seconds before the vibration recommenced. This particular phenomenon was of considerable concern and it was belived that, in time, it might have a serious effect on the aircraft's structure. Similar high-frequency vibra- tion had also been experienced with the Typhoon and although modifications to the engine mountings reduced this characteristic, it was not entirely eradicated.

The stall speed with flaps and undercarriage up was 82 mph IAS, reducing to 61 mph IAS with flaps and undercarriage down. Characteristics at the stall were similar to the Typhoon, but the actual stall speeds were considerably lower. The best approach speed was 90 mph IAS and the landing was straightforward and easy to perform.

As P5224 was only at A&AEE for a limited period, climbing trials consisted of one climb in MS gear and one in FS gear. The results were combined to produce the Tornado's climb performance with supercharger gear being changed at 10,000 ft. The maximum rate of climb was found to be 3500 ft/min up to full throttle height in MS gear at 3200 ft and the time to reach 20,000 ft was 7.2 minutes. The full throttle height in FS gear was 16,800 ft which was achieved in 5.8 minutes with a rate of climb of 2550 ft/min. The service ceiling was 34,900 ft, this height being reached in 29 minutes, by which time the rate of climb had reduced to 100 ft/min. The full results were as follows:

| Height | 1000 ft | 5000 ft | 10,000 ft | 15,000 ft | 18,000 ft |
|---|---|---|---|---|---|
| Rate of climb – ft/min | 3500 | 3250 | 2580 | 2550 | 2390 |
| Time from start – min | 0.3 | 1.4 | 3.2 | 5.1 | 6.3 |

| Height | 20,000 ft | 23,000 ft | 26,000 ft | 30,000 ft | 32,000 ft |
|---|---|---|---|---|---|
| Rate of climb – ft/min | 2120 | 1710 | 1310 | 760 | 500 |
| Time from start – min | 7.2 | 8.8 | 10.8 | 14.7 | 17.9 |

During the climb, oil-cooling requirements were met for temperate summer conditions, but not for tropical summer conditions. The performance of the radiator did not fulfil either requirement.

Level speed runs were only made in FS gear and during these trials boost was limited by the automatic boost control to 8 lb/sq.in instead of 9 lb/sq.in. Ballast was added to obtain the correct weight of 10,690 lb. The maximum speed was recorded as being 398 mph at 23,300 ft, but it was considered that had full boost been available a top speed of 400 mph would have been achieved. Other results are included in the table:

| Height | 16,500 ft | 18,000 ft | 20,000 ft | 23,300 ft |
|---|---|---|---|---|
| TAS – mph | 381 | 385 | 390 | 398 |
| IAS – mph | 313 | 309 | 303 | 292 |

| Height | 26,000 ft | 28,000 ft | 30,000 ft |
|---|---|---|---|
| TAS – mph | 392 | 387 | 381 |
| IAS – mph | 274 | 260 | 246 |

Although the Rolls-Royce Vulture performed reasonably well in the Tornado, it had also been selected to power the twin-engined Avro

Manchester bomber but suffered chronic reliability problems. The Manchester had been rushed into service in November 1940. However, a spate of engine failures did not bode well and as little improvement had been made by the middle of the following year, future contracts for the aircraft were cancelled and the decision was also taken to terminate production of the Vulture. Had the Tornado programme gone ahead, it would have been produced by Avro at its factory at Yeadon near Leeds, as Hawker was fully occupied with the Hurricane. Before cancellation, the first production Tornado (R7936) was flown on 29 August 1941. This aircraft was subsequently used for trials work with Rotol and de Havilland contra-rotating propellers. A third Tornado prototype (HG641) had also been ordered and this was flown for the first time on 23 October 1941. It was powered by a 2210 hp Bristol Centaurus CE.4S 18-cylinder radial engine and was used as a development aircraft for the Typhoon II, which became the Tempest (see Chapter 7).

With the demise of the Tornado, this left just the Typhoon, which was itself beset by development difficulties, many of which were also engine related. The first Typhoon to be tested by A&AEE was P5212, which was put through its paces as the Battle of Britain was reaching its climax. The aircraft was flown by Flight Lieutenant Sammy Wroath from the Hawker airfield at Langley near Slough, his subsequent report being generally favourable.

Access to the cockpit was via hinged 'car-type' doors on either side of the fuselage. In addition, the roof panel could also be opened. A retractable handhold was located on the outside of each door and was connected to the locking handle on the inside. This was considered to be an unsatisfactory arrangement, as it was felt that the handhold might be used by a member of the ground crew when climbing down from the wing, which could lead to the door being unlocked without the pilot being aware. A problem had already occurred during the first dive to limiting speed by Philip Lucas, when one of the handles had been sucked out by air pressure, thereby unlocking the door.

The view to either side was good, but that ahead was blocked by the engine. Of more significance was a complete lack of vision to the rear, caused by solid fairings behind the pilot's head and the fact that no rear view mirror was fitted. The curved side panels of the windscreen gave rise to some slight distortion, as did the moulded roof, which was particularly bad at the edges. Large side windows were provided, operated by a cable and sprocket gear, and these formed excellent clear view panels. However, the operating mechanism left something to be desired as it was not robust enough, and could not be shut at speeds above 250 mph IAS, as the upper edge did not enter its locating groove as a result of distortion caused by suction.

The cockpit itself was roomy and comfortable, all the flying controls could be moved freely and the rudder bar was easily adjusted. The controls for the throttle, propeller, two-speed supercharger, radiator shutter, flaps and undercarriage were all located on the left-hand side of the fuselage and fell easily to hand. The elevator and rudder trim controls were also positioned to the pilot's left but were considered to be too close to the fuselage side for easy operation. The indicators were also rather small and the readings were difficult to distinguish. There was a 'spongy' feel to the elevator trimmer, which was very sensitive and would have benefited from lower gearing. A hand pump was provided to the left of the pilot's seat in case of failure of the engine-driven hydraulic pump, and for emergency operation of the undercarriage a trip mechanism could be operated to allow the wheels to drop to the down position by gravity. The fuel cocks, switches and indicators were all located on the right-hand side of the cockpit.

The noise levels in the cockpit were very low in comparison with other fighter aircraft of the period, even when flying at limiting speed in dives, and this was considered to be one of the best features of the Typhoon. Should it be necessary to make an emergency exit, the pilot had first to release both door latches, before pulling down on a lever on each side of the cockpit to withdraw the hinge pins of the cabin doors which, together with the roof, were jettisoned. The system had been tried in the air at a speed of about 350 mph IAS and had worked well. Should the aircraft overturn on the ground, it was thought that the side doors would open sufficiently for the pilot to be able to get out.

Flight trials were carried out at a take-off weight of 10,620 lb. Ground handling was good, the Dunlop brakes operated smoothly and the aircraft showed no tendency to 'peck'. On take-off, there was a strong swing to the right, especially at full throttle, but this could be controlled by rudder, which was moderately light and effective. Prior to take-off, the rudder trim was normally set to one-half left to help counteract the swing. Although the optimum flap setting to achieve the shortest take-off run was 45–50 degrees, it was recommended that the flaps be set to 30 degrees to combine an acceptable take-off performance with reasonable safety. Once airborne, no difficulty was experienced in maintaining directional control and there was sufficient rudder bias to allow the aircraft to be climbed 'feet off'.

In level flight the aircraft was stable about all three axes, the controls being light, effective and well harmonised. Because of the torque effect of the propeller, the Typhoon was easier to bank to the right than to the left, and during tight turns, less back stick was required to maintain a turn to the right. Like the Tornado, some vibration was experienced, particularly during steep turns at about 320 mph IAS (3150 rpm, +3 lb/sq.in boost), which was attributed to the engine mountings. Some trouble was experienced with the fuel system, which consisted of four self-sealing tanks (two main tanks in the wings and two in the nose) with a total capacity of 154 gallons. When drawing fuel from the main tanks, the port tank tended to empty first, as a result of which air was sucked into the system and the engine cut. However, if the supply was quickly switched to the nose tanks, it picked up again immediately.

Several dives were made up to 475 mph IAS, during which the aircraft was extremely steady with no tendency towards wing drop so that it could be held on a target with ease. The ailerons were moderately light and effective up to this speed and there was no sign of over-balancing or snatching. The elevator and rudder controls were also moderately light and well harmonised with the ailerons, yaw being applied at speeds of 430–50 mph IAS without any sign of the rudder over-balancing. As the aircraft exhibited a degree of tail heaviness in the dive requiring a moderate push force to overcome, the level of acceleration forces on recovery was not excessive.

No comprehensive stalling tests were carried out at this stage, but stall speeds with flaps and undercarriage up and down were 88 and 70 mph IAS respectively, which were somewhat higher than the figures recorded on the Tornado. Slow speed turns could be made with ease and, with the flaps and undercarriage down, turns of 30 degree angle of bank were made down to 80 mph IAS with a low fuel load. The best speed to lower the wheels on the approach was 160 mph IAS and although this led to some fore-and-aft pitching, it was not considered serious. When in the landing configuration, the best approach speed was 100 mph IAS, with touchdown occurring at 72 mph IAS. The tail could be easily lowered and full braking did not cause any swing, neither was there any indication of nose heaviness.

The Typhoon was fitted with a de Havilland Hydromatic three-blade propeller of 14 ft diameter, but performance testing was complicated to a certain extent by a temporary limitation of 3150 rpm for the change over from MS to FS gear so that climbing trials were carried out in FS supercharger from 8000 ft. A maximum rate of climb of 2730 ft/min was achieved at full throttle height of 15,500 ft. The best climbing speed was 200 mph IAS up to 16,000 ft, reducing by 4 mph per 1000 ft thereafter. One climb was made to 29,000 ft, although this had to be abandoned owing to ignition trouble. Further testing had to be discontinued due to failure of the radiator which had to be removed for repair by the manufacturers. The estimated absolute ceiling was 33,000 ft. The full results were as follows:

| Height | 8000 ft | 10,000 ft | 13,000 ft | 15,000 ft | 18,000 ft |
|---|---|---|---|---|---|
| Rate of climb – ft/min | 2615 | 2650 | 2690 | 2725 | 2340 |
| Time from 8,000 ft – min | – | 0.75 | 1.9 | 2.6 | 3.75 |

| Height | 20,000 ft | 23,000 ft | 26,000 ft | 28,000 ft | 30,000 ft |
|---|---|---|---|---|---|
| Rate of climb – ft/min | 2020 | 1550 | 1070 | 760 | 450 |
| Time from 8,000 ft – min | 4.7 | 6.4 | 8.7 | 10.9 | 14.3 |

The take-off run was measured at 525 yards when corrected for zero wind and ISA conditions, with 845 yards being needed to clear 50 ft. In comparison with the Tornado, the Typhoon was faster by around 10 mph, with a maximum speed of 410 mph TAS at a full throttle height of 19,800 ft in FS gear. The maximum speeds were recorded from 10,000 ft.

| Height | 10,000 ft | 13,000 ft | 15,000 ft | 16,500 ft | 18,000 ft |
|---|---|---|---|---|---|
| TAS – mph | 377 | 387 | 393 | 399 | 403 |
| IAS – mph | 343.5 | 336 | 331.5 | 329 | 324.5 |

| Height | 20,000 ft | 23,000 ft |
|---|---|---|
| TAS – mph | 410 | 404 |
| IAS – mph | 320 | 300.5 |

After his experiences with P5212, Sammy Wroath compiled a reasonably favourable assessment praising in particular its speed, its light and well harmonised controls, and its relatively quiet cockpit. However, he criticised the Typhoon's lack of altitude performance, its poor rearward vision, oversensitive elevator trimmer and inadequate cockpit heating as height was gained. Problems had also been experienced with the radiator, as there had been inadequate engine cooling, even when operating in temperate conditions.

Further testing with P5212 looked at aileron response, stalling, the effect of gun-firing and behaviour in the dive. The method of testing aileron response involved placing the aircraft in a 45-degree bank, then applying one quarter opposite aileron and measuring the time taken to roll back through level flight to 45 degrees opposite bank. This particular test was carried out over a wide speed range from 240–460 mph IAS with very consistent results. The time taken varied from 4¾–5¾ seconds, which reflected the lack of heaviness of aileron control as speed was increased. Just before the stall the nose was very high with general vibration and tail buffeting. As the aircraft stalled, the starboard wing dropped sharply to an angle of about 45 degrees, followed by the nose, but there was no tendency to spin. Once the control column was moved forward, recovery was immediate and only around 300 ft in height was lost. Both the rudder and elevator remained effective up to the stall, but the ailerons began to lose their effectiveness, though they remained adequate if large angles were used.

Firing the twelve Browning machine-guns did not produce any vibration or change in handling qualities, and from the pilot's point of view their operation was hardly noticeable. On one occasion, when only the guns on the port side fired, only a very slight yaw to port was recorded. During diving trials it was found that the cabin roof opened slightly at speeds above 470 mph IAS, but even after the locking mechanism was tightened, a fractional gap could still be seen. In the dive the aircraft behaved in similar fashion to that noted in the first series of tests with the 'sponginess' of the elevator trimmer being particularly bad. The engine and propeller functioned satisfactorily, with the constant speed unit keeping rpm at 3700 throughout, and the cabin doors stayed firmly shut, unlike on some early test flights. The maximum endurance was measured at 2¼ and 1½ hours for flight at 15,000 ft and 25,000 ft respectively which, although meeting the requirements of the time, was considered to be a little disappointing.

Although the Typhoon had an impressive turn of speed at low to medium levels, it was obvious at an early stage that its thick wing was not conducive to high levels of performance at altitude. Its relatively high wing loading at 38½ lb/sq.ft also conspired against manoeuvrability. At the time that P5212 was being tested, the first examples of the Messerschmitt Bf 109F were seen in the skies over Britain. This aircraft was capable of fighting effectively at higher altitudes than its predecessor, the Bf 109E. If this trend was to be repeated in bomber design, as seemed likely with Junkers Ju 86P reconnaissance aircraft regularly flying over the UK at altitudes up to 40,000 ft, Fighter Command would have had to fight at a serious disadvantage, should attacks on the scale of the Battle of Britain be repeated. Sydney Camm was quick to offer a 'thin wing' F.18/37, which was to evolve into the Tempest, but in the meantime the RAF would have to make do with the Typhoon and more advanced versions of the Spitfire.

Despite the fact that the Typhoon was the RAF's fastest fighter by a considerable margin when it entered service with 56 Squadron in September 1941, there was no guarantee that it would remain in that position for very long, as the development programme was in serious trouble in several respects. Napier was struggling with the Sabre engine, in particular with frequent failures caused by uneven wear of the sleeve valves. Even by the end of 1942 the time between overhauls

(TBO) was still only twenty-five hours. The Typhoon was also badly affected by carbon monoxide (CO) contamination, although this tended to vary between individual aircraft. Improved sealing of the cockpit did not completely eradicate the problem and as a result pilots had to be on oxygen whenever the engine was running. There were also a worrying number of in-flight break-ups caused by failure of the rear fuselage at the transport joint. A modification programme was initiated to re-inforce this particular area, but structural failures continued to occur and were to do so throughout the Typhoon's career, albeit with reduced frequency. Other possible causes of these accidents were failure of the elevator mass-balance or elevator flutter, but a conclusive answer was never found.

For a considerable time the future of the Typhoon was in doubt, with 'pro' and 'anti' factions within Fighter Command arguing their respective cases. A suitable role was needed for the Typhoon and for a time it was considered as a night-fighter, working with twin-engined Havocs equipped with Turbinlite aerial searchlights. But the difference in speed between the two aircraft proved to be too great and the whole concept was soon abandoned. It was also suggested that the Typhoon be fitted with Airborne Interception (AI) radar and R7881 was fitted with AI.VI in early 1943. To assess the suitability of the Typhoon for night flying R7617 was delivered to Boscombe Down for testing in August 1942.

As tested, R7617 weighed 10,770 lb and was powered by a Sabre II with a fully balanced crankshaft. The instrument panel was illuminated by floodlights low down on each side of the cockpit, with dimmer switches being fitted on the panel itself. The compass had its own light with a dimmer. Landing lights were located in each leading edge and could be dipped by a lever fitted to the engine control box. Unfortunately, the cockpit lights tended to dazzle the pilot and cause reflections, but when the intensity was lowered to overcome this there was then insufficient light to read the instruments. In addition, the fuselage to the side of the pilot was not illuminated so that the elevator and rudder trimmers were in darkness.

It was almost impossible to see through the curved side panels of the windscreen at night and the view directly forward was only moderate, but with the side windows wound down the pilot could see adequately to the side and down. When flying at full throttle, the exhaust could be seen as a yellowish-blue flame if the pilot moved his head to one side, but it did not interfere significantly with his night vision. The Typhoon's stability in the air made night flying relatively easy, the greatest difficulty being experienced on landing, owing to the poor forward view, which meant that the aircraft had to be put down further to one side of the flare path than was usual with other types. In the event, R7881 was the only Typhoon to be fitted with AI radar, as by mid 1943 the night-fighter role was being adequately fulfilled by the Mosquito, which offered only marginally reduced performance, but with the advantages of greater endurance, twin engines and a two-man crew to share the workload.

In December 1942 Typhoon IB R7673 arrived at A&AEE for spinning trials to determine the best method of recovery. The take-off weight was 11,040 lb and the aircraft was in full operational trim apart from lacking an aerial mast and aerials. Spins were made to the right and left from 15,000 ft and 25,000 ft, the method of entry being from a turn at a speed of about 95 mph IAS. When spinning to the left from 15,000 ft, the aircraft was reasonably steady, although some fore-and-aft pitching was apparent. The rate of rotation was considered to be rather slow for such a heavy aircraft with a high wing loading, the nose position being well below the horizon. On the first spin full opposite rudder was applied after two turns, followed by a slow forward movement of the control column, but after three more turns there was still no sign of recovery. The throttle was therefore opened, whereupon the aircraft responded immediately. Two more spins were made to the left and on both occasions recovery commenced as soon as anti-spin controls were applied, leading to the assumption that in the first case 'full' opposite rudder had not been quite full enough. The total height loss in a two-turn spin, including recovery, was 3300 ft. Spins to the right were very similar, except that the height loss was around 3800 ft.

Spins to the left from 25,000 ft were very much the same as those carried out at the lower height, but spins to the right were somewhat different. On entering the spin, the nose fell below the horizon, as was to be expected, but it then rose again so that after one turn it was above the horizon. As the aircraft commenced its second turn the nose fell once more, after which a recovery was attempted but without success as the nose stayed down and the rate of rotation increased. There was also considerable 'kicking' on the rudder control. In this instance the use of engine was not attempted as opening the throttle would only cause the aircraft to yaw to the right, i.e. into the spin. Instead, the control column was moved backwards and forwards in an attempt to make the aircraft pitch. Although this appeared to have no effect initially, a slow recovery was commenced after about another three turns. Considerable height was lost during this procedure, level flight eventually being regained at 17,000 ft.

By mid 1942 the Typhoon was in service with Nos 56, 266 and 609 Squadrons of the Duxford Wing and was also replacing Hurricanes with Nos. 1, 257 and 486 Squadrons. As the only aircraft at the time capable of catching the Focke-Wulf Fw 190A, which was being used for low-level hit-and-run raids on coastal towns, it was important to have precise figures for climb and level-speed performance. In addition, an Fw 190 had just been presented to the RAF by an errant *Luftwaffe* pilot and was thus available for comparison. R7700 was used to assess the Typhoon's capabilities, the trials being carried out from June to September 1942. The aircraft was powered by a Sabre II of 2180 hp and was fitted with a transparent fairing to the rear of the cockpit instead of the solid fairing, which had been the subject of much criticism. The maximum permissible settings for the Sabre II at the time of testing were 3500 rpm, +6 lb/sq.in (climb); and 3700 rpm, +7 lb/sq.in (level flight, limited to five minutes).

The aircraft was climbed to 31,000 ft with the radiator shutter open at the best climb speed, which was 185 mph IAS decreasing by 3 mph per 1000 ft above 16,000 ft. The supercharger was changed from MS to FS gear at 12,600 ft. The maximum rate of climb was 2790 ft/min in MS gear at 6300 ft and 2000 ft/min in FS gear at 17,800 ft. The service ceiling was estimated to be 32,200 ft with an absolute ceiling of 33,000 ft. Other results were as follows:

| Height | 2000 ft | 4000 ft | 6000 ft | 10,000 ft | 14,000 ft |
|---|---|---|---|---|---|
| Rate of climb – ft/min | 2790 | 2790 | 2790 | 2320 | 2000 |
| Time from start – min | 0.7 | 1.45 | 2.2 | 3.7 | 5.6 |

| Height | 18,000 ft | 20,000 ft | 24,000 ft | 28,000 ft | 32,000 ft |
|---|---|---|---|---|---|
| Rate of climb – ft/min | 1,970 | 1,710 | 1,180 | 660 | 130 |
| Time from start – min | 7.6 | 8.7 | 11.5 | 15.95 | 28.5 |

The maximum speed performance in level flight was tested with radiator shutters in the closed position and in MS gear the best figure achieved was 376 mph TAS at 8500 ft with 394 mph TAS being recorded in FS gear at 20,200 ft. Other speeds at selected heights were as follows:

| Height | 1000 ft | 2000 ft | 4000 ft | 10,000 ft | 14,000 ft |
|---|---|---|---|---|---|
| TAS – mph | 345.5 | 349.5 | 357.5 | 375 | 370 |
| IAS – mph | 362 | 362 | 359.5 | 344 | 317.5 |

| Height | 18,000 ft | 20,000 ft | 22,000 ft | 24,000 ft | 26,000 ft |
|---|---|---|---|---|---|
| TAS – mph | 384 | 393.5 | 391 | 384 | 371 |
| IAS – mph | 309 | 306.5 | 293.5 | 278 | 258.5 |

On 19 August 1942 the Duxford Wing took part in the ill-fated Dieppe operation. One Dornier Do 217 was claimed destroyed for the loss of two Typhoons of No. 266 Squadron. Several important lessons were learned after this particular shambles, one of which was that overwhelming tactical air power would be necessary if an invasion of Northern France was to stand any chance of success. The desperate need for fighter-bombers was to put an end, once and for all, to the calls for the Typhoon to be taken out of service. From the beginning of 1943 its role was to be geared very much towards ground attack, initially with 250-lb and 500-lb bombs mounted on racks under the wings, but ultimately with 1000-lb bombs. Trials were carried out at Boscombe Down in September 1942, to determine whether carrying underwing stores affected the aircraft's handling characteristics.

The aircraft used, Typhoon IB R7646, was flown with 500-lb medium case bombs on faired racks, although it was also tested with the fairings removed. With both bombs and fairings in place, the take-off weight was 12,155 lb. The first tests were made with bomb racks and fairings but no bombs, to check for vibration which had been experienced on all aircraft previously flown by the establishment. Vibration levels were found to be more pronounced but, in addition, a further vibration was felt which had not been noted on other aircraft. This occurred only at speeds between 110–140 mph IAS with the engine throttled right back and with flaps and undercarriage up, and was quite violent, being felt throughout the aircraft. It was not experienced with the engine on, or with flaps and undercarriage down, and there was also a marked reduction when the flaps were lowered by 20 degrees.

With two 500-lb bombs in place on faired racks the take-off run was noticeably longer, but the characteristics were generally the same, except that any bouncing or bucketing was slightly more pronounced. In the air, the handling was very much the same, although lateral control was rather heavier and vibration levels were more intense, which made the aircraft unpleasant to fly. At climbing speed the aircraft was unstable, becoming just stable at cruising speed and stable at maximum speed. It was also stable when gliding on the approach with the flaps and undercarriage down. The stalling characteristics were also similar, although the actual speeds were, as expected, a little higher at 93 mph IAS and 70 mph IAS respectively with the flaps and undercarriage up and down. With the aircraft trimmed for maximum level speed, dives were carried out up to 400 mph IAS. Up to 350 mph IAS the Typhoon's behaviour was normal, but above this speed buffeting was experienced. This was slight at first but tended to increase with speed and was quite marked between 380–400 mph IAS, although as it did not affect the steadiness of the aircraft, it was considered acceptable. The left wing tended to drop with increases in speed and the ailerons became slightly heavier, but, even at limiting speed, control remained good. The speed performance in level flight at 8000 ft with two 500-lb bombs was 336 mph IAS, which was 36 mph IAS less than that achieved with the aircraft in the clean configuration.

The aircraft was also flown with a bomb carried under the port wing only, to assess the handling characteristics in the asymmetric condition. When the starboard bomb was dropped at 240 mph IAS, the pilot could hardly detect when it left the aircraft as there was no immediate change in lateral trim. At moderate to fast speeds the aircraft was only slightly out of trim (left wing low), there was no tendency to overbank to the left, nor was any difficulty experienced in banking quickly to the right. At slower speeds the effect of the asymmetric load became more pronounced and at speeds near the stall, or on the approach glide, the stick had to be held over to the right to keep the port wing up.

The characteristics at the stall were the same as with both bombs attached and even with the bomb on the port wing, the right wing still tended to drop. In the dive the Typhoon's behaviour was very similar to the two-bomb case, except that there was slightly less buffeting. The aircraft was not landed in the asymmetric condition, but it was felt that the level of control was sufficient in an emergency. However, it was recommended that the aircraft be put down on a runway to avoid the possibility of a bounce causing the left wing to drop, as there might not be enough aileron control to raise it. The aircraft was also flown with a single bomb under the starboard wing with similar results. When flown without fairings fitted, the Typhoon handled in similar fashion, except in the dive when a slight but continuous pitching set in above 300 mph IAS, together with slight lateral and directional instability, which made it impossible to keep the aircraft steady. This became worse with increase in speed and the dive was discontinued at 360 mph IAS.

Just as the Tornado had been intended for production by Avro, the Typhoon was produced by Gloster, another firm in the Hawker Siddeley group of companies, at its factory at Hucclecote. The Typhoon continued to be developed throughout its life, in particular the hood, which was revised several times. The final design incorporated a sliding 'bubble' canopy in place of the original doors, which were often likened to those from an Austin 7 car. To reduce drag, the aerial mast was replaced by a whip aerial and fairings were added to the cannon barrels and exhausts. Late production machines also featured a four-blade de Havilland propeller, which was tested on DN340 at A&AEE in September 1943. Particular attention was paid to longitudinal and directional stability and control as adverse comments had been received from the squadrons.

The characteristics on take-off were similar to those of previous

Typhoons, except that the swing to the right appeared to be slightly less strong. Directional stability was tested in the climb by trimming the aircraft and then displacing the rudder through a small distance in either direction, to see if it would return to its original position when released. But in the event, it tended to remain in the displaced position and the aircraft would skid along with the nose about 3 degrees removed from the direction of travel. When larger rudder displacements were made, the nose made some effort to return to the trimmed state, but tended to take up the same position noted above. In terms of longitudinal stability, if the elevator was moved to give a speed change of around 10 mph IAS and then released, a sharp divergence in speed, either up or down, occurred.

The instability in yaw and pitch was also apparent in cruising flight up to 230 mph IAS, after which the effect decreased with speed, although it was still present to some extent even at maximum speed. Turns without the use of rudder showed no sign of tightening, although stick force was very light, but if right rudder was used in a turn to the right the aircraft did tighten up due to the gyroscopic forces of the propeller. DN340 was only dived to 450 mph IAS instead of its limiting speed of 525 mph IAS due to bad weather. As the instability tended to decrease with speed, high-speed dives were not too much of a problem, the aircraft tending to return to its trimmed position when the rudder was displaced. However, rudder trimming was found to be very sensitive and a change in yaw produced a most unpleasant fore-and-aft pitching motion.

The four-blade propeller brought about a big improvement in the level of vibration, which significantly reduced, although there was a regular engine 'beat' about once every second between 2900–3200 rpm. Although stability had worsened slightly, the reduced level of vibration far outweighed this. However, it was felt that the tendency to skid might introduce difficulties as regards aiming at a target. As part of the investigations into structural break ups, it had been proposed to fit an inertia weight to the Typhoon's control column and this system had already been tested on R7700. It was found that the high levels of vibration experienced on this aircraft were transmitted via the weight to the pilot's hand on the stick. This was considered unacceptable, but the reduced vibration with the four-blade propeller meant that this complaint was no longer valid and later aircraft were fitted with an inertia weight and a carefully mass-balanced elevator (late production Typhoons were also fitted with the enlarged Tempest tail to improve longitudinal stability, especially when carrying two 1000-lb bombs).

The Typhoon was to be fitted with a wide variety of underwing stores, including smoke bombs, long-range tanks, anti-personnel bombs and napalm. However, it will forever be remembered for its use of one particular weapon, the 3 in rocket projectile or RP, a rather crude, simple device that could pack a devastating punch. Each rocket consisted of a 3 in diameter cast iron pipe containing the propellant, with four cruciform stabilising fins at one end and a 60-lb semi-armour piercing warhead at the other.

In April 1944, brief handling trials were performed by EK497 at Boscombe Down at a take-off weight of 12,245 lb with eight RP in place. In many areas the RP installation did not affect the handling characteristics; the take-off, although noticeably longer, was similar and the controls were not adversely affected in any way. Longitudinal stability was actually improved over that of the clean aircraft, which made it more pleasant to fly. This was due to a forward shift in CG of approximately 1½ in when RPs were fitted. Stall speeds of 95 mph IAS and 78 mph IAS were recorded with the gear up and down, the nose and starboard wing dropping, as was to be expected. Recovery was immediate on relaxation of back pressure on the control column.

Dives were made up to 480 mph IAS with the engine set to 3500 rpm, +6 lb/sq.in boost and the aircraft trimmed for level flight. Very little buffeting was experienced, which was in marked contrast to the carriage of other stores where buffet had been the limiting factor. Owing to additional drag over that of the clean aircraft, acceleration in the dive was extremely slow, especially at speeds above 450 mph IAS. It was this that imposed a practical limit of 480 mph IAS, rather than any undesirable handling characteristics. When approaching to land, it was recommended that a speed of 110 mph IAS be used, which was 5 mph above that for a clean aircraft.

The vibration levels encountered with EK497 were extremely bad and were well above the average in intensity. It was present over the whole range of engine speeds and was especially noticeable when any force was applied to the control column. However, this was not considered to be due in any way to the presence of the RP installation, rather that the machine being used was inherently worse than the norm. A&AEE stated that it was 'most unsatisfactory' that Gloster should deliver an aircraft for service in such a condition.

The tactics used by RP Typhoons depended to a large extent on the type of target. When attacking concentrations of tanks, gun positions, observation posts and the like, a dive of around 60 degrees would be commenced from 8000 ft, with the rockets being fired in a salvo when passing around 4000 ft. For attacks against smaller targets such as individual tanks, a shallow dive of about 25 degrees would be used from an initial height of 3500 ft, the rockets being ripple-fired when the range had decreased to 500–1000 yards. The Typhoon's steadiness in the dive made it an excellent launch platform, but wind drift and gravity drop would tend to compound pilot-induced errors caused by any slight pitch or yaw of the aircraft at the point of firing. In addition to the actual destruction caused by the rocket-firing Typhoons, their use severely restricted the movement of German forces in daylight hours and also had a profound effect on the morale of the *Wehrmacht*.

With the invasion of Northern France in June 1944 the Typhoon came into its own and was to be the premier Allied fighter-bomber for the rest of the war. It was often employed in 'Cab Rank' patrols over the front line, to be called down at any time to deliver its massive firepower of two 500/1000-lb bombs or eight 60-lb RPs and four 20-mm Hispano cannon. It was also to achieve fame in several famous actions, none more so than that at Falaise in Normandy.

On 7 August 1944 the German 7th Army launched an attack from Mortain, comprising four *Panzer* divisions to split the American forces, but the Allies had already been forewarned by Ultra decrypts and the full weight of tactical air power was soon unleashed. The advance quickly faltered and turned into a retreat, which, by 15 August was centred on Falaise. It was here that the rocket-firing Typhoons began to decimate the German Tiger tanks, which were trapped in a relatively small pocket, unable to move. Nowhere was the devastating effect of the Typhoon's 'aerial artillery' demonstrated more clearly and less than 10 per cent of the tanks committed to battle were to escape. In addition to close support duties, the Typhoons of 2nd Tactical Air Force ranged well behind the front line on interdiction sorties, attacking transport and communications as well as 'high value' targets such as bridges and enemy HQ buildings.

Although the Typhoon was less than successful as an interceptor, it was to find its true role as a fighter-bomber. Its subsequent record vindicated those who had supported its continued existence in the face of numerous attempts to kill it off by the 'Spitfire lobby' and factions within Engineering. Ironically, the Germans were to play a role in saving the Typhoon. For a period of twelve months (until the arrival of the Spitfire IX in appreciable numbers in late 1942), it was the only aircraft on the RAF's inventory capable of dealing with the Focke-Wulf Fw 190A, which was becoming an increasing embarrassment in the low-level *Jabo* role. Having survived into 1943, the technical difficulties that afflicted the Typhoon were gradually overcome and it was ready to take its place in history. Although 3330 Typhoons were built, only one (MN235) has survived and is currently displayed at the RAF Museum at Hendon.

CHAPTER SEVEN

# Hawker Tempest

The Hawker Tempest was, perhaps, what the Typhoon should have been all along. Although the Typhoon had the potential for very high performance, its relatively thick wing (19.5 per cent thickness/chord ratio at the root and 12 per cent at the tip) made for handling difficulties at the top end of the speed range, due to excessive drag rise and the formation of localised shock waves which, especially during high-speed dives, could lead to loss of control. The development of a thinner wing section as early as 1940 was considered, but it was not until the following year that work finally got under way. The thickness/chord ratio was reduced to 14.5 per cent at the wing root and 10 per cent at the tip and the maximum wing thickness now occurred at 37.5 per cent chord, instead of 30 per cent as on the Typhoon. The wing's profile was also altered to semi-elliptical.

As the internal wing space had been considerably reduced, fuel now had to be accommodated elsewhere and the front fuselage was extended by 21 in to allow a 76-gallon tank to be inserted between the engine firewall and the oil tank, which was situated immediately in front of the cockpit. To compensate for the extended forward fuselage, a fillet was added to increase the fin area and the horizontal tail surfaces were also of increased span and chord. A revised undercarriage was incorporated, the main wheels now being fully covered when retracted. The tailwheel was also retractable. The name initially given to the new fighter was Typhoon II, but by mid 1942 this had been changed to Tempest, reflecting the large number of changes incorporated in the design. Furthermore, as the Typhoon's future was still in doubt at the time, a change of name was beneficial in that it tended to disassociate the new aircraft from its troubled predecessor.

Continuing difficulties with the Napier Sabre engine meant that it was necessary to consider alternative powerplants, namely the Bristol Centaurus 18-cylinder radial that was under development, and the Rolls-Royce Griffon. To simplify the various engine options, Mark numbers were allocated as follows: Mark I (Sabre IV), Mark II (Centaurus IV), Mark III (Griffon IIB), Mark IV (Griffon 61), Mark V

(Sabre II). In the event, neither of the Griffon-engined prototypes were completed, although one (LA610) later appeared as a Fury with a Griffon 85 and contra-props. The Tempest I was also abandoned as the Sabre IV was far from being fully developed, but only after the first flight of the prototype (HM599) on 24 February 1943. Before the axe fell, performance testing showed it to have a top speed of 466 mph at 24,500 ft, due in no small part to its reduced frontal area as a result of Sydney Camm's decision to use wing-mounted radiators.

The first Tempest to fly was the Mark V prototype (HM595) on 2 September 1942 and the following February the aircraft was delivered to Boscombe Down for preliminary performance measurements by A&AEE test pilots. It was looked upon favourably and was considered to be manoeuvrable and pleasant to fly, although the elevator appeared to be rather heavy. A full handling assessment was carried out on the third production Tempest V (JN731) over a five-week period commencing on 25 October 1943 with a typical service loading of 11,480 lb, including service equipment and full internal fuel (132 gallons).

Entry to the cockpit was made from the starboard side and involved a certain amount of mountaineering, the pilot being provided with a foot stirrup, handhold and two retractable steps in the side of the fuselage. Access was relatively easy, although the handhold was a little on the high side and a jump was necessary to be able to reach it. The seat had a sprung back and the seating position was comfortable, with all the essential controls coming nicely to hand when the pilot was strapped in. The height of the seat could be adjusted by a lever located on the right-hand side of the cockpit. Cold air was available through two small ventilators, one on each side of the panel. Hot air was supplied via two pipes near the pilot's feet. The aircraft was reasonably quiet in flight, although a high-pitched note or resonance was apparent, which made it fatiguing to fly for long periods. Otherwise, the aircraft was free from excessive vibration at all speeds and engine settings.

The windscreen and hood were a big improvement on the arrangement previously seen on early Typhoons. Although the windscreen had a narrower centre panel, the solid members between this and the two side panels were much thinner. The 'bubble' hood had no obstructions and was almost completely free from distortion, giving an excellent view in flight. On the ground, the view forwards was completely obstructed by the engine cowling, but in flight the nose attitude was well down, allowing the pilot to see directly ahead. There was no clear view panel, but the hood could be opened via a rotating lever up to 250 mph IAS, although at this speed it was not an easy task.

In an emergency, the hood could be jettisoned by pulling on a red-painted handle located to the bottom right of the cockpit, a panel in the right-hand side of the fuselage coming away at the same time. The position of the jettison lever forced the pilot to lean forward so that his head was well clear when the hood departed. Should the aircraft over-turn on the ground, the armour plate behind the pilot's head provided protection, and with the canopy open or jettisoned, it was considered that the pilot should have been able to vacate the cockpit in most normal circumstances. However, if the canopy had been locked in an intermediate position, it could not be opened from outside and it was felt that this facility should be deleted.

Ground handling of the Tempest was relatively easy; the brakes were smooth in action and turns could be made in either direction. Take-offs were normally made with the flaps in the up position, and with elevator and rudder trimmers set to 'take-off' and 'full left' respectively. With these settings, the tail could be raised quite early in the run. The aircraft tended to swing to the right, but this could be held with moderate left rudder. Stability on take-off was good, even on grass, with very little pitching being experienced, a moderate backward pressure being needed on the control column to lift the aircraft off the ground. The undercarriage could be raised immediately after take-off, producing a slight change of trim to tail heavy, but this could easily be held. The climb away was reasonably steep.

In flight, the ailerons were pleasantly light at slow speeds and on the glide, but were heavier at normal flying speed, although they remained smooth and progressive in action. Despite an increase in heaviness with speed, the ailerons could still be moved to a useful extent, even up to the limiting speed of 550 mph IAS. However, control was not good and the rates of roll obtained were fairly low. The elevator control proved to be light, effective and smooth in operation at all normal flying speeds, except on the glide with the flaps and undercarriage down, when control became less effective with rather sluggish response. The rudder was quite heavy at all times. This was not too much of a hindrance as it was little used, although it became rather more notice-able if the aircraft was out of trim directionally.

The Tempest gave the impression of being unstable longitudinally, as it required great concentration on the part of the pilot to fly the aircraft accurately fore-and-aft. This was particularly noticeable during manoeuvring flight, when it was easy to obtain higher normal acceler-ations than had been intended. The lightness of the elevator combined with longitudinal instability made the aircraft quite tiring to fly. At an aft CG there was no sign of tightening when carrying out a steady turn, but if the aircraft was pulled quickly into a fairly high 'g' turn there was a tendency to tighten, although this characteristic died away as the turn progressed and was not present at forward CG. For 4 g turns between

200 mph IAS and maximum level speed, the pull force required on the stick was light, but not unduly so for a fighter.

Longitudinal behaviour was tested at aft CG by disturbing the aircraft by about 10 mph from its trimmed speed before releasing the control column. In most conditions of flight, with the flaps and under-carriage up a phugoid of gradually increasing amplitude was noted, the only occasion when trimmed speed was regained being in the glide with the flaps and undercarriage down. With CG forward, the aircraft was slightly more stable but its behaviour was similar.

Determination of the Tempest's longitudinal stability was not helped by a marked change in directional trim with alteration in speed and power. When power was decreased, the aircraft yawed strongly to the left, a characteristic that was also noted with an increase in speed. Because of the heaviness of the rudder control, it was almost impossible to keep the aircraft sighted on a target if the throttle was opened or closed rapidly, as might be expected in combat. It was for this reason that some lightening of the rudder was considered desirable. To make matters worse, any yaw to the left produced a nose-down pitch.

Lateral and directional stability were not tested fully, but from the flying carried out, the aircraft did not appear to have any particular problems in these respects. If a wing was depressed and the control column released, it would return very slowly to its original position, or it could be raised by use of rudder. Likewise, if the aircraft was disturbed directionally from a trimmed condition and the rudder released, it returned to its original heading.

Stall speeds with the undercarriage up and down were 85 mph IAS and 74 mph IAS respectively. Due to the aircraft's longitudinal instability, any uncorrected backward movement of the control column produced a speed divergence towards the stall. In the landing con-figuration, the first warning of an approaching stall was aileron snatching, which became apparent at 95 mph IAS. This was accom-panied by the port wing going down, about half aileron being required to counteract this particular tendency. At the same time, the aircraft was prone to yaw to the left, with progressive use of rudder being needed to keep straight, until about three-quarters right rudder was in use at the point of stall requiring a heavy foot load. Although the elevator control was light down to 95 mph IAS, it became progressively heavier right up to the stall, which occurred with the stick about three-quarters back from the central position. Some lateral instability was noted as the stall was approached.

With the flaps and undercarriage down, aileron snatching commenced at 80 mph IAS and was continuous below that speed. As speed was reduced, full right rudder trim and almost full right rudder was needed to hold the aircraft straight. The elevator control was light, but the response was sluggish. The stall occurred with the control column about halfway back and was characterised by a sharp yaw to the left, followed by a slight drop of the nose. The stick could be pulled back with no further effect, as the control was completely ineffective. There was no tendency to spin and the aircraft recovered immediately when back pressure on the control column was relaxed.

Dives were carried out with careful monitoring of the indicated airspeed to ensure that Mach 0.80 was not exceeded (the same limitation as that used by Hawker in their trials). This corresponded to 370 mph IAS at 30,000 ft or 540 mph IAS at 10,000 ft. The Tempest was found to be steady and smooth in the dive, with no control surface instability or buffeting. The aircraft accelerated rapidly up to 480 mph IAS, the speed then increasing slowly to a maximum of 535 mph IAS. Acceleration was dependent to a large extent on the yaw/pitch couple and any degree of mishandling could seriously affect performance. With increasing speed the aircraft tended to yaw to the left, which if not corrected fully (due to the heavy force required) resulted in a slight reduction in the push force needed on the control column to maintain balance. The rudder trimmer was extremely effective at high speed and had to be used with great care if a rapid yaw and consequent pitch was to be avoided.

When the undercarriage was lowered on the approach there was a slight nose-down change of trim, the wheels coming down unevenly, which caused some yawing and pitching. When the flaps were lowered, there was a further moderate nose-down change of trim, but this could easily be held by a backward movement of the stick whilst re-trimming. The best approach speed with the flaps and undercarriage down with the engine throttled back, was 110 mph IAS, which produced a steep glide, but with rather sluggish response to control movements. The elevator was particularly bad in this respect, which meant that it was difficult to get the tail down for landing. This characteristic was at its worst when CG was in the forward position. When the engine was used on the approach, the speed could be reduced to 90 mph IAS, the increased airflow tending to improve elevator control so that a three-point landing could be made without difficulty. The landing was straightforward, although some tailwheel shimmy was experienced when landing on grass.

If the throttle was advanced with the flaps and undercarriage down, as in the case of a baulked landing, there was a nose-up change of trim, which could be held prior to re-trimming. The aircraft also tended to yaw to the right, which needed firm pressure on the left rudder pedal. With the engine set to 3700 rpm, +4 lb/sq.in boost, the aircraft could be climbed away before retracting the undercarriage, the flaps being kept down until a speed of 160 mph IAS had been reached. When the flaps were raised, there was no appreciable sink, just a slight nose-up change of trim as also occurred when raising the undercarriage. Although the handling characteristics were generally found to be acceptable, A&AEE called for improved longitudinal stability, lighter aileron control, greater elevator effectiveness with the engine off and a lighter rudder to provide better control when confronted with the large change of directional trim with change of engine power.

Performance testing was also carried out using JN731, beginning in November 1943. Although it was fitted with a Sabre IIA of 2180 hp, the same engine as fitted to the Typhoon, it demonstrated a much-improved rate of climb and top speed. The propeller used was a four-blade, de Havilland of 14 ft diameter and the engine operating limits were: climb – 3700 rpm, +7 lb/sq.in boost (1 hour maximum), combat – 3700 rpm, +9 lb/sq.in boost (5 minutes maximum). Full climbs were made using combat power, since the rpm limitation was the same as that for normal climbing power and the combat boost restriction fell below the normal boost limit of +7 lb/sq.in well within the permitted period. The supercharger gear change was made when boost in MS gear fell to +4 lb/sq.in which occurred at 8700 ft.

With full combat power selected, a maximum rate of climb of 4380 ft/min was recorded in MS gear at sea level (full throttle height). With the supercharger in FS gear, the best rate of climb was 3000 ft/min at 13,500 ft, which was reached in 4½ minutes. Other results were as follows:

| Height | 4000 ft | 10,000 ft | 15,000 ft | 18,000 ft | 20,000 ft |
|---|---|---|---|---|---|
| Rate of climb – ft/min | 3740 | 3000 | 2785 | 2380 | 2110 |
| Time from start – min | 1.0 | 2.8 | 4.5 | 5.65 | 6.55 |

| Height | 22,000 ft | 26,000 ft | 30,000 ft | 32,000 ft | 34,000 ft |
|---|---|---|---|---|---|
| Rate of climb – ft/min | 1835 | 1300 | 755 | 485 | 215 |
| Time from start – min | 7.6 | 10.15 | 14.0 | 17.25 | 23.15 |

The service ceiling was 34,800 ft with an estimated absolute ceiling of 35,600 ft. The climb rate when using normal boost rating was 3815 ft/min at sea level, with full throttle heights of 3500 ft (3815 ft/min rate of climb) and 15,800 ft (2680 ft/min rate of climb) in MS and FS supercharger.

Level speed tests showed a maximum of 432 mph TAS at 18,400 ft, which was approximately 20 mph faster than the best speed recorded on a Typhoon. The full results were as follows:

| Height    | Sea Level | 4000 ft  | 6600 ft   | 10,000 ft | 12,800 ft |
|-----------|-----------|----------|-----------|-----------|-----------|
| TAS – mph | 376       | 397      | 411       | 409       | 407       |
| IAS – mph | 398       | 397      | 396       | 375       | 358       |

| Height    | 16,000 ft | 18,400 ft | 20,000 ft | 24,000 ft | 28,000 ft |
|-----------|-----------|-----------|-----------|-----------|-----------|
| TAS – mph | 421       | 432       | 431       | 423       | 405       |
| IAS – mph | 353       | 349       | 338       | 311       | 276       |

The full throttle heights as tested were thus 6600 ft and 18,400 ft, which were approximately 4–500 ft higher than expected, as full combat boost was not obtainable due to slight inaccuracies of the automatic boost control. The top speed was not affected.

Heavy lateral control at high speed was greatly improved with the introduction of spring-tab ailerons. Although it was still outclassed by the Fw 190 and Mustang in terms of rate of roll, at speeds above 350 mph IAS the Tempest was superior to the Spitfire. Reduced wing thickness compared with the Typhoon contributed to a significant improvement in dive and zoom climb capability, acceleration in the dive being one of the Tempest's greatest advantages. It was also an excellent gun platform due to its steadiness in an attacking dive. At low to medium levels few aircraft could stay with a well flown Tempest V and comparative trials carried out at AFDU showed it to be 15–20 mph faster than the Mustang III and Spitfire XIV up to 15,000 ft. Above this height, its superiority was gradually reduced and above 25,000 ft both the Mustang and Spitfire were faster.

The Tempest V was introduced to RAF service by No. 486 Squadron in early 1944, which together with Nos 3 and 56 Squadrons, formed the Newchurch Wing under the leadership of Wing Commander Roland Beamont DSO DFC. The Tempest V's low-level speed performance was put to good use during the V-1 flying bomb campaign, destroying a total of 638, representing 36 per cent of the RAF's total claims. The Tempest was widely used by 2nd Tactical Air Force in support of the Allied advance in northern Europe, its main duty being to achieve low-level air superiority so that the fighter-bombers could go about their business without interference from the *Luftwaffe*. When the opportunity arose, armed reconnaissance missions were also flown, looking for suitable targets well behind the front line. The Tempest V was one of the most deadly low-level fighters of the late war period and was responsible for destroying twenty Messerschmitt Me 262 jet fighters in air combat.

While the Tempest V was entering service, the Tempest II was being tested at Boscombe Down. The prototype (LA602) was flown for the first time on 28 June 1943 and was followed into the air by LA607 on 18 September 1943. Like the prototype Tempest V, a Typhoon tail was initially fitted but a revised fin with dorsal fillet was soon added. Power came from a 2520 hp Centaurus IV. The airframe was basically the same as that of the Tempest V, except for a revised forward end to accommodate the new engine, with air intakes in the leading edges of the wings for the carburettor and oil cooler. Following development delays with the Centaurus XII, which had been the preferred engine for production aircraft, plans eventually centred on the Centaurus V.

Performance and handling trials were carried out on LA602 at Boscombe Down in early May 1944. The noise level of the Tempest II was considerably lower than the Mark V, which made it much less tiring to fly. However, there was excessive vibration throughout most of the rpm range. At engine speeds above 2400 rpm a harsh high-frequency vibration developed, which worsened with increasing rpm up to the maximum of 2700 rpm. Below 2000 rpm a similar vibration occurred, which reached its peak at 1750 rpm and then fell off rapidly as engine revs were reduced. The vibrations tended to increase with the application of normal accelerations, but were not greatly affected by changes in speed. At speeds above 200 mph IAS buffeting was also experienced when the cooling gills were fully open, which felt very like the engine vibration.

The pilot's throttle control received mixed reviews. It was rated better than that on the Mark V, being easy to move without any tendency to slip, but the 'gates' on the quadrant, which were meant to indicate the positions for cruising, rated and take-off boost, could barely be felt. The forward view on the Tempest II was slightly worse than the V due to the wider nose and the undercarriage also seemed less smooth, especially when taxying on rough ground. The take-off was similar to the Tempest V, but in the climb there was insufficient left rudder trim available to fly 'feet off' below 210 mph IAS, though the foot loads were not large. The best climbing speed was 190 mph IAS.

General flying showed the ailerons to be even heavier than on the Mark V. The rudder was moderately light for small deflections, becoming heavier when moved through greater angles. Although similar to the Tempest V, the fact that changes in directional trim with speed and power were less marked, meant that the pilot did not have to re-trim directionally during manoeuvres at cruising speeds, though it was still necessary at high speeds. A degree of longitudinal instability was still present in the Tempest II when flown at the normal full service load of 11,360 lb (aft CG), although any deviation from steady trimmed flight was not rapid if flown 'hands off', the aircraft being rated as easy to fly. No tightening was experienced in turns, even when the aircraft was pulled quickly into a turn. Similarly, recoveries from trimmed or out-of-trim dives did not produce excessive accelerations, unless they were induced by the pilot due to the light elevator forces present. It was, however, considered that some improvement in longitudinal stability still needed to be made, in case CG was moved further aft in service when carrying additional loads.

The stalling speeds for the Tempest II were virtually identical to the Mark V, the actual results with the flaps and undercarriage up and down being 86 mph IAS and 75 mph IAS respectively. The approaching stall was announced by gradually increasing buffet and although the port wing usually dropped, on occasions the starboard wing would go down. Recovery was immediate on pushing the control column forward and there was no tendency to spin. Although the limiting speed in the dive was 580 mph IAS, tests were only carried out to 515 mph IAS owing to a cracked hood. All the controls became heavier, particularly the ailerons, and like the Tempest V, the aircraft yawed to the left with a nose up pitch, although this particular characteristic did not appear to be quite as pronounced. If the control column was released at high speed, the aircraft continued in the dive, which was only to be expected as no force was needed to maintain the desired attitude.

The recommended approach speed was 100 mph IAS, but if the aircraft was held off too high on landing the right wing tended to drop quite sharply as the aircraft stalled. Once again, with the engine off there was insufficient elevator control to achieve a three-point landing, although this situation was improved slightly by using a little engine to improve the airflow over the tail to generate improved effectiveness. The approach and landing had to be made with the cooling gills closed, as the stall speed was around 5–7 mph higher with them open and there was a further reduction in elevator effectiveness.

Climbing performance at combat power showed further improve-ment over the Tempest V, the Mark II taking 2½ minutes less to get to 30,000 ft. The full throttle heights in MS and FS gear were 5000 ft and 14,900 ft, with rates of climb of 4400 ft/min and 3220 ft/min respec-tively. Other results were as follows:

| Height | 2000 ft | 7000 ft | 11,400 ft | 16,000 ft | 20,000 ft |
|---|---|---|---|---|---|
| Rate of climb – ft/min | 4400 | 3970 | 3220 | 3070 | 2530 |
| Time from start – min | 0.25 | 1.6 | 2.85 | 4.3 | 5.7 |

| Height | 22,000 ft | 24,000 ft | 26,000 ft | 28,000 ft | 30,000 ft |
|---|---|---|---|---|---|
| Rate of climb – ft/min | 2260 | 1990 | 1730 | 1460 | 1180 |
| Time from start – min | 6.55 | 7.5 | 8.55 | 9.85 | 11.35 |

The increase in level-speed performance was slightly more modest, with a maximum of 440 mph TAS at full throttle height in FS gear of 17,500 ft. The best speed achieved in MS supercharger was 422 mph TAS at 8400 ft, with the gear change being made at 13,700 ft. The full results were as follows:

| Height | Sea level | 4000 ft | 11,000 ft | 13,700 ft | 20,000 ft |
|---|---|---|---|---|---|
| TAS – mph | 372 | 396 | 421 | 419 | 439 |
| IAS – mph | 386 | 388 | 374 | 356 | 338 |

| Height | 22,000 ft | 24,000 ft | 26,000 ft | 28,000 ft | 30,000 ft |
|---|---|---|---|---|---|
| TAS – mph | 437 | 434 | 430 | 423 | 414 |
| IAS – mph | 326 | 313 | 300 | 284 | 267 |

The problem with excessive vibration was eventually overcome by the use of flexible engine mounts in place of the original rigid mounting and, on later aircraft, by the use of a five-blade propeller. As the Tempest II had been selected for use in the Far East, tropical trials were carried out at Khartoum in April 1945. Shortly after, MW754 was delivered to the Air Fighting Development Squadron (AFDS) at Tangmere for a full tactical evaluation.

The take-off weight with full internal fuel and ammunition was 11,700 lb, which resulted in a wing loading of 38 lb/sq.ft, the same as for the Tempest V. The Centaurus V developed 2300 hp at 2700 rpm and +8 lb/sq.in boost in MS gear at 5000 ft and 1950 hp at 16,500 ft in FS gear. The maximum power (2700 rpm and +12 lb/sq.in boost) at sea level was 2650 hp using 150-octane fuel. The power was trans-mitted through a 0.4 to 1 reduction gearing to a four-blade Rotol metal propeller of 12 ft 9 in diameter. Cooling air for the engine entered between the cowling and the spinner (no cooling fan was employed) and exited through adjustable gills on each side at the rear of the engine.

Fuel was carried in four self-sealing tanks. The main tank in the fuse-lage, just aft of the forward firewall, held 76 gallons and was augmented by two inter-spar tanks, one in the inner portion of each wing, containing 28 gallons and a nose tank in the port wing with a further 28 gallons, giving a total fuel capacity of 160 gallons. The arm-ament was similar to the Tempest V and consisted of four wing-mounted 20-mm Hispano cannon. Each gun had its own ammunition box, the inboard guns having 162 rounds, with 156 rounds for the outer guns. They were controlled electro-pneumatically from a push switch on the spade grip of the control column and could be fired

1. Hurricane prototype K5083 being flown by P. W. S. Bulman in its original form with strutted tailplane, retractable tailwheel and unstiffened canopy.

(Author)

2. A later view of K5083 with modified conopy, cantilever tailplane and radio mast. The stub exhausts are shown to advantage.

(Philip Jarrett)

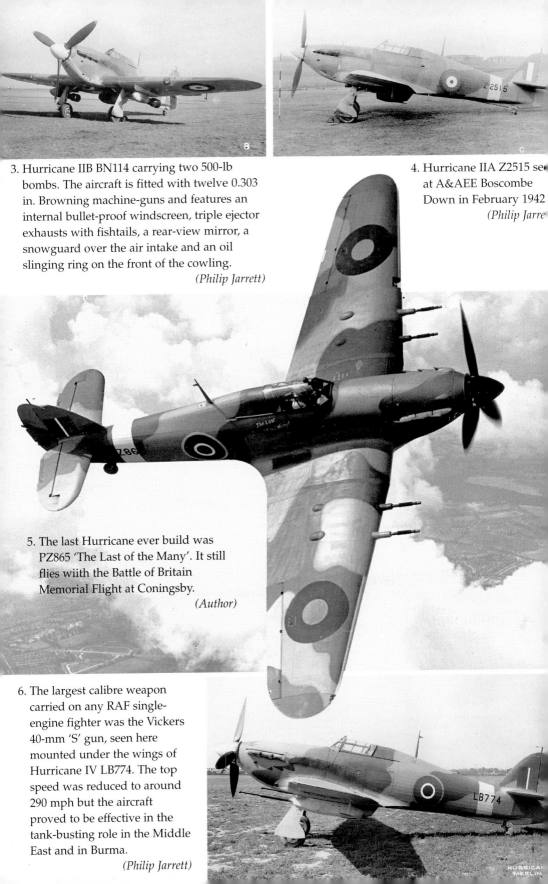

3. Hurricane IIB BN114 carrying two 500-lb bombs. The aircraft is fitted with twelve 0.303 in. Browning machine-guns and features an internal bullet-proof windscreen, triple ejector exhausts with fishtails, a rear-view mirror, a snowguard over the air intake and an oil slinging ring on the front of the cowling.
*(Philip Jarrett)*

4. Hurricane IIA Z2515 se· at A&AEE Boscombe Down in February 1942
*(Philip Jarre·*

5. The last Hurricane ever build was PZ865 'The Last of the Many'. It still flies wiith the Battle of Britain Memorial Flight at Coningsby.
*(Author)*

6. The largest calibre weapon carried on any RAF single-engine fighter was the Vickers 40-mm 'S' gun, seen here mounted under the wings of Hurricane IV LB774. The top speed was reduced to around 290 mph but the aircraft proved to be effective in the tank-busting role in the Middle East and in Burma.
*(Philip Jarrett)*

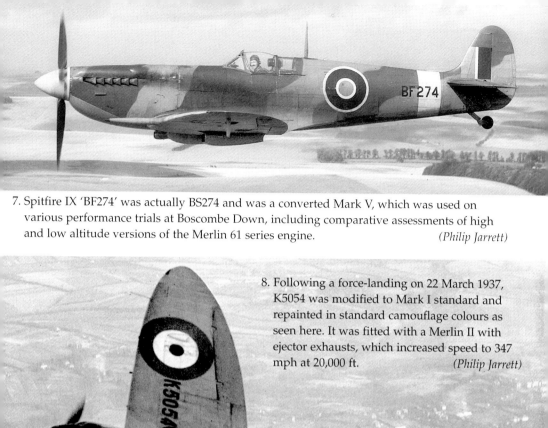

7. Spitfire IX 'BF274' was actually BS274 and was a converted Mark V, which was used on various performance trials at Boscombe Down, including comparative assessments of high and low altitude versions of the Merlin 61 series engine. *(Philip Jarrett)*

8. Following a force-landing on 22 March 1937, K5054 was modified to Mark I standard and repainted in standard camouflage colours as seen here. It was fitted with a Merlin II with ejector exhausts, which increased speed to 347 mph at 20,000 ft. *(Philip Jarrett)*

The clean lines of the prototype Spitfire are immediately apparent in this view of K5054. It is still fitted with small wheel doors to the undercarriage legs, but these were soon deleted. *(Author)*

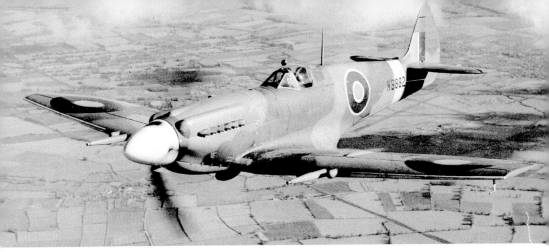

10. The Griffon was introduced to operational use by the Spitfire XII, its single-stage supercharged engine excelling at low level. MB882 flew with No. 41 Squadron before ending its days at the Fighter Leader School at Milfield. *(Author)*

11. Spitfire XIV RB146 seen during trials at Boscombe Down with a rudder guard for spin tests at various CG loadings. *(Author)*

12. Spitfire F.21 LA188 was used for high-speed trials and was dived to Mach 0.89 during investigations into compressibility. This work continued after the war and the aircraft was eventually struck off charge on 16 June 1954. *(Philip Jarrett)*

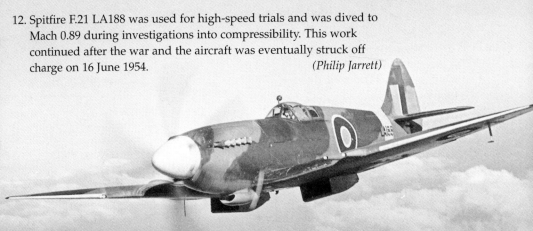

3. The Defiant II prototype N1550 seen during testing at Boscombe Down with a tropical oil cooler in an enlarged fairing under the nose. *(Philip Jarrett)*

14. The prototype Defiant K8310 in natural metal finish and without the turret, which was still being tested in Overstrand K8175. Ballast was fitted to maintain the correct CG position. *(Philip Jarrett)*

5. Defiant I N1551 was converted to a Mark II and was used at Boscombe Down for performance and handling trials. It survived until 14 February 1943, when it was abandoned after control was lost. *(Philip Jarrett)*

16. K8620 was the second Defiant prototype and was flown for the first time on 18 May 1938. *(Philip Jarrett)*

17. The first prototype Skua I, K5178, seen at Brough in 1937. On completion of its allotted test schedule the aircraft was used for ditching trails from HMS Pegasus in February 1939.

*(Philip Jarrett)*

18. Skua II L2883 was the first aircraft to be fitted with an arrester hook and also featured a modified tailwheel oleo to prevent juddering. It was delivered to Worthy Down on 10 January 1939.

*(Philip Jarrett)*

19. Skua I K5179 was the second prototype and featured the extended nose, which increased its length by 2 ft 4¾ in. It is seen here at Brough in May 1938 with Flight Lieutenant Henry Bailey, Blackburn's chief test pilot, in the cockpit.

*(Philip Jarrett)*

20. A formation of Blackburn Rocs in echelon starboard. The aircraft are fitted with light series bomb carriers under the wings.

(Philip Jarrett)

21. Blackburn Roc L3084 was delivered to 27 MU Shawbury on 31 August 1939 and was subsequently converted to a target tug.

(Philip Jarrett)

22. The first production Fulmar N1854 was used for performance and handling trials at Boscombe Down. On its return to the manufacturers, it was modified as a Mark II and it is currently preserved at the Fleet Air Arm Museum at Yeovilton. *(Philip Jarrett)*

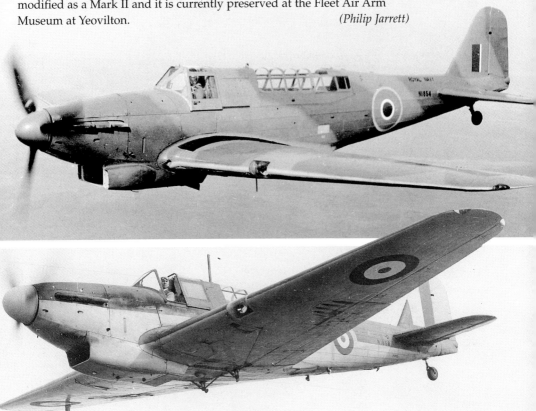

23. Another early production Fulmar, N1858 undertook speed trials at Boscombe Do[v] before being used by Fairey to test double-split flaps and geared tab ailerons. It w[as] later fitted with powered ailerons similar to those intended for the Fairey Spearfis[h] torpedo/ dive-bomber. *(Philip Jarre[tt])*

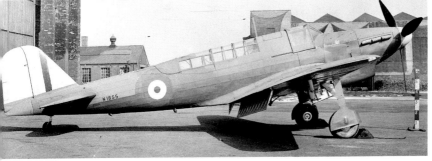

24. N1855 was also involved in the te[st] programme at A&AEE and was used for diving trials. *(Philip Jarre[tt])*

25. A Fulmar II, possibly N4021. The fitting of the 1300 hp Merlin XXX required a revised Rotol propeller, a new radiator and oil cooler, and revisions to the fuel system. The aircraft also had a modified rudder mass-balance. *(Philip Jarrett)*

TORNADO PROTOTYPE
VULTURE
OCT. 1941

26. The prototype Tornado P5224 is easily identified by the twin exhaust stacks of its Rolls-Royce Vulture 24-cylinder 'X' engine. It is seen here at Boscombe Down in October 1941.

*(Philip Jarrett)*

27. Typhoon prototype P5212 pictured at the Hawker airfield at Langley soon after roll out. It has the original small tail and triple exhaust stubs. The lack of rearwards view was criticised during initial trials at A&AEE.

*(Philip Jarrett)*

28. Tornado P5224 in the air. No guns were fitted during the trials at Boscombe Down, ballast being added to obtain the correct weight. *(Philip Jarrett)*

29. Typhoon R7579 was the third production aircraft and features the enlarged tail and revised exhaust stacks. It was used by Hawker before being struck off charge on 1 April 1943. *(Philip Jarrett)*

30. JR128 of No. 183 Squadron shows the Typhoon in its final form, with fully blown hood and whip aerial. It later flew with No. 181 Squadron and was shot down by flak at Livarot near Falaise on 18 August 1944. Flt Lt W. Grey baled out and became a PoW. *(Author)*

31. Typhoon IB EK183 displays black and white underwing identity stripes and a white cap to the spinner. These markings were one of several attempts to avoid 'friendly fire' incidents, owing to the Typhoon's similarity from certain angles to the Focke-Wulf Fw 190. EK183 flew with Nos 56 and 609 Squadrons and eventually became instructional airframe 5232M. *(Philip Jarrett)*

32. EJ846 was one of 305 Tempest V aircraft of the second
production batch produced by Hawker in 1944. It was
eventually converted to a target tug and was still in
use at Sylt in 1954. *(Philip Jarrett)*

33. Tempest V prototype HM595 seen at Langley in September 1942 with
a Typhoon canopy and tail unit. *(Philip Jarrett)*

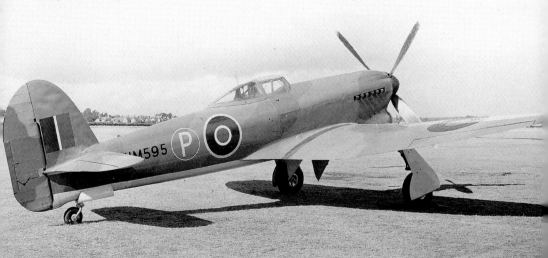

34. The prototype Tempest II LA602 at Langley in June 1943, fitted with a Typhoon tail unit.

*(Philip Jarrett)*

35. Tempest V NV768 was fitted with an experimental annular radiator and is seen here with Tempest VI NX121.

*(Philip Jarrett)*

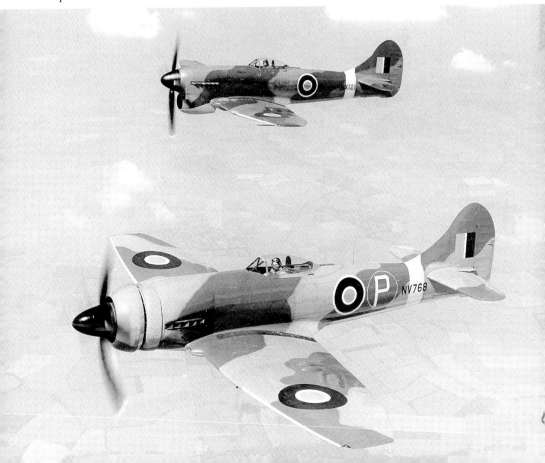

36. Formerly of II/JG 54, Messerschmitt Bf 109E-3 AE 479 was captured by the French and subsequently tested in the UK at Boscombe Down and Farnborough. It was shipped to the USA in June 1942. *(Philip Jarrett)*

37. DG200 was a Bf 109E-4 and was used for a comparative assessment against the Spitfire and Hurricane. It is seen here being flown with the canopy removed. *(Philip Jarrett)*

. The Bf 109G or Gustav was built in greater numbers than any other variant and was powered by a Daimler Benz DB 605A of 1475 hp. *(Philip Jarrett)*

39. Another captured Bf 109, NN644 is an 'F' model, which is readily identifiable by its rounded wing tips. *(Philip Jarrett)*

40. Len Thorne of AFDU posed with Bf 109G TP814 after his take-off accident on 22 November 1944 at Wittering. *(Author)*

41. Focke-Wulf Fw 190A-3 Werke Nummer 313 shortly after its arrival at Pembrey on 23 June 1942. Its subsequent evaluation confirmed that is was superior to the Spitfire V in nearly all aspects of performance. *(Author)*

42 The Pembrey Fw 190 after the application of RAF markings and with the serial number MP499. *(Author)*

all together, or in pairs. Pressing the top of the button fired the inboard cannon, the bottom fired the outer guns and all four were fired by pressing the centre of the button. At the time of test, MW754 was fitted with a GM.2 reflector gunsight.

A number of flying limitations were in place at the time of test. As the aircraft was fitted with an underwing pressure head instead of a pitot mounted in the leading edge of the wing, the maximum speed was limited to 520 mph IAS. Intentional spinning was prohibited and the aircraft was restricted to a speed of 300 mph IAS with the hood open. Although drop tanks of 45-gallon capacity had been cleared by A&AEE up to 450 mph IAS, the larger 90-gallon tank had still not been approved.

Ground handling was straightforward and as the aircraft was tail-heavy, the tail showed no inclination to lift, even when taxying over rough surfaces. The brakes were extremely powerful and had to be handled with care. The forward view was considered to be slightly worse than that from a Tempest V. On take-off, full port rudder trim was needed and the throttle opened slowly as the aircraft tended to swing to starboard. Although the swing was a little worse than the Tempest V, it could easily be held with rudder. At an engine setting of +8½ lb/sq.in boost and taking off into a headwind of 10–15 mph, the run was approximately 350 yards. The aircraft became airborne at around 100 mph IAS, but there was a tendency for the starboard wing to drop if pulled off too early.

The best technique for landing was to leave a small amount of power on, as in a glide there was insufficient elevator authority to allow a three-point touchdown to be made. Although A&AEE had warned that the right wing was liable to drop if the aircraft was held off too high, AFDS found the landing to be normal. After touchdown a swing to the left was the most likely outcome, however, this could easily be controlled by using the brakes, provided care was taken not to over-correct.

General handling tests showed the elevators to be the lightest of the three controls and they were adequate at all times except in a glide landing. The rudder was described as 'pleasantly heavy', its action was positive and it required less re-trimming than the Tempest V with changes in speed and power. The ailerons were also quite heavy, but the response was immediate throughout the speed range. It was felt that some more port trim was needed for take-off and there was also insufficient port trim to be able to fly 'feet off' when carrying out a maximum rate climb.

The Tempest II proved to be slightly unstable in pitch at heights above 15,000 ft at all speeds. In a tight turn there was a tendency for the aircraft to tighten up, especially at altitude, but this characteristic was

not sufficiently pronounced as to cause the pilot any real embarrassment. The aircraft was stable directionally. Generally, the Tempest II
was easy and pleasant to fly. There was plenty of warning of a high-
speed stall, with increased buffeting and aileron snatch. Some
problems were experienced with high oil temperatures during
prolonged climbs, or when operating at high throttle settings for any
length of time. Pilots also had to monitor the cylinder head temperature gauge closely, as certain combinations of mixture strength and
boost were liable to cause detonation, although generally the
Centaurus engine was found to be extremely reliable. Between
1600–2000 rpm, and to a lesser extent at maximum power, considerable
vibration was experienced. However, it was not of sufficient intensity
as to cause any serious mechanical problem, although it was annoying
for the pilot and tended to affect his ability to hold his sight on a target.

No difficulties were encountered during low-flying or aerobatics
and the nose did not wander when manoeuvring in the rolling plane.
Formation flying was straightforward as regards general handling,
although the rough running of the engine as mentioned above meant
that pilots were either throttling back to avoid the period, or opening
up beyond it. Under these conditions, aircraft in formation were either
going too slow or too fast and constant throttle juggling was necessary.
If the rough-running was found to be too fatiguing over a long period
and the pilot increased engine revs to 2000 rpm by moving the propeller
control lever forward, this had the effect of reducing range by around
10–15 per cent.

The Tempest II was also flown at night and pilots commended its
almost total lack of exhaust glare. The only difficulty was its inclination
to swing on landing, which was not dangerous to a pilot who had flown
the aircraft and was aware of this particular characteristic. One aspect
of the Tempest II that needed improvement was a lack of ventilation
in the cockpit, especially at low altitudes. This was a particular concern
as the aircraft was intended for use in the Far East. When taxying,
exhaust fumes also tended to seep into the cockpit, a problem that had
been around for a long time, going back to the early days of Typhoon
development.

The Tempest II was flown against a Tempest V for a tactical comparison. Consumption tests were carried out, which showed that the
Tempest II had a very similar radius of action to that of the Mark V. On
average, the Tempest II was 15 mph faster than the Mark V, the
advantage varying from 10–20 mph depending on height, and this
could be maintained up to the aircraft's operational ceiling, which was
considered to be 30,000 ft (the level at which the climb rate fell below
1000 ft/min). In terms of acceleration, the Tempest II was markedly
superior when opening up from cruising speed to full throttle and it

pulled away rapidly. The Tempest II could also climb at a better rate, being 350 ft/min better up to 3000 ft, but by the time that 8000 ft had been reached its advantage was 1000 ft/min. This figure had dropped once again to 400 ft/min by 12,500 ft, but this could be maintained up to the service ceiling.

In zoom climbs at equal power settings the two aircraft were very similar, but at full throttle the extra power of the Centaurus gave the Tempest II a definite edge. The dive performance was virtually identical and there was little to choose between the two as regards turning circles, although if anything the Tempest V had a slight advantage. During the trials, the rate of roll of the Tempest II was shown to be better than that of the Mark V, although as the two aircraft shared the same airframe there was no aerodynamic reason why this should be so. It was assumed that the ailerons on MW754 were performing above the average and might not be representative of production aircraft.

The Tempest II was highly commended by AFDS, as its very high speed had been achieved with moderate wing loading so that a high degree of manoeuvrability had been retained. The fire power of the Tempest II was formidable as a result of the increased rate of fire of the Mark V 20-mm Hispano cannon and, if required, a bomb could be carried under each wing. There was also provision for the carriage of RP. Like all high-powered, single-engine fighters (without contra-props) it was sensitive to changes in speed. This meant that the pilot had to continually trim the rudder, or apply heavy foot loads to prevent skid, which was the major source of inaccuracy during ground-attack sorties.

The Centaurus engine performed well during the trials and was extremely reliable. As an air-cooled engine it was well suited to the Tempest II, which was intended for use in South-East Asia Command in the low-to medium-level air superiority role and for ground attack, as it would have been less vulnerable to ground fire than equivalent liquid-cooled engines.

Relatively few recommendations were made. Although the armour protection for the pilot (and vulnerable parts of the engine) was considered adequate for air combat, ideally, more was required to protect against ground fire. A fully automatic carburettor control to maintain the correct mixture between economical cruising and rated boost was urgently needed to reduce the pilot workload. It was also felt that the lack of a rack under the centreline for a bomb or drop tank was a major omission. A contra-rotating propeller to remove the need for directional trim changes due to alterations in speed would have been nice. Failing that, however, a rudder trim indicator, along the lines of that developed for the Spitfire, would have allowed the pilot to pre-select his rudder trim with reasonable accuracy before going in to a dive.

The Tempest II entered service with No. 54 Squadron at Chilbolton in November 1945 and was also flown by No. 247 Squadron at the same base. It was used by three squadrons attached to BAFO in Germany (Nos. 16, 26 and 33) and by four squadrons in India (Nos 5, 20, 30 and 152). Despite the fact that the Tempest II was to have been used in the Far East, only one unit was to fly it in this region, No. 33 Squadron, which transferred from Gutersloh to Kai Tak in July 1949. Here, it was used on anti-terrorist operations armed with rocket projectiles, until it was replaced by twin-engined de Havilland Hornets in 1951. Production of the Tempest II totalled 472, of which 422 were built by Hawker and fifty by Bristol.

The last Tempest was the Mark VI, which was powered by a Sabre V of 2340 hp. The prototype was HM595, which was converted and flown for the first time in its new guise on 9 May 1944. To provide greater cooling the carburettor intake was repositioned in the wing leading edge, the freed up space in the nose scoop allowing a larger radiator. The oil cooler was also moved to a position behind the radiator, but tropical trials showed a need for additional oil cooling, which was provided by a subsidiary unit located in the leading edge of the starboard wing. The maximum speed was 438 mph TAS at 17,800 ft and service ceiling was estimated at 38,000 ft. The Tempest VI was used in the Middle East, where it was flown by Nos 6, 8, 39, 213 and 249 Squadrons, all the remaining aircraft being withdrawn in early 1950.

# PART TWO

# German Fighters

# CHAPTER EIGHT

# Messerschmitt Bf 109E/G

One of the most famous aircraft of all time, the Messerschmitt Bf 109 was to be built in larger numbers than any other fighter aircraft, with a production run in excess of 30,000, its advanced design and high performance providing the benchmark by which other types were measured for much of its existence. A low-wing cantilever monoplane with a flush-riveted skin, the Bf 109 showed considerable ingenuity in design as Willy Messerschmitt had gone to great lengths to keep its size and weight to the absolute minimum. The first Bf 109 (D-IABI) was flown on 28 May 1935 by *Flugkapitän* Hans Knoetzsch and was powered by a Rolls-Royce Kestrel V of 695 hp. Subsequent machines were fitted with a 610 hp Junkers Jumo 210 12-cylinder, inverted-vee, liquid-cooled engine, but in 1937 the first test flights were carried out with the new Daimler Benz DB 600A engine of 960 hp, which endowed exceptional performance with a top speed of 323 mph. In late 1937 a specially boosted DB 601 engine of 1650 hp propelled Bf 109 V13 to a new world speed record for landplanes of 379 mph.

After the early Jumo-powered Bf 109B/C, the first main variant was the Bf 109E or *Emil*, which was fitted with a 1100 hp DB 601A. Although based on the earlier DB 600, it featured direct fuel injection instead of a carburettor, and improved supercharging. The first *Emils* were delivered to JG 132 at Dusseldorf in December 1938 and by September 1939 the *Luftwaffe* had taken delivery of over 1000 Bf 109s, including the early variants used in the Spanish Civil War. Experience during the latter conflict and in the initial stages of the Second World War had shown the Bf 109 to be a supreme fighter, but its true test would come when it encountered the Hurricanes and Spitfires of the RAF. Clashes began in earnest after the German invasion of the Low Countries on 10 May 1940, with French-based Hurricanes hopelessly outnumbered by large numbers of Bf 109Es and Bf 110 twin-engined long-range fighters. RAF Fighter Command's Spitfires, which had been kept well away from the defensive actions over France, were finally drawn into the air battles that were soon raging in the skies over Dunkirk, but the main confrontation was yet to come.

RAF Fighter Command already knew much about their principal adversary as a result of the Bf 109E-3 captured intact by the French in late 1939. Following the comparative assessment with the Hurricane made by pilots of No. 1 Squadron (see Chapter 1), the aircraft was flown to the UK for evaluation and a series of handling trials were carried out at Farnborough in May/June 1940. The aircraft was flown by three RAE pilots, who all commented on the cramped, narrow cockpit and lack of headroom. The location of the rudder pedals also meant that the pilot sat in a slightly reclined attitude, which was not particularly comfortable. The positioning of the controls was good, in particular the elevator trim and flap controls on the pilot's left and the throttle control, which was not gated and was described as being 'marvellously simple' in operation.

Several aspects of the cockpit design were unusual to British pilots; toe instead of stick-operated brakes and the lack of a blind flying panel being two of the more notable omissions. The absence of an Artificial Horizon was particularly felt when flying in cloud. There was also no klaxon to warn the pilot should he forget to lower the undercarriage prior to landing. The hood was hinged on the starboard side and could not be opened in flight, although sliding windows were fitted on each side. However, these were difficult to open at high speed and cockpit noise (already high) increased appreciably. In an emergency, a jettison lever released the whole hood for the pilot to bale out.

When on the ground the forward view was extremely poor due to the aircraft's steep tail-down attitude, but in the air it was no worse than in a Hurricane or Spitfire. The cramped seating position in the Bf 109 did, however, make it difficult to clear the area downwards and to the rear. A direct vision panel was provided, which proved to be of great value when flying in bad visibility. It was draught-free at all speeds, which meant that a Bf 109 could fly faster in such conditions than a Spitfire, whose pilot had to resort to opening the hood and peering out around the windscreen, a task that could only be done at relatively slow speed due to the slipstream. The direct vision panel was also of use when landing, due to the aircraft's high nose position on touchdown.

On take-off with 20 degrees of flap set, the throttle could be opened quickly without fear of the engine choking, thanks to the fuel-injected DB 601's smooth response. Initially, the control column was held forward, but the tail came up quickly and it could then be eased back. Pilots soon became accustomed to holding the aircraft down on take-off, until they were sure that flying speed had been attained, as the left wing was liable to drop if pulled off too soon. The take-off run was extremely short and the initial rate of climb was significantly better than the early Spitfires equipped with two-pitch propellers (this advantage was largely nullified with the introduction of constant-speed propellers on later Spitfires). The best approach speed was 90 mph IAS with the flaps and undercarriage down and as the glide was quite steep, the view ahead was reasonably good. Landing required a greater degree of skill than either the Hurricane or Spitfire, as the aircraft had to be rotated through a large angle to adopt the correct three-point attitude. If a wheeled landing was attempted, there was a tendency for the left wing to drop. As CG was well behind the main wheels, full braking could be used immediately after touchdown without risk of the tail lifting.

The stall speed with the flaps and undercarriage up was 75 mph IAS. When gliding at 1.2 × stall speed, a forward or backward movement of the control column produced a very slowly damped pitching oscillation of long period when the stick was released, before the aircraft eventually settled to its trimmed speed. About 1 in of backward stick movement, requiring hardly any force, was required to bring about a stall. The slots opened at about 110 mph IAS and as they did so the ailerons snatched slightly and there was slight aileron vibration. If both the ailerons and rudder were held fixed, the left wing dropped suddenly through about 10 degrees at 83 mph IAS and the aircraft went into a gentle left-hand spiral. Aileron could be used to lift the wing. If this was attempted, with the rudder fixed, the aircraft became laterally unsteady and there was some aileron buffet which increased as speed was reduced. Below 77 mph IAS the aircraft could not be controlled by aileron alone.

If the rudder was used to raise the wing (ailerons fixed) the lateral oscillations could not be checked at speeds below 81 mph IAS. Control could be retained down to the stall speed of 75 mph IAS by vigorous use of aileron and rudder. By the time stall speed was reached, the aileron buffet was very marked and the aircraft was very unsteady laterally. If the stick was pulled further back at the stall, the ailerons and rudder were still slightly effective, but the aileron buffeting and lateral unsteadiness was of such violent proportions that a sustained stalled glide was impossible. At no time did the aircraft show any tendency to spin.

With the flaps and undercarriage down the stall speed was 61 mph IAS. Any fore or aft movement of the stick at 1.2 × stall speed led to a quickly damped pitching oscillation when the stick was released, and the aircraft was far more stable than in the clean configuration. No aileron snatching occurred when the slots opened at about 90 mph IAS and there was very little stall warning. If both the ailerons and rudder were held fixed, the aircraft maintained a straight path down to the stall when the left wing dropped suddenly through about 10 degrees followed by the nose, with a left-hand spiral once again the result. There was complete control until the stall was reached, but neither the rudder nor ailerons were effective at the stall, and the dropped wing could not be raised until speed had increased. As in the previous case, there was no risk of a spin developing.

Aileron control when flying at approach speed was very good; there was a positive feel and the response was quick. This was in marked contrast with the Spitfire, in which aileron control lightened with loss of speed to the point where feel was lost. As speed was gained, the ailerons of the Bf 109E tended to become heavier, but the response remained excellent up to 200 mph IAS. Above this speed the ailerons became unpleasantly heavy and were nearly immovable above 400 mph IAS. A pilot applying all his strength at this speed could only generate about one-fifth aileron movement, or about the same as a Spitfire in similar circumstances. Unlike Allied fighters, the Bf 109 did not have a rudder trimmer and during high-speed dives the pilot had to exert considerable pressure on the left rudder to keep the aircraft straight. This characteristic, together with heavy aileron control, tended to limit evasive manoeuvres in dives to right turns only.

Following the initial handling trials, a number of mock combats were carried out with a Spitfire I at around 6000 ft. The Bf 109 had a considerably heavier wing loading (32.2 lb/sq.ft compared with 24.8 lb/sq.ft) and so it was no great surprise to discover that the Spitfire could easily stay with its German rival during sustained turns up to 220 mph IAS. The Bf 109 would stall if the turn was tightened to generate more than 4 g, the leading edge slats tending to open shortly before this figure was reached, causing some aileron snatch and loss of sighting view. If the control column was pulled back further, a shuddering would be felt. The aircraft would then either come out of the turn or drop its wing even more, oscillating in pitch and roll and rapidly losing height. The stall itself was fairly benign and the aircraft made no attempt to flick into a spin.

Paradoxically, there were a number of occasions when the Bf 109 was able to stay with a Spitfire in a turn, despite its supposed inferiority in this respect. This was due to concerns on the part of the Spitfire pilot as regards his aircraft's handling as it approached its limit. With its extremely light elevator control, a high-speed stall was a distinct possibility, in which case it was likely to flick and enter a spin. Many pilots were wary of this and as a result did not utilise the Spitfire's turn performance fully.

During dives, it was found that the Spitfire could match the Bf 109 (more so if it had a constant-speed propeller), but the latter could initiate a diving manoeuvre much quicker due to its fuel-injected engine. Pilots of the Bf 109 found they could push over straight into a dive without their motors cutting, as was the case with both the Hurricane and Spitfire and their carburettor-equipped Merlins. The best climb speed of the Bf 109 was lower than the Spitfire, but its climbing angle was much steeper, which gave it an advantage in offensive and defensive manoeuvring in the vertical plane.

A good evasive manoeuvre for a Spitfire pilot was a half roll and dive, thus taking advantage of his aircraft's light elevators to bring about a rapid recovery. A Bf 109 pilot trying to follow this was faced with his aircraft building up speed quickly in the dive, followed by a decrease in elevator effectiveness as the control forces rapidly built up. Considerable height could be lost in this manoeuvre and if carried out at too low a level, could result in the aircraft flying into the ground.

Aerobatics were also flown but the Bf 109 did not find favour. As looping manoeuvres had to be started at around 280 mph IAS, the heavy elevator control at this speed was not ideal and as the speed diminished at the top of the loop, the slats could sometimes pop out, the resulting aileron snatch affecting directional control. During rolls below 250 mph IAS, there was a tendency for the nose to drop in the final stages, involving considerable backward movement of the control column. Upward rolls also suffered, due to the heaviness of the elevator control and resultant difficulty in setting up the required vertical axis.

The maximum speed of the Bf 109E was recorded as 355 mph TAS at 16,400 ft with the radiators closed and 330 mph TAS with the radiators open. A height of 23,000 ft was reached in just over ten minutes and the absolute ceiling was 32,000 ft. The trials were carried out at a take-off weight of 5580 lb, which included full internal fuel tanks and a full war load.

Trials were also carried out by A&AEE, the findings being broadly in agreement with RAE Farnborough as the following extracts from their report indicate.

All controls in level flight are light, quick in response and effective up to a speed of 250 mph IAS after which they become extremely heavy. This is particularly the case with the elevator which is out of harmony with the other controls to start with, becoming noticeably heavier, and in the dive almost immovable. It is to be particularly stressed that the controls are pleasantly light at all speeds up to 250 mph IAS and they appear to tighten up very suddenly so that at high speed they are practically immovable. Experienced pilots state that in the event of an attack from behind by a 109, the attack can easily be broken off by the attacked by pulling up quickly from a dive. The 109 cannot follow due to the heaviness of its controls.

Loops – It is impossible to execute a loop in the normal manner due to the heaviness and ineffectiveness of the elevator. If a normal loop is attempted, the aeroplane flicks on the top of the loop. The only way in which a loop can be done is by winding the tail trim back. Even then great care must be taken to ensure that the aeroplane does not flick out of the loop at the top.

Slow-rolls – It is very easy to slow-roll the aeroplane at speeds up to 250 mph IAS but at higher speeds the controls are so heavy that difficulty is experienced. A great deal of rudder has to be used in the rolls and this is unusual in the modern fighter. Very tight rolls can be executed at speeds up to 190 mph IAS. Slight snatching of the aileron is noticeable in rolls at speeds of 120–140 mph IAS.

Half roll off a loop – This manoeuvre is difficult for the same reason as given above. When rolling off to the left the aeroplane has to be checked as it tends to flick out in the opposite direction. To the right the difficulty is overcoming a tendency towards a high speed stall. Provided the control column is eased forward, however, the manoeuvre can be completed successfully.

Summary of flying qualities – General reports on the handling of the aeroplane which were received before the arrival of the aeroplane itself led one to believe that numerous faults existed, but these have been found to be untrue. The aeroplane is pleasant to fly at speeds up to 250 mph IAS, the only objection being the lack of space in the cockpit. This objection is a very real one in the case of a large pilot. At speeds in excess of 250 mph IAS the controls suddenly become very heavy and at 400 mph IAS recovery from a dive is difficult because of the heaviness of the elevator. This heaviness of the elevator makes all manoeuvres in the looping plane above 250 mph IAS difficult, including steep climbing turns. No difference was experienced between climbing turns to the right or left. In general the flying qualities of the aeroplane are inferior to both the Spitfire and Hurricane at all speeds and in all conditions of flight. It does not possess the control which allows good quality flying and this is particularly noticeable in aerobatics.

After use by A&AEE and RAE, the Bf 109E (by now carrying the serial number AE479) was flown by AFDU at Northolt and Duxford and was delivered to the USA in 1942.

In many respects the testing that was carried out at Boscombe Down and Farnborough in 1940 tended to compare the Bf 109 and Spitfire as pure flying machines and the respective reports left the reader in no doubt as to which was considered to be the better machine. Unfortunately, the Bf 109 and Spitfire were both weapons of war and delicate handling characteristics or the purity of an aerobatic manoeuvre would count for nothing in an aerial dogfight. Despite certain similarities in design and performance, the Bf 109 and Spitfire were poles apart. With its lightly loaded wing, the Spitfire was always going to come out on top in a turning fight, whereas the excellent vertical penetration of the Bf 109 meant that it was ideally suited to dive and zoom tactics, a situation that was aided by its fuel-injected Daimler Benz DB 601 engine. Despite such inconsistencies, the outcome of many air battles still depended to a large extent on which pilot saw the other first.

The Messerschmitt Bf 109 was heavily developed throughout the Second World War, the next major variant after the *Emil* being the Bf 109F or *Friedrich*. Although early variants were powered by the DB 601N of 1200 hp, the more powerful DB 601E of 1300 hp was fitted from the Bf 109F-3. The airframe was tidied up considerably with revised supercharger and radiator intakes, rounded wing tips, a cantilever tailplane and a fully retractable tailwheel. The Bf 109F showed its superiority over the Spitfire V as a high-altitude fighter in 1941/42, but was supplanted from the summer of 1942 by the Bf 109G or *Gustav*, which was basically an F-series airframe fitted with the new DB 605A of 1475 hp. The *Gustav* was virtually identical to the Bf 109F, the only distinguishing features being two small intakes behind the propeller spinner and the deletion of the two triangular-shaped windows on the fuselage sides below the windscreen.

A number of captured examples of the Bf 109G were flown by British testing establishments, including AFDS at Wittering. The aircraft tested was Bf 109G-6/U-2 *Werke Nummer* 412951, which also carried the serial number TP814. It was powered by a DB 605A-1, which developed 1550 hp at 22,000 ft and was armed with two MG 131 machine-guns mounted above the engine, a single MG 151/20 cannon firing through the propeller hub and two MG 151/20 cannon carried in underwing gondolas. Fittings were provided under the fuselage to enable an overload fuel tank to be carried or a 250 kg bomb. The all-up weight with a full war load was approximately 7488 lb, giving a wing loading of 43.6 lb/sq.ft.

The cockpit was as narrow and cramped as ever, but the instrument panel had been tidied up with superfluous instruments and controls having been removed. The usual flying instruments were installed, but a combined Artificial Horizon and Turn and Bank Indicator was of particular note. The engine instruments were standard, with the permissible limits marked on the dials. Two wheels were positioned on the left-hand side of the pilot's seat, the outer wheel controlling the operation of the flaps and the inner wheel the tailplane incidence. A gauge was provided for the latter, the position of the flaps being indicated by lines painted on the port wing flap. Operating switches for the undercarriage were also located on the left side of the cockpit.

Engine revs and boost were interconnected and were operated under normal conditions by the throttle control. Provision was made, however, for independent operation of engine rpm in an emergency situation, by a switch installed below the throttle quadrant. Revs could then be controlled by a two-way pivot switch attached to the top of the throttle lever, but this system had only to be used in the event of the Constant Speed Unit failing.

The view forwards and downwards out of the Bf 109G was even worse than on earlier aircraft due to the bulges on each side of the forward fuselage that covered the ammunition feed chutes for the MG 131 machine-guns. Willy Messerschmitt had paid particular attention to streamlining in the design of the Bf 109. Great difficulty was therefore experienced in accommodating the subsequent need for more guns of a heavier calibre. Not only did the various bulges and appendages restrict the pilot's view, they also tended to increase drag and reduce overall performance.

When manoeuvring on the ground, the Bf 109G was not particularly nose heavy. The brakes were positive, but the tailwheel did not caster easily and so sharp turns were difficult. Because of the high nose and poor forward visibility, extreme care had to be taken when taxying in the vicinity of other aircraft or obstructions. One disturbing aspect noted with TP814, was its tendency to disgorge exhaust fumes into the cockpit when taxying at low revs.

Unless taking off directly into wind, the aircraft showed a strong inclination to weathercock and as a result the throttle had to be opened slowly. Once in the air, the rudder was noted as being fairly heavy, but not uncomfortably so. As with earlier aircraft, there was no rudder trimming and it was necessary to apply right rudder for take-off and left rudder at high speeds. With increase in speed, the ailerons became increasingly stiff and were especially so at speeds in excess of 350 mph IAS. At speeds below 180 mph IAS, it was noted that the ailerons were not particularly positive and as the stall was approached they were almost non-effective. The elevators also became increasingly difficult to operate as speed increased and this was accentuated above 350 mph IAS by the fact that the elevator trimmer control was practically impossible to operate.

A number of tactical comparisons were carried out, including an evaluation of TP814 and a Spitfire LF.IX with a low-altitude rated Merlin 66. The two aircraft were compared for speed and all-round manoeuvrability at heights up to 25,000 ft. With the Spitfire being flown at 18 lb/sq.in boost it held a slight advantage up to 16,000 ft, but was then overtaken by the Bf 109 from 16–20,000 ft. Above this height, the Spitfire was again the faster by about 7 mph. At 25 lb/sq.in boost the Spitfire was 25  mph faster up to 15,000 ft, becoming 7 mph faster above that height.

During sustained climbs, the Spitfire was found to be superior to the Bf 109G at all heights. It had a particular advantage below 13,000 ft using 18 lb/sq.in boost and was, naturally, even more in the ascendant when using 25 lb/sq.in boost. When both aircraft were pulled up into a climb following a dive, the performance was almost identical, but when climbing speed was reached the Spitfire began to slowly pull away. The Spitfire also had the advantage in rate of roll and turn performance, in which it was greatly superior, but the Bf 109G could leave its rival without any difficulty during dives.

The Bf 109G was also compared with a fully operational Spitfire XIV powered by a 2050-hp Griffon 65 using 18 lb/sq.ft boost. The Spitfire proved to be superior in every aspect of performance, being approximately 25 mph faster at all heights up to 16,000 ft. As this was the rated altitude of the Bf 109G, the performance gap shrank to 10 mph at this height. However, it then increased progressively with altitude, the Spitfire being 50 mph faster by the time that 30,000 ft had been reached. In terms of climb performance, there was little to choose between the two aircraft at the Messerschmitt's best operating height of 16,000 ft, but at all other heights the Spitfire had a pronounced superiority in rate of climb. The Bf 109G's former ascendancy over the Spitfire in dive performance was largely nullified against the Mark XIV, as although it held a slight initial advantage, this was lost as soon as speed was increased above 380 mph IAS.

The Spitfire's famed turn performance was still apparent, although the use of the Griffon engine, which turned in the opposite direction to the Merlin, meant that the advantage was more marked when turning to the right. The rate of roll of the Mark XIV was, like its predecessors, superior at all speeds.

Before TP814 could be compared with a Tempest V, it suffered a fate similar to many other Bf 109s when it was wrecked as a result of a take-off accident. Its pilot on that fateful day was Len Thorne, but it was later ascertained that the crash had occurred as a result of under-carriage failure as he recalls:

During the Autumn of 1944 a Bf 109G was allocated to AFDU under the number TP814. Most of the flying was carried out by other unit pilots; my experience was limited to five flights during October and November, but as an aircraft, I didn't enjoy it. I found the cockpit cramped and, with the up-and-over canopy, very claustrophobic. Great care had to be taken when taking off and landing due to the Gustav's inclination to swing and ground-loop at the slightest provocation. When taking off at Wittering on the grass on 22 November 1944 I managed to avoid such trouble, but could do nothing when the port oleo support strut fractured as the aircraft was about to unstick. The port wing tip struck the ground and TP814 carried out a complete cart-wheel. Once again I was quite lucky as I was doing about 120 mph at the time. Luckily it came to rest the right way up but was rather badly bent. As other Bf 109s were available it was decided not to undertake repairs.

A trial had, in fact, already taken place between a Tempest V and another Bf 109G of 1426 (Enemy Aircraft) Flight. This trial had shown that the Hawker fighter using 9 lb/sq.in boost had a speed advantage of 40–50 mph at heights below 20,000 ft, but this superiority rapidly diminished above this height. Generally, the climb of the Bf 109G was superior to that of the Tempest at all heights, but this advantage was not pronounced at heights below 5000 ft. When both aircraft commenced a dive at the same speed and were then put into a climbing attitude, the Tempest was slightly superior and this could be maintained if the Tempest possessed an initial speed advantage and was able to keep its speed above 250 mph IAS.

Comparative dives between the two aircraft showed that the Tempest would pull away from the Bf 109G. Although the gap did not widen markedly in the early stages of the dive, in a prolonged descent the Tempest was greatly superior. At speeds below 350 mph IAS there was practically nothing to choose between the two aircraft as regards rate of roll, but when this speed was exceeded it was found that a Tempest pilot could out-manoeuvre a Bf 109G by banking quickly and changing direction. Turn performance was evenly matched, the Tempest being marginally the better machine.

The Bf 109 remained in production until the end of the war and was the subject of further development. The fastest of all the *Gustav* variants was the Bf 109G-10, which achieved a top speed of 428 mph powered by a DB 605G engine with MW-50 water-methanol injection. The last production series was the Bf 109K, which entered service towards the end of 1944. The final variant to see service (albeit in very small numbers) was the Bf 109K-14, which was powered by a DB 605L of 1475 hp with MW-50 and was armed with two MG 131 machine-guns and a single MK 108 cannon. Had the war continued, it is likely that further advanced variants of the Bf 109 would have been produced, including the L-series, which would have featured a 1750 hp Junkers Jumo 213E engine in place of the DB 605. The estimated top speed of the Bf 109L was 474 mph, approximately 20–25 mph faster than the Spitfire F.21.

CHAPTER NINE

# Focke-Wulf
# Fw 190A

The arrival of the Focke-Wulf Fw 190A in the skies over northern France in the late summer of 1941 heralded a particularly difficult period for RAF Fighter Command. Already committed to a policy of taking the air war to the enemy, the performance advantage of the newcomer over the Spitfire V caused great anxiety in the upper echelons of the RAF. Ultimately, it led to losses not seen since the Battle of Britain. Initially, the Fw 190 was only in service in small numbers and was also beset by teething troubles, notably engine failures as a result of overheating. By early 1942, however, most of its problems had been rectified and the pilots of JG 26 had sufficient confidence in their new mount to extract its full potential.

By mid 1942, the level of dominance that the Fw 190 had achieved over the Spitfire V led some in the British military hierarchy to seriously consider acquiring an example by clandestine means. A seemingly outlandish scheme formulated by Captain Philip Pinkney, a Commando officer, involved stealing an Fw 190 from a *Luftwaffe* airfield in northern France. However, happily for all involved (not least test pilot Jeffrey Quill who had been 'volunteered' to fly it) the issue was suddenly resolved in an action that took place on the evening of 23 June 1942 over the western end of the English Channel.

Following a raid by Bostons of No. 107 Squadron on the airfield at Morlaix (No. 10 Group Ramrod 23), a number of Fw 190A-3s of JG 2 attacked the bombers and their Spitfire escorts over the Channel. In a blatant disregard of orders, two Fw 190s flown by III *Gruppe* adjutant *Oberleutnant* Arnim Faber and his wingman *Unteroffizier* Wilhelm Reushling followed the RAF formations to the south coast of England, harrying them all the way. Reushling shot down Wing Commander Alois Vasatko, leader of the Czech Wing, in BM592, but his moment of glory was short-lived, as his aircraft was damaged by debris from Vasatko's Spitfire and he was forced to bale out. He was rescued from the sea off Brixham, but the body of the Czech was never found.

Meanwhile, Spitfires had been scrambled from Bolt Head, but only two managed to get airborne following a collision between two others prior to take-off. Flight Sergeant Frantisek Trejtnar in BL517 spotted a solitary Fw 190 flying north about 10,000 ft above him. He gave chase, but was still below his intended target when he had reached 18,000 ft. This was the Fw 190 flown by Faber, who had been watching the Spitfire in its climb. Choosing the right moment to strike, Faber dived to attack head-on, his fire hitting the Spitfire's starboard wing and wounding its pilot in the right arm. Severely damaged, Trejtnar's aircraft was pitched into a spin, which had still not been recovered at 5000 ft, at which point he baled out.

Having circled his victim as he descended on his parachute, Faber then made the elementary mistake of flying a reciprocal course, which took him north instead of south. Eventually a coastline appeared, which he assumed to be that along the English Channel, but in fact was the north coast of Devon. When land appeared after an appropriate amount of time, he was confident that he was back over northern France, but in reality he was flying along the south coast of Wales. Selecting the first airfield that presented itself, he performed an immaculate victory roll prior to landing at Pembrey, a training station near Llanelli, where he was promptly arrested. Not surprisingly, the arrival of one of the *Luftwaffe*'s prized fighters acted like a magnet for RAF fighter pilots in the area, including Wing Commander M.V. 'Mindy' Blake DSO DFC, leader of the Portreath Wing, and Flight Lieutenant Dave Glaser of No. 234 Squadron. Glaser later recalled that Faber offered to fly the Fw 190 on minimum fuel in mock combat with a Spitfire, but his offer was refused, as it was obvious that he would take to his parachute at the earliest opportunity.

Wearing RAF roundels and the serial number MP499, the Fw 190 was flown to RAE Farnborough the following month for a full structural examination. In the tradition of the German aircraft industry, the build quality was of an extremely high standard and as a second-generation monoplane fighter, it had a number of unusual features, including an electrically operated undercarriage. The fuselage was of stressed skin construction with twenty-one L-section stringers with one wide top hat section stringer at the top. Transverse formers (also of L-section) were used about 18 in apart. Two self-sealing fuel tanks were located in the lower front fuselage, containing 64 gallons and 51 gallons.

The wing main spar was a built-up I-section member of substantial construction in the centre section, but with rapidly tapering top and bottom booms, while the web was a solid plate of the same thickness throughout its length. Bending was taken entirely by the main spar (near the centre section) while further out, where the spar flanges became of negligible size, bending loads were shared by the many L-section stringers. Throughout the wing, shear forces were taken by the main spar and the trailing edge member, which also had a solid plate web. The ribs were small in number and consisted of plate webs with their edges turned over to form flanges riveted to the skin. The rib flanges were cut away to clear the stringers and the webs were pierced with lightening holes with turned-over edges for stiffening. The main spar and the trailing edge members formed a torsion box with the top and bottom wing skin.

The wings were assembled as one unit, the single main spar being continuous through the fuselage. The wing was attached to the fuselage at five points, two vertical bolts passed through attachments at the top of the main spar, and there were two horizontal pins at the roots of the light trailing edge members, which were not continuous. A further horizontal pin joint was located at the centre of the main spar bottom boom. This latter connection was made to support the bottom spar boom laterally, as the bottom central engine mounting tube was connected to the front side of the spar boom at this point.

Following its evaluation at Farnborough, MP499 was delivered to AFDU at Duxford for an assessment of its performance and handling characteristics, and for comparative trials. In its report, AFDU confirmed that, in most respects, the Fw 190 was greatly superior to the Spitfire V. The aircraft was found to be difficult to taxy due to excessive weight on the self-centring tailwheel when on the ground. For take-off, 15 degrees of flap was required and it was necessary to keep the control column back to avoid a swing developing during the initial stages of the run. Once airborne, however, the pilot immediately felt at home and the aircraft was pleasant to fly, all controls being light and positive. Retraction of the flaps and undercarriage was barely noticeable, although some sink occurred if the flaps were raised before a reasonably high airspeed had been attained.

The Fw 190 handled well during high-speed manoeuvres and an excellent feature was that it was seldom necessary to re-trim for differing flight conditions. The stalling speed was relatively high at approximately 110 mph with the undercarriage and flaps retracted and 105 mph with the gear and flaps down, but all controls remained effective until the point of stall. The best approach speed for landing was around 130–140 mph IAS, reducing to about 125 mph when crossing the edge of the aerodrome. Owing to a steep angle of glide, the view during the approach was good and the actual landing was straightforward, with touchdown occurring at approximately 110 mph. Once the Fw 190 was in the tail-down attitude the view was poor, but locking the tailwheel assisted in preventing a swing during the landing run. The landing run was similar in length to that of the Spitfire IX.

Only brief performance tests were carried out; but these showed a maximum speed of 390 mph TAS at 1.42 ata (atmospheres) boost, 2700 rpm, at the maximum power altitude of 18,000 ft. All flights at this power setting were for a duration of two minutes only. During the trial, pilots reported that the BMW 801D engine was running very roughly and as a result they had little confidence in its reliability. The AFDU report mentioned that interrogation of PoWs who had flown the Fw 190 had confirmed that the roughness of the engine was usual. German pilots also had little faith in its reliability and disliked having to fly the Fw 190 over the sea, not that this had stopped Faber and Reushling!

Fuel capacity amounting to a total of 115 gallons was carried in two self-sealing tanks, each tank being fitted with an immersed pump for use at altitude. There was also a protected oil tank containing 9 gallons. The approximate endurance under operational conditions, including dogfights and a climb to 25,000 ft, was 1 hour 20 minutes. A red warning light was fitted in a prominent position in the cockpit and illuminated when there was only fuel left for 20 minutes' flying. The rate of climb up to 18,000 ft under maximum climbing conditions of 1.35 ata boost, 2450 rpm, and 165 mph was around 3000–3250 ft/min. The Fw 190 had a high rate of climb when the entry was made from a fast cruising speed and the climb angle was steep. When pulling up from a dive, the rate of climb was described as phenomenal. It was noted that the power of the BMW 801D began to fall away at around 22,000 ft and was considerably reduced at 25,000 ft.

The Fw 190 also had exceptional performance in the dive, with high initial acceleration. The maximum speed obtained in a dive was 580 mph TAS at 16,000 ft and at this speed the controls, although slightly heavier, were still remarkably light. It was during diving tests that the lack of any need to re-trim was particularly noted and this characteristic was present at all times, even during the entry and subsequent pull-out. Due to the fuel injection system, it was possible to enter a dive by pushing the control column forward without the engine cutting.

During the trials AFDU pilots praised the canopy design of the Fw 190, which allowed lookout the like of which had not been seen before. The hood was of moulded plexiglas and offered an unrestricted view all round. Unlike most British fighters, there was no rear view mirror, but this was considered unnecessary as the view over the tail was so good. The hood was not to be opened in flight as tail buffeting was likely to occur and there was also the possibility that it might be blown off due to the slipstream. This was not a problem when flying in visual conditions as the quality of the plexiglas was so good, but it was an obvious disadvantage when flying in bad visibility or rain, or when the canopy had been contaminated with oil.

Although the Fw 190 was extremely light on the controls, it was reasonably easy to fly on instruments, but as it lacked an Artificial Horizon and Vertical Speed Indicator it had to be flown on a limited panel comprising gyro compass, turn and bank indicator, altimeter and air speed indicator, (ASI). With its excellent all-round view, particularly over the nose, the Fw 190 was well suited to low flying and ground strafing. Its gunsight was also depressed slightly, which tended to prevent pilots from flying into the ground during low-level attacks. Formation flying was easy, thanks to the excellent view and the aircraft's wide speed range made regaining formation relatively easy, although it was slow to decelerate.

MP499 was not flown at night, but it was inspected with the engine running on a dark night with no moon. The exhaust flames when seen from ahead at a distance of 100 yards appeared as a dull red halo and from the side the flames could be seen up to 500 yards away. From astern, the flames could be seen up to a distance of 200 yards. Although the Fw 190 was fitted with sufficient instrumentation for night flying, it was considered that the exhaust glare would badly affect the pilot's night vision, especially during take-off and landing. The cockpit lighting was adequate and did not reflect on the canopy.

In its conclusions, the AFDU report gave the Fw 190 credit for being a formidable low- to medium-altitude fighter. It was obvious that Kurt Tank, its designer, had given much thought to the environment in which the pilot had to work, as the cockpit was extremely well laid out and there was a general absence of large levers and unnecessary gadgets. The pilot was also given a comfortable seating position and was well protected by armour. Although it had advanced performance, its simplicity enabled new pilots to be thoroughly conversant with all the controls very quickly.

The engine was easy to start but required a lengthy run-up period, even when warm, before the oil temperature was within limits for take-off. This delay, compounded by difficulties experienced during taxying, meant that the Fw 190 was inferior to Allied fighters when it came to quick take-offs. Once in the air, however, it was a different story, one of the Fw 190's most outstanding qualities being its remarkable aileron control. It was possible to change direction with incredible speed and when viewed from another aircraft, the change appeared as if a flick roll had been performed. If RAF fighters were to stand any chance against the Fw 190; they had to be flown at high speed when in a combat area to give them any chance of achieving an element of surprise or, more likely, to avoid being bounced.

The AFDU trial also made a comparative assessment of the Fw 190's performance against several Allied fighters, including the Spitfire VB, Spitfire IX, and Mustang IA. Against the Spitfire VB, it came as no surprise to discover that the Fw 190 was 20–35 mph faster at all heights and also possessed a clear advantage in climb performance. Although the best climb speed of the two was very similar, the angle of climb of the Fw 190 was much steeper, so that its climb rate was approximately 450 ft/min better. When climbs were made from high cruising speed, or after a pull up from a dive, the Fw 190's superiority was even more marked. When the two aircraft were dived, it was found that the Fw 190 could draw away with ease, especially during the initial stages of the dive.

In terms of manoeuvrability, the Fw 190 was superior in all respects, except that of turning circles. However, when it was attacked, even this deficiency could be overcome to an extent by using the Fw 190's better rate of roll. Its large ailerons allowed very quick turn reversals that a Spitfire had great difficulty in following and if this was followed by a dive, the Focke-Wulf's excellent acceleration often allowed it to increase range to the point where the Spitfire was forced to break off. Other than utilising the Spitfire's superior turn performance, the most effective defence when attacked by an Fw 190 was to enter a high-speed shallow dive, which forced the Fw 190 into a long stern chase. Although it caught up eventually, a considerable distance was covered and it was thought that this tactic was liable to draw the Fw 190 too far away from its base. The only other crumb of comfort for Spitfire V pilots was that the Fw 190 was prone to flick during a high-speed stall, which could have dire consequences if it occurred at low level.

At the time of the AFDU trial the Spitfire V was still the mainstay of RAF Fighter Command, but the first examples of the Spitfire IX had already been delivered to No. 64 Squadron at Hornchurch. Powered by a two-stage, two-speed Rolls-Royce Merlin 61, much was required of the Spitfire IX and during comparisons with MP499, it lived up to expectation. Although the Fw 190 was 7–8 mph faster at 2000 ft, this situation had been reversed by 8000 ft and the Spitfire IX maintained its superiority up to 18,000 ft, where the Fw 190 held a slight advantage. At 21,000 ft the two aircraft were evenly matched but the Spitfire IX was 5–7 mph faster by the time that 25,000 ft was reached. In continuous climbs up to 23,000 ft, there was little to choose between the two, although at this height the performance of the Fw 190 was beginning to fall off, whereas that of the Spitfire IX was increasing. In climbs from high cruising speed and in a pull up from a dive, the Fw 190 held a slight advantage. Due to its particularly good acceleration, the Fw 190 was faster in the dive but this superiority was not as marked as with the Spitfire VB. In manoeuvring flight the Fw 190 once again held the advantage (except in turning circles), but if a Spitfire IX pilot decided to 'cut and run' the Fw 190 stood little chance of closing to gun firing range if it had been seen early enough and the Spitfire had been flying at a high cruising speed.

When measured against a Mustang IA, the Fw 190 had a slight speed advantage at 2000 ft but at medium levels (i.e. 10–15,000 ft) the Mustang was 15 mph faster. Above this height band, however, the initiative swung once more in favour of the Focke-Wulf, which was 5 mph faster at 20,000 ft and above. In the climb, the Fw 190 was superior to the Mustang at all heights, as the best climb speed for the latter was around 10 mph slower and its best angle of climb was not as steep. Performance was much more even in the dive, and if anything, the Mustang held a slight advantage. The Fw 190 was generally more manoeuvrable but, as with the Spitfire, it lost out to the Mustang when it came to turning circles. Against the Mustang, the Fw 190's superiority in rate of roll was not as marked as it had been with the Spitfire. As a result, its initial defensive manoeuvre of a diving turn reversal was not as effective, particularly if both aircraft were flying at high speed. The best defence for the Mustang was once again to operate within the combat area at high cruising speed and to dive away at full throttle. As far as the Fw 190 was concerned, a dive was best followed by a steep climb, which the Mustang could not match.

Following the present of Faber's Fw 190A, several other examples fell into the hands of the RAF. On the night of 16/17 April 1943 no fewer than three Fw 190A *Jabos* of SKG 10 arrived at West Malling following an attack on London. Of these, only A-4/U-8 *Werke Nr* 7155 flown by *Feldwebel* Otto Bechtold could be returned to the air. However, two more Fw 190As were acquired soon after when SKG 10 pilots landed in error at Manston on 20 May and 20 June 1943. The first to arrive was *Unteroffizier* Heinz Ehrhardt in A-4/U-8 *Werke Nr* 5843, which became PN999 and was used by the RAE before being sent to 1426 (Enemy Aircraft) Flight on 28 September 1943. During its time at RAE, PN999 was flown by Squadron Leader Johnny Checketts DFC, who at the time was OC No. 485 (New Zealand) Squadron at Biggin Hill. His impressions of the Fw 190 were given in a letter to 11 Group HQ dated 27 August 1943.

This flight was made by me to find the differences in the Fw 190 and the Spitfire LF.IX (Merlin 66) in regard to flying qualities. The Fw 190 number PN999 which I flew was not taken higher than 4,000 ft so that the experience I gained was very limited in the 30 minutes I flew. I found the cockpit and controls extremely well laid out and that every switch and all the flying controls were very convenient and easy to work. I should imagine that scramble times would compare with the Spitfire. Taxying is reasonably easy, but the toe brakes are strange after hand brake control and overall I think the Spitfire is much better for taxying.

The take-off was terrifying and I had considerable difficulty in keeping the aircraft straight in spite of the fact that I held the stick back to lock the tailwheel. I think I opened the throttle too slowly, because I saw the same aircraft take-off before I flew it in a perfectly normal manner. The electrical undercarriage is very simply raised and the tail trim is quite effective. The machine is beautiful to fly and quite fast at normal cruising revs and boost which I did not exceed. I had been warned about an extremely rough engine but under cruising conditions I found that the engine behaved perfectly and compared with most radials.

When I was about eight miles south of base, two Mustangs saw me and made attacks, dummy or real, I don't know. I did not give these aircraft any chance but owing to their insistence I let them see my RAF roundels and they formated on me and then tried to play. In the resulting steep turns at maximum cruising boost and revs I found no difficulty in getting on the tail of these aircraft and could have easily shot them down. I found the Revi gunsight very pleasant to use and the gun buttons in a comfortable position on the control column. The rate of climb of the Fw 190 was greatly superior to the Mustangs but inferior to the Spitfire LF.IX. I should imagine that at lower than 22,000 ft the Fw 190 would be slightly better than the Spitfire IX with Merlin 61. When the Mustangs sheered off I tried rolls and general defensive flying. The Fw 190 is remarkable and really beautiful to aerobat in the rolling plane, but in the looping plane it is greatly inferior to the Spitfire. Visibility is exceptionally good all round and is greatly superior to that in the Spitfire. I found the cockpit slightly small for defensive fighting and the back parachute was uncomfortable, which might account for the fact that attacks on the Fw 190 from below and behind often catch the Fw pilot unawares.

On my first approach I found the vital actions easy and comfortable, although landing with the hood closed was strange. I was forced round again by a Spitfire cutting in and the overshoot procedure was normal and the aircraft behaved perfectly. On my second approach I came in at 130 mph and used motor. The landing position is very blind and uncomfortable, but if the aircraft is motored in at 120–130 mph, a three point landing is easily made although swing after landing is noticeable. I enjoyed the experience and should like to fly this aircraft at 22,000–30,000 ft to gain experience at its combat heights. I am convinced through experience that the Spitfire with the Merlin 66 engine is much superior at all levels, but the Fw 190 could be a very aggressive aircraft in the hands of an experienced fighter pilot.

The later examples of the Fw 190 that ended their days in RAF service were the fighter-bomber version that were employed in the west on hit-

and-run attacks and, in the case of SKG 10, on night attacks aimed mainly on London. The *Jabo* variant of the Fw 190A was flown from Farnborough by Wing Commander Jamie Rankin DSO DFC, a vastly experienced fighter pilot, who identified several handling differences compared with the fighter version. On the Fw 190 bomber, much more tail trimming was required for climbs and dives and the lateral control, although still good, was not nearly as light at high speeds as in the fighter tested previously. Slight buffeting was also experienced on the elevators at speeds of more than 350 mph, possibly due to inter-ference of the airflow by the fuselage bomb rack.

Following its initial evaluation and comparative testing, AFDU continued to use captured Fw 190s for further trials work, including tours of fighter airfields to show the aircraft to the resident pilots and allow them the chance to fly against it in mock combat. Flight Lieutenant Len Thorne was heavily involved in this work, taking over the responsibility from Flight Lieutenant H.S. 'Susie' Sewell when he was rested after a crash at White Waltham. Sewell and Thorne were carrying out fuel consumption tests in a Mosquito (HJ666) on 30 July 1943 when an engine cut. An emergency landing had to be aborted due to personnel crossing the perimeter track, but when full power was selected, the good engine also quit and the aircraft crash-landed on the airfield. Although both crew members were able to walk away from the accident, Sewell was badly affected by the crash and was off flying for some time. In contrast, Len Thorne was back in the air the very next day and went on to make over eighty sorties in Fw 190 PM679, amounting to over 100 hours flying time.

> On 1 August 1943 I was made up to Flight Commander and given the job of flying the Fw 190 which I always thought of as 'my' 190. I spent two days looking at it because 'Susie' Sewell had gone, there was no-one else to ask about it and the Germans had very unkindly not left us a set of Pilot's Notes. The time was spent going over it point by point, studying as much of it as I could but Squadron Leader Dyson, who was our C.O. at the time, got very impatient because I was taking so long to start the flying. The Air Ministry was getting hot under the collar as they wanted the demonstrations to start so I was put under some pressure and finally took it into the air.
>
> The Fw 190 handled well and was a delight to fly, although it had to be watched on take-off and particularly on landing. If you held off too high, the stall when it came, was very sudden and it would literally fall out of your hands. With its high wing loading (44 lb/sq.ft) and high approach speed it was almost frightening after our docile Spitfires. Demonstrations and mock combats

were carried out at North Weald, Northolt, Hornchurch, Kenley, Biggin Hill, Tangmere, Ibsley, Portreath, Exeter and Colerne. At Kenley I remember having to land on the short runway and at Biggin the Group Captain worked me so hard that I ended up landing on the flare path in the gathering gloom. Although I was normally escorted by two or more Spitfires, there were one or two 'hairy' moments. The Polish pilots were reputedly trigger happy and were apparently unimpressed by RAF roundels on a German aircraft. In the course of one of the dogfights, one of the Spitfires suddenly streamed black smoke and went straight down with an engine failure. I thought 'Christ, they'll think I've shot him down' so I was more scared that day than most!

Some of the mock combats seemed very realistic to me. It was during one of these that the 190 showed its teeth when, without warning, it flicked off a tight turn into an inverted spin. Recovery was straightforward but took about 3–4,000 ft of altitude. At Hornchurch I arrived just as the Wing was returning from a Sweep. One of the Squadron Commanders arriving in the circuit saw this 190 below him and came screaming down behind me only to realise that I had my wheels and flaps down and a Spitfire on each wing tip. He hauled off at the very last moment but it was rather frightening all the same. After this episode I started to have four Spitfires as escort instead of two! At the request of the Army there were glorious (authorised) beat ups of various gun posts. The Army were always asking us to do these so they could train their light Ack-Ack crews. Having made your dive you then pulled up and in the 190 you could do seven or eight upward rolls before the speed fell off, so an approved beat up was something to look forward to. At Portreath the coastal defence guns opened up at me but fortunately they were way behind.

During a visit to Benson I had the honour of meeting a great gentleman in the person of Air Commodore John Boothman who was then AOC of the Photographic Reconnaissance Unit (PRU). With the permission of the Air Ministry I showed him the taps and sent him off for a short trip in PM679, one of the two Fw 190A-4s which had landed in error at Manston. In return he allowed me to fly any of the various PRU aircraft so I rather foolishly chose a Spitfire XI instead of one of their P-38 Lightnings which would have been another type for my logbook. There followed further visits to Coltishall, Aston Down, Great Massingham, Syerston, Rednal and Eshott. It was during the flight to the latter that trouble developed. The BMW radial engine always felt and sounded a bit harsh, but on this flight it was really rough with considerable vibration. Despite hard work by the ground-crew there was no improvement. With some trepidation I flew the 190 back to Wittering [AFDU had moved to Wittering from Duxford in March 1943]. When the engine was stripped down one of the pistons was found to have a fist-sized hole through the crown. In spite of this the engine had continued to function with negligible loss of power.

The final visits were to North Weald and Hartford Bridge after two months of repairs and servicing. At the end of November 1943 it was back home at Wittering for a well-earned rest for aircraft and pilot. During the course of the foregoing exercises and demonstrations the 190 was flown against Spitfires, Typhoons, Tempests, Mosquitos and Bostons. At Benson the trials were carried out at heights above 26,000 ft against PRU Spitfires, Mosquitos and Lockheed P-38 Lightnings.

Having mastered the technique of take-off and landing, I thoroughly enjoyed the eight months of that assignment. The high cruising speed, well in excess of 300 mph, compared very favourably with the Spitfire and was similar to the Merlin-engined Mustang, Thunderbolt, Typhoon and Tempest. The cockpit was roomy, well laid out, and the tear-drop canopy gave excellent visibility. In my estimation the Fw 190A is classed with the Spitfire VIII and IX and the Mustang III. It was one of the best fighters of the Second World War.

On 18 March 1944 I did a comparative trial in PM679 against Spitfire XIV RB179 and at the end found the engine rougher than usual. After adjustments I took her up for an air test the following morning but suffered a near engine failure and successfully put down again at Wittering. There was a delay of several weeks and I believe a new engine was taken from one of the damaged arrivals. On 24 June I again tried an air test but as soon as I was airborne it was obvious that there was something dramatically wrong with the engine so I did a tight circuit and on the downwind leg the engine quit completely. I had no alternative but to do a 'dead-stick' landing and as I came over the airfield boundary I jettisoned the hood. This was operated by a cartridge system and when you fired it, the hood was blown straight off and away. Apart from that there was no damage to the aircraft as I managed to put it down without breaking anything. By then there were a number of other Fw 190s around so it was decided that they wouldn't try to repair mine.

PM679 was not flown again and was used for spares for PE882 and PN999, which were in service with No. 1426 (Enemy Aircraft) Flight at Collyweston. Not long after, PE882 was written off in a crash on 13 October 1944, which claimed the life of the unit's C.O., Flight Lieutenant E.R. 'Lew' Lewenden. It was seen to be on fire before coming down on the Stamford to Kettering road near the airfield, eventually coming to rest in the garden of a nearby house.

Like most other fighters of the period, the Fw 190 was constantly developed in terms of performance and weapons capability. After the prolific A-model, produced in numerous sub-variants to fulfil fighter, fighter-bomber and bomber-destroyer roles, the next major version was the Fw 190D, the first of the long-nosed Fw 190s. This version was powered by a Junkers Jumo 213A engine of 1750 hp, although this could be increased to 2240 hp with MW-50 water-methanol injection. Introduced in the autumn of 1944, the Fw 190D came as a nasty shock to many P-51 Mustang and Spitfire IX pilots, as the greatly increased power of the Jumo endowed a much better altitude performance when compared with the Fw 190A. The top speed was 426 mph at 21,336 ft and even at 33,000 ft (which could be attained in seventeen minutes) the Fw 190D-9 was still capable of 397 mph. The service ceiling was nearly 40,000 ft.

The ultimate Fw 190 was given a completely new designation, the Ta 152, after its designer Kurt Tank. Although it only saw service in small numbers, its performance was superior to every other piston-engined fighter of the time. With MW-50 and GM-1 nitrous oxide boost it was capable of 472 mph at 41,000 ft and its service ceiling was over 48,000 ft. It had a climb rate of around 3000 ft/min and possessed superb acceleration and agility, to the extent that some *Luftwaffe* pilots preferred the Ta 152 to the Messerschmitt Me 262 jet fighter. Had it been available a year earlier, the Ta 152 may well have had some influence on the air battles taking place over the *Reich*. As it was, its appearance caused little more than a minor irritation to the Allied air forces, although it did show what the German aircraft industry would have been capable of had the controlling authorities actively promoted the development of high performance aircraft, instead of relying for so long on outdated designs.

# PART THREE

# American Fighters

43. (Above) Fw 190A-4 PM679 carries out a low level beat up with a P-47D Thunderbolt of the 334th Fighter Squadron, 4th Fighter Group, Eighth Air Force.
*(Philip Jarrett)*

44. One of the Fw 190A-4/U-8 Jabos of SKG 10, which landed in error after attacks on London in early 1943.
*(Author)*

45. Focke-Wulf Fw 190A-4/U-8 PN999 is former, Werke Nummer 5843 of SKG 10. After testing by RAE Farnborough, it was flown by No. 1426 (Enemy Aircraft) Flight and was last recorded as being in store at 47 MU Sealand in November 1947.
*(Philip Jarrett)*

47. The Buffalo's extensive cockpit glazing is emphasized in this view of AS417.    *(Philip Jarrett)*

46. Buffalo AS426 displays its unusual undercarriage and large aerial mast mounted on the forward fuselage.
*(Philip Jarrett)*

48. Buffalos of No. 453 Squadron lined up at Sembawang, Singapore with AN185 in the foreground.
*(Philip Jarrett)*

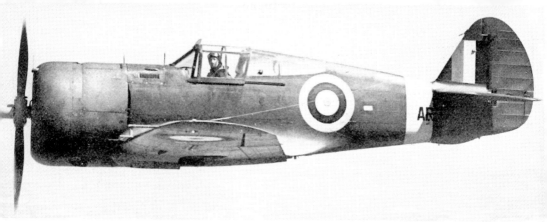

49. Although outclassed by contemporary fighters in the west, the Curtiss Mohawk performed well in the Far East and remained in first-line service in small numbers until early 1944.

*(Philip Jarrett)*

50. Mohawk III AR634 during testing at A&AEE and already looking somewhat weather-beaten. The aircraft is fitted with a ring and bead sight.

*(Philip Jarrett)*

51. Mohawk IV, possibly AR645. The Mohawk IV was equivalent to the French Hawk H-75A-4 and was powered by a Wright Cyclone of 1200 hp. *(Philip Jarrett)*

53. DS174 (formerly 40-2983) was one of three P-39Cs delivered in July 1941 for initial trials and flown by AFDU to assess the type for fighter operations. *(Philip Jarrett)*

55. Bell Airacobra I AH573 was used for trials work at A&AEE and AFDU and was struck off charge on 11 February 1942. *(Philip Jarrett)*

52. A view of Airacobra I AH573 in the air. The protruding barrel of the 20 mm cannon firing through the propeller boss is clearly evident. *(Philip Jarrett)*

54. Unusually for an American aircraft, the cockpit of the Airacobra was relatively cramped and tall pilots had little or no head room. *(Philip Jarrett)*

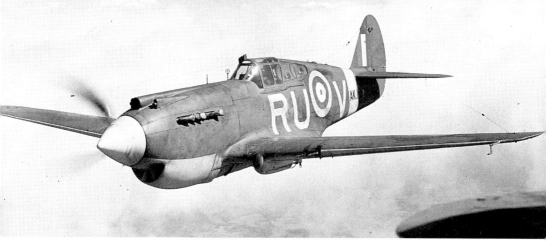

56. The Tomahawk IIB was the equivalent of the USAAF P-40C and was fitted with an American radio and oxygen system. It was also capable of carrying a 43-gallon drop tank. *(Philip Jarrett)*

. A pleasant air-to-air view of Tomahawk I AH925. After testing at A&AEE it was used by No. 30 OTU and was withdrawn from use at the end of 1944. *(Philip Jarrett)*

58. Tomahawk I AH769 was one of the first ex-French machines to arrive in January 1941 and flew with No. 268 Squadron and No. 1686 Flight before being struck off charge on 31 May 1944. *(Philip Jarrett)*

59. Kittyhawk I photographed at Boscombe Down in January 1942.     *(Philip Jarrett)*

60. Kittyhawk IIA FL 220 was powered by a Packard-Merlin V-1650-1 and was used by A&AEE in August 1942 for performance and handling trials. It was relegated to instructional use in August 1943.     *(Philip Jarrett)*

61. Allison-engined Kittyhawk IV FX594, photographed in October 1944. *(Philip Jarrett)*

62. Kittyhawk IIIs of No. 260 Squadron at Castel Benito in early 1943. *(Philip Jarrett)*

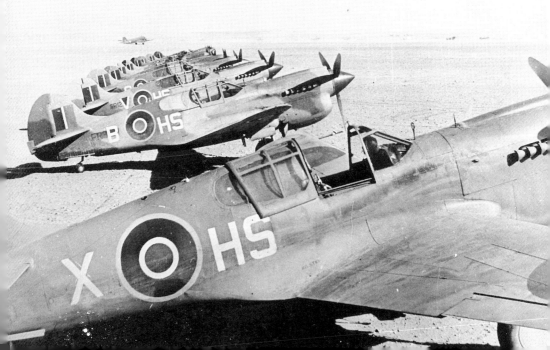

63. Air-to-air view of Mustang X AM208, showing the original under-nose air intake position.
*(Philip Jarrett)*

64. AG346 was the second production Mustang I and flew with several units before being shot down by flak on 20 August 19944 when serving with No. 168 Squadron. *(Philip Jarrett)*

65. Mustang I AL 975/G was used as an engine test bed by Rolls-Royce for development of the Merlin-powered variants, and as such was re-designated Mustang X. It was also flown by AFDU and was finally struck off charge on 5 April 1945. *(Philip Jarrett)*

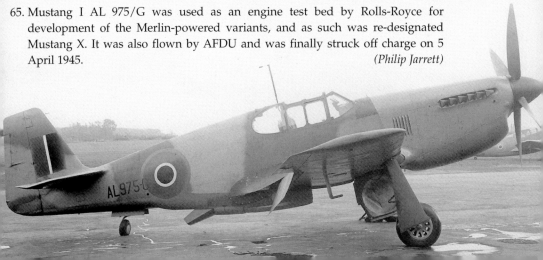

66. Mustang III FX 893 at Boscombe Down, fitted with a bulged Malcolm hood and underwing
rocket rails. *(Philip Jarrett)*

67. A late production Mustang IV, showing the moulded bubble canopy that improved all-round
vision. *(Philip Jarrett)*

THUNDERBOLT
DOUBLE WAS
MAY 1944

68. Thunderbolt I FL844 (ex 42-25792) was used at Boscombe Down for evaluation and handling
   trials with various sizes of drop tanks. *(Philip Jarrett)*

69. KJ346 was a Thunderbolt II, which was equivalent to the USAAF P-47D-30-RE with bubble
   canopy. It is seen here shortly after roll out from the Republic plant at Farmingdale. A total of
   830 Thunderbolts saw service with the RAF, of which 590 were of the Mark II variant.
   *(Philip Jarrett)*

70. Thunderbolt I HD118.                                          *(Philip Jarrett)*

71. Thunderbolt II HD265 RS-G of No. 30 Squadron fitted with long-range drop tanks.

*(Philip Jarrett)*

72. BJ513 was one of the initial batch of 91 ex-French Martlet Is. The downward vision panel can be seen in the bottom of the fuselage aft of the main wheels.
*(Philip Jarrett)*

74. Martlet V JV337 was powered by a Pratt & Whitney Twin Wasp and pictured in June 1943.
*(Philip Jarrett)*

73. Martlet I BJ570. Note the forward rake of the aerial mast.
*(Philip Jarrett)*

75. The Wildcar VI featured a taller fin and rudder, which significantly improved directional control. JV642 was the sixth production aircraft and was used for performance and handling trials at Boscombe Down in April 1944. *(Philip Jarrett)*

76. Hellcat I FN322 was used for brief performance trials at Boscombe Down from July to August 1943. *(Philip Jarrett)*

77. Hellcat I FN376. The Hellcat offered a significant improvement in performance over the Wildcat, being around 50 mph faster, with a much superior rate of climb. *(Philip Jarrett)*

79. The Hellcat II was powered by a Pratt & Whitney R-2800-10W Double Wasp incorporating water injection. Deliveries of the Hellcat II to the Fleet Air Arm amounted to 930 out of a total of 1182. *(Philip Jarrett)*

78. Hellcat II JV270 fitted with underwing rocket rails in March 1945. *(Philip Jarrett)*

80. A Corsair I in the air and seen here with the original canopy design.     *(Philip Jarrett)*

81. An early Corsair I showing the flaps in the fully extended position.     *(Philip Jarrett)*

82. A Corsair I showing the original rounded wing tip shape. To fit into the below deck hangars of British aircraft carriers, the wings had to be clipped by around 8 in. *(Philip Jarrett)*

83. Goodyear-built Corsair IV KD300 displays clipped wings, raised canopy and a lengthened tailwheel leg. *(Philip Jarrett)*

CORSAIR M
DOUBLE W
OCTOBER

# CHAPTER TEN

# Brewster Buffalo

O f all the piston-engined fighters of the Second World War, the Brewster Buffalo has to be a candidate for being the most unloved. Although its handling characteristics were pleasant enough and it possessed no real vices, its relatively poor performance and inadequate hitting power meant that it would have been hope-lessly outclassed had it been pitted against modern high performance fighters such as the Bf 109E.

The aircraft that would be known in the UK as the Buffalo, was designed by Dayton Brown of the Brewster Aeronautical Corporation in 1936 and proved to be of considerable interest to the US Navy, who applied the designation F2A. Its portly fuselage accommodated a 950 hp single-row, nine-cylinder Wright Cyclone radial engine. It featured a mid-set wing, with an inward retracting undercarriage (the wheels being housed in the lower fuselage), and a large glazed canopy, which provided excellent rearwards vision. Following comparative testing, the US Navy began to favour the rival Grumman F4F Wildcat and Brewster's corpulent offering was eventually foisted onto the Marine Corps. With the rapidly worsening political situation in Europe, orders began to come in from overseas and forty-four of the original F2A-1 aircraft for the US Navy were de-navalised as the Brewster B-239 and delivered to Finland for the war against the Soviet Union. An order was also placed by Belgium for the up-rated (1100 hp Wright Cyclone GR-1820-G) B-339, but these aircraft had not been delivered by the time that the country capitulated after the German invasion of May 1940.

The Belgian order was taken over by the RAF and three Brewster Buffalos were delivered to Church Fenton in September 1940 to be taken over by the newly re-formed No. 71 Squadron, which was the first of the so-called 'Eagle' Squadrons manned by US volunteer pilots. The unit's first CO was Squadron Leader Walter Churchill DSO DFC, who had become an 'ace' whilst flying Hurricanes of No. 3 Squadron during the air battles over France. His evaluation of the Buffalo was less than complimentary. Indeed, he went so far as to recommend that the aircraft should on no account be considered as a fighter until considerable modifications had been carried out to eradicate certain deficiencies as highlighted by recent operational experience.

Churchill considered that the armament of two 0.5-in and two 0.303-in machine guns was entirely inadequate, a situation that was exacerbated by the lack of a reflector gunsight. He also criticised the thickness of the armour protection to the rear and the fact that it did not protect the pilot's head. The shoulder straps of the Sutton harness also passed over the top of the seat instead of through slots in the back, which meant that they tended to give way when the aircraft was inverted and could lead to the pilot hitting his head on the hood. The undercarriage actuating lever was too small and difficult to operate. This criticism also applied to the flap-operating lever and the seat adjustment. As the R/T controls were located on the right-hand side of the cockpit, this required the pilot to change hands to operate the radio. He was also liable to hit his elbow on the seat every time he had to change from send to receive. The oxygen system was regulated automatically, instead of being a manual operation, and it was felt that the latter would have been preferable as this system at least allowed the pilot the opportunity to turn up the amount of oxygen he was receiving if he was in a dogfight. Churchill also considered that the Buffalo's stick-type control column, with the firing button located on the top, was not as good as the articulated spade grip as used on most RAF fighters.

Criticism was also levelled at some of the Buffalo's structural aspects. The wings were not bolted to the fuselage centre section as was normal practice on British fighters, but had a straight through spar. It was felt that they would be difficult and time-consuming to repair following an accident or as a result of battle damage. As the fuel tanks were of the integral type, another lengthy maintenance job was in the offing should they take any hits. The elevators were activated by a push-pull tube instead of the more normal twin-cable arrangement, and although these provided an excellent level of control, it was felt that the tubes might succumb to enemy fire to a greater extent than a cable system. As there was no automatic boost control, the pilot had to continuously adjust the throttle during a climb, to avoid exceeding maximum permissible boost. As the flaps only extended through 60 degrees, the aircraft tended to glide in a fairly flat attitude, as a result of which its landing roll could be excessively long. After landing the tailwheel was also liable to wobble on its caster, which on occasion was severe enough to strip the rubber from the tyre. Churchill concluded that the Buffalo would make an excellent 'trainer' aircraft as it was relatively simple to fly and delightful for aerobatics.

At the same time as Walter Churchill was evaluating the Buffalo at

Church Fenton, another example was being tested at RAE Farnborough. The best technique on take-off was to hold the stick fully forward for about thirty yards to bring the tail up, after which the aircraft ran smoothly and showed no tendency to bounce. As speed increased there was a slight tendency to swing to the left, but this was easily controlled by rudder, which was effective, but not so sensitive as to cause over-correction. The aircraft flew itself off without assistance after a take-off run shorter than both the Hurricane and Spitfire. When airborne, it accelerated quite rapidly and had a good initial rate of climb. The elevator control was excellent and not too sensitive, as on the Spitfire, or too sloppy, as on the Hurricane.

The best approach speed was around 90–95 mph IAS and the hydraulically operated split flaps took nine seconds to come down. Lowering the flaps caused a nose-down trim change of around 17 degrees, which required re-trimming, but even with the trimmer wheel fully aft (tab angle 17 degrees) there was still slight nose heaviness. There was also a marked sensation of sinking at speeds below 75 mph IAS. The approach glide was steep, which allowed an excellent view of the aerodrome and because of the slight sinking, pilots found that they tended to flatten out slightly higher than usual. The landing itself was easy and the aircraft settled down after a small float with no bounce or swing. The brakes could be used soon after touching down and they were smooth and effective in operation. Once on the ground, the Buffalo was very manoeuvrable and could readily be turned in its own space with the aid of a little braking.

With the engine set to 1850 rpm, the stall speeds were 76 mph IAS with the flaps and undercarriage up and 64 mph IAS with the flaps and undercarriage down. The stall was marked by the sudden drop of a wing, followed by the nose, but the aircraft tended to quickly un-stall itself when back pressure on the control column was relaxed. With the flaps and undercarriage down the wing dropped rather more quickly, however the stall was still quite mild. Longitudinal trim was maintained by the elevator trim tabs, which were controlled via a 1¾ in diameter wheel, which rotated about an axis parallel to the wing span and operated in the natural sense, i.e. winding back on the wheel brought the nose up. Full tab range (+17 to −8 degrees) required nine complete turns of the wheel. Directional trim was provided by a 3-in diameter wheel, nine turns of which rotated the rudder trim tab through its full travel of +/−5 degrees.

The ailerons were tested in the speed range 90–400 mph IAS. They were proved to be exceptionally effective, crisp and powerful; stick forces were neither too light at low speeds or too heavy at greater speeds. Pilots considered them to be a definite improvement over the fabric-covered ailerons of the Hurricane and Spitfire. A comparison of the Buffalo and Spitfire in terms of aileron response and stick force makes interesting reading.

| | | Buffalo | | Spitfire | |
|---|---|---|---|---|---|
| EAS | ASI | Time to bank 45° (sec) | Max force (lb) | Time to bank 45° (sec) | Max force (lb) |
| 214 | 200 | 1.7 | 10.5 | 1.8 | 10 |
| 267 | 250 | 1.7 | 14 | 1.8 | 18 |
| 320 | 300 | 1.7 | 17 | 2.1 | 35 |
| 372 | 350 | 1.8 | 20 | 2.6 | 55 |
| 413 | 390 | 1.6 | 24 | 3.5 | 80 |

The elevator was tested at speeds between 80–400 mph IAS, with the response and feel being rated as excellent. At 80 mph IAS the response was exceptionally good, but at the same time the stick forces were not too light. With increase in speed the weight increased steadily, but even at 400 mph IAS, the stick force was not unduly heavy and the response remained good. At 80 mph IAS the rudder was effective, but the response was poor for the first quarter movement. This improved above 100 mph IAS and the response and feel were good until fairly high speed (over 300 mph IAS), when the rudder tended to become too light. Even a small displacement gave a large response, which caused a snaking tendency that had to be corrected. Apart from this, the control harmony was good. RAE pilots were highly complimentary about the handling characteristics of the Buffalo and all agreed that a definite advance had been made in fighter controls.

AFDU (then at Northolt) also produced a report on the Buffalo in November 1940. As the aircraft was not fitted with guns, the findings were somewhat complimentary, as its performance was rather better than an aircraft in operational trim. Pilots were particularly impressed by the aircraft's roomy and comfortable cockpit and the excellent view afforded by the extensive glazing, particularly to the sides and rear, which was vastly superior to that offered in both the Hurricane and Spitfire. The hood could be opened easily at all speeds, but proved to be difficult to close at high speed. One item in the cockpit that was criticised, however, was the mechanism to raise and lower the pilot's seat, as it was found to be almost impossible to raise the seat when in the air.

As Farnborough had already discovered, the take-off in a Buffalo was completely straightforward. It was rated as being superior to that in a Hurricane. For landing, it was recommended that a little engine be left on instead of employing a full glide approach, and despite the aircraft's comparatively fast approach speed it pulled up very quickly after touchdown. The pedal-operated brakes were very efficient at shortening the landing run and as an aid to taxying. The Buffalo's main asset in the air was its excellent manoeuvrability, brought about by its excellent aileron control and relatively stubby wings which, at a span of 35 ft, were 5 ft shorter than the Hurricane. The elevator control was also light and positive and although the rudder was heavier, this did not produce any real harmonisation problems and directional control was readily available. Trimmers were provided for all three controls and these were found to be quite sensitive and very effective, and materially aided the aircraft's excellent controllability.

Brief comparative trials were flown against a Hurricane at the Buffalo's rated altitudes and during level speed tests the Buffalo was found to be 15 mph faster at 6000 ft. At 14,700 ft the maximum speed of the two aircraft was virtually identical. However, it was later calculated that had the Buffalo been carrying its full war load, as was the Hurricane, the speeds would have been approximately the same at the lower height and the Buffalo would have been slower by around 12 mph at the higher altitude. Owing to the disparity in weight the Buffalo also out-performed the Hurricane in climbs to 15,000 ft and it could easily turn inside the British aircraft. Pilots were of the opinion that the Buffalo would be a good gun platform.

With a maximum speed of around 300 mph and a rapidly deteriorating performance above 15,000 ft, there was no possibility of the Buffalo being used in the European theatre and most aircraft were shipped to the Far East. The first unit to become operational was No. 67 Squadron at Kallang, Singapore in May 1941. The Buffalo was also flown by Nos 146, 243, 453, 488 and (RAAF) 21 Squadrons. Carrying full fuel and armament, the Buffalo's performance was reduced still further. Following the Japanese invasion in December 1941, it was hopelessly outclassed by the nimble Mitsubishi Zero, which benefited from a vastly superior power-to-weight ratio. A story that did the rounds at the time told of Buffalo pilots having to suffer the ignominy of the Blenheim twin-engined bombers they were escorting being forced to slow down so that they could keep up. In an effort to improve performance, some aircraft had their all-up weight reduced by having two of their 0.5-in guns replaced by 0.303-in Brownings, together with a smaller ammunition load and less than full fuel. This accounted for around 900 lb, which reduced the performance gap with the Zero. However, general wear and tear on the airframes and down-on-power engines countered this and following the withdrawal of units to India, the Buffalo was quickly replaced by the Hurricane.

At the same time as the dispatch of the Buffalo to the Far East, a number of aircraft were delivered to the FAA, which was suffering from a desperate shortage of fighters, to the point that even obsolescent machines had to be considered. It served with No. 805 Squadron during the defence of Crete in March 1941, alongside the Fairey Fulmar, and also flew with No. 885 Squadron. Prior to its naval service, the Buffalo was flown by Eric Brown, who was to become a renowned test pilot and CO of the Aerodynamics Flight at Farnborough. Like many pilots before him, he found the view directly ahead to be extremely poor because of the high sit of the nose when on the ground, but despite this taxying was easy and the efficient brakes allowed the aircraft to be weaved gently to clear the path ahead. As there was no automatic boost control, the throttle had to be opened carefully on take-off and plenty of forward stick had to be applied to raise the tail to allow the aircraft to accelerate. The rudder control was deemed excellent and the gentle swing to the left during the take-off run could easily be controlled.

Once airborne, the Buffalo climbed steeply with an initial climb rate of around 2000 ft/min, but it was found that this figure soon diminished as altitude was gained. At a cruising speed of 160 mph IAS, the aircraft was unstable longitudinally, which caused problems if it had to be flown on instruments in cloud. Laterally, the Buffalo was neutrally stable and it had positive stability directionally. The maximum speed was noted as being 290 mph IAS at 16,500 ft and the service ceiling was 25,000 ft. Although Brown was not impressed with these levels of performance, he was delighted by the aircraft's handling, particularly the ailerons, which were highly effective throughout the whole speed range. The elevators were nearly as good and the rudder, although the heaviest of the three controls, was entirely adequate.

The Buffalo's low-speed characteristics were mild-mannered and the stall with the undercarriage and flaps up occurred at 76 mph IAS, together with a gentle wing drop and a lowering of the nose. With the gear and flaps down the stall came at a very low 67 mph IAS, although it was noticeable that the wing drop was slightly more pronounced. Prior to landing, the undercarriage was lowered at 95 mph IAS followed by the flaps, the operation of which was considered to be a little on the slow side. The best approach speed was around 80 mph IAS. This allowed a reasonable view ahead, but to achieve this almost full backward elevator trim was required. A distinct pull on the control column was needed to set the aircraft in the correct attitude for a three-point landing, which occurred at 75 mph IAS. The landing run could be controlled easily by gentle use of the brakes and there was little danger of a swing developing.

After his flight, Brown had mixed emotions as regards the Buffalo. On the one hand, the aircraft was a delight to fly. The handling characteristics and control responses were as good, if not better, than any other fighter he had flown, but as a weapon of war it was seriously flawed due to its laboured performance at altitudes above 10,000 ft. At a time when the RAF/FAA were looking towards the 20-mm Hispano cannon as the primary weapon in fighter combat, the Buffalo's fire-power also left something to be desired.

Of the Buffalos that were sent to the Far East, the vast majority were lost in action in Malaya and Singapore, or were destroyed in the face of the Japanese advance. A handful made it to serve with second-line units and the last few RAF machines were struck off charge in late 1943 to become instructional airframes. Although the aircraft was to achieve fame in the war in Finland, where it fought at low level (where it was at its best) and against mediocre opposition, elsewhere it was a different story. Sadly, Brewster's gallant effort to compete with more established names in the world of fighter aircraft production was doomed to failure, and the Buffalo has unfortunately gone down in history as one of the world's worst aircraft. This is all rather unfair, as there was nothing particularly wrong with the Buffalo as a flying machine, quite the opposite. However, the rapidly advancing technology of the day meant that many other types were soon able to surpass its relatively modest performance.

# CHAPTER ELEVEN

# Curtiss Mohawk

The Curtiss Hawk 75A (Mohawk in RAF service) was a close contemporary of the Brewster Buffalo and was similar in several aspects of its design, in particular the fitment of a Wright Cyclone GR-1820-G 205A engine of 1200 hp in the later variants. Despite this, it was to fare somewhat better than the Buffalo in its operational career and was to remain in first-line service in the Far East until January 1944.

The Hawk 75A was the export version of the Curtiss P-36A that had entered US Army Air Corps service in April 1938 and was a development of the Hawk 75, which was outwardly similar, but with a fixed undercarriage. Early aircraft were fitted with a Pratt & Whitney Twin Wasp R-1830-13 of 1050 hp and the type was selected by France to complement the Morane MS.406, Dewoitine D.520 and Bloch 152 fighters of the French Air Force. By the time that war was declared, France had 108 Hawks in service and another 183 had been delivered by the time of the armistice. The most popular version in French service was the H-75A–3, which was armed with six 7.5-mm machine-guns and had slightly improved performance compared with the early variants.

Further orders were placed for the Wright Cyclone-powered H-75A-4, but only six of these had reached Europe by the time of the French collapse. After the fall of France, all outstanding contracts were transferred to Britain and a total of 227 were delivered, plus ten more that were obtained from other sources. Of these, only five were powered by the Twin Wasp (Mohawk III), the rest being equivalent to the H-75A-4 and designated Mohawk IV. Initial deliveries were made to the UK in the summer of 1940. After reassembly, these airframes were held in reserve until the immediate crisis of the Battle of Britain had passed. Having been originally ordered by the French Air Force, there was much work to do to change over to British instrumentation and radios. This work was entrusted to Westland Aircraft, who were to carry out similar work with the Mohawk's successor, the Curtiss P-40 Tomahawk.

The first example to be tested in the UK was a French Hawk 75A

(No. 188), which was also used for comparative trials with a Spitfire I (K9944). The trial was carried out at RAE Farnborough over a two-week period, commencing 29 December 1939, and was brought about by worrying reports of Spitfire ailerons becoming almost immovable at speeds above 300 mph IAS. A Hawk had already been flown by Sam McKenna (a pilot from A&AEE) in France and from this it was known that the American aircraft possessed remarkably good controls. The ailerons in particular were light, which was in marked contrast with the Spitfire. It was hoped that a closer inspection would shed some light on how the problems with the British fighter might be put right.

During the trials at Farnborough, the Hawk was flown at a take-off weight of 6025 lb. The aircraft was found to be unusually manoeuvrable on the ground, owing to its steerable tailwheel. This was coupled to the rudder bar through a spring system and was steerable through 30 degrees in either direction, after which the mechanism automatically declutched, leaving the wheel to castor freely. Although pilots had been warned to be wary of this feature, they experienced no difficulty in doing quite sharp turns, as the turn could be stopped quickly when desired by using the brakes. As the pilot's seat was quite high, the view ahead was fairly good, but in any event the aircraft could be easily swung from side to side to clear the area ahead when taxying. The brakes were operated from pedals on the rudder bar and were very powerful.

Take-offs were simple and no flap was required. There was a tendency to swing to the left, but this could easily be held by the application of opposite rudder. The acceleration was good and the ground run was free from bouncing or wing drop. As soon as the aircraft was airborne, the pilot had a feeling of complete control, the ailerons being pleasantly crisp and the elevator not unduly light. The initial climb was very good. On raising the undercarriage (which took about twenty seconds to retract completely), the aircraft became slightly tail heavy.

On lowering the flaps prior to landing, the nose tended to pitch down and a slight pull was needed on the control column to maintain the correct speed. The approach was normally flown at 80–85 mph IAS and in this condition all three controls were effective and had positive feel, which was conducive to pilot confidence. When trimmed in the glide at 85 mph IAS, the aircraft was markedly stable (stick-free) and normal gliding turns could be made with no risk of stalling or loss of height. If the engine had to be opened up as in a go-around, the aircraft became tail heavy, but this could be held with one hand while the trim was being adjusted. Care had to be taken not to raise the flaps too quickly, as the nose tended to rise quite rapidly and height could be lost. On landing, there was only a small float and the control column did not have to be pulled right back to produce a three-point touchdown. The aircraft tended to settle on the ground quite firmly and there was no swing until the latter part of the ground run, when the brakes were easily capable of maintaining a straight course. Heavy braking could be applied soon after landing, without fear of lifting the tail.

Elevator trimming was controlled by a 3-in diameter wheel on the pilot's left. At full throttle with the flaps and undercarriage up, the Hawk was just stable (stick-free) at all speeds from 100–400 mph IAS. Pilots considered the longitudinal stability characteristics to be ideal for a fighter, thus confirming the widespread view that stick-free longitudinal stability for this type of aircraft at climbing speeds and above should be 'just on the right side of neutral'. The rudder trim tab was operated by a similarly positioned wheel and could be used for take-off, or when steep prolonged climbs or fast dives were being carried out. Directional control was aided by the fin being set at 1½ degrees to the plane of symmetry to counteract propeller slipstream. No lateral trim was provided, except for fixed tabs that could be preset when the aircraft was on the ground.

Tests were carried out in high-speed dives up to 400 mph IAS, whereby each control in turn was given a slight displacement and released. When rudder was applied at the highest speeds attained, the nose dipped downward quite sharply and the aircraft tended to yaw. On releasing this control input, however, the nose came up again and the aircraft swung back quickly with no oscillation. The dipping of the nose was found to be more pronounced when yawing to the left than to the right. At no stage did any vibration, flutter or snaking develop.

The ailerons had exceptionally nice feel over the whole speed range, being light and powerful, but not over-sensitive. At low speeds they were not excessively light, the pilot feeling a definite resistance to stick movement, and were responsive, if a little sluggish near the stall. As speed increased, the ailerons did not harden up unduly and were still light and very effective at 250 mph IAS. An increase in heaviness was apparent above 300 mph IAS, but even at 400 mph IAS (the highest speed attained) well over half aileron could be applied without excessive effort and the aircraft could be banked quickly from side to side. There was no sign of snatching or vibration at any speed. In general, more stick movement was required in lateral manoeuvres than was usual with British aircraft. This was due to the low gearing between the stick and ailerons. It was found that this did not lessen the ease or pleasantness of the Hawk's lateral control when turning; but rather, as the control was effective and smooth, it made for definite and well-controlled manoeuvres.

The elevators also exhibited a similar balance in control forces throughout the speed range. The gearing between the stick and elevator (2.75 degrees per inch) was fairly low and as a result the elevator was not unpleasantly sensitive. There was also no appreciable alteration in effectiveness when the engine was throttled back. At low speeds with the engine off, the rudder was a little sluggish. However, with the engine on, the rudder response was normal. Heaviness increased with speed, becoming most marked above 300 mph IAS, but it was still effective, even with small displacements. Control harmony was rated as being exceptional and features that pilots praised most highly were the positive feel on all three controls at very low speed and the absence of any significant stiffening up at high speeds.

During mock aerial combat between the Hawk and a Spitfire I, the Curtiss proved to be superior in several respects. The aircraft were flown by two pilots of Aerodynamics Flight, RAE, who alternated the flying tasks to eliminate any differences in piloting skill. If the Spitfire dived on the Hawk with both aircraft flying at 350–400 mph IAS, the pilot of the Hawk could easily avoid being shot down by quickly applying aileron to set up a banked turn that the Spitfire could not follow. This was due to the fact that the Hawk could apply about three-quarters aileron at 400 mph IAS, whereas the Spitfire could only apply around one-fifth aileron at the same speed. As a result, it could not bank as quickly and tended to overshoot the Hawk, leaving it behind and above. If the Hawk dived on the Spitfire and managed to get within gun-firing range, the pilot had no difficulty in following the Spitfire round until the superior performance of the latter allowed it to draw away. The difference between the two aircraft in the amount of force needed to obtain lateral control was most marked.

Although the elevator of the Hawk became fairly heavy at high speeds, this was not considered to be detrimental, as it lessened the danger of inadvertently applying excessive 'g'. The Spitfire elevator was much lighter at speeds around 300–400 mph IAS and more sensitive to small control displacements, so that the pilot had to concentrate hard during manoeuvring to avoid a high-speed stall or the possibility of blacking out. Both pilots involved in the trials considered the Spitfire elevator to be 'too touchy'. Dogfights were also carried out at speeds of around 250 mph IAS. Once again, the Hawk came out on top due to its excellent manoeuvrability and superior all-round view from the cockpit. The Spitfire pilot, however, did have the advantage of being able to break off combat at any time due to his mount's superior top speed as a result of its aerodynamically cleaner design. The Hawk also lost out to the Spitfire in the dive, as it was rather slow to pick up speed and considerable height was lost in the process.

As the Spitfire tested was fitted with a two-pitch propeller, the take-off and initial climb of the Hawk was considerably better than the Spitfire, which was also prone to swing more during its take-off run. During the climb the controls of the Hawk were effective without being too light, in contrast to both the Spitfire and the Hurricane. On the Spitfire, the elevator was over-sensitive and the aileron too light and on the Hurricane the elevator was rather sluggish. It was naturally desirable that the aircraft be kept steady on the climb as the under-carriage was raised, hood closed, propeller adjusted etc, but this was a difficult task in both British aircraft.

With the flaps and undercarriage down, the gliding angle of the Hawk was steeper than either the Spitfire or Hurricane, and the view very much better. When trimmed for the approach glide, there was a high degree of longitudinal stability and the elevator control was effective, but not too light. The Hurricane was particularly bad in this respect, as it was about neutrally stable and had a light and sluggish elevator at low speeds with the flaps down. The general feel of the controls during the approach in the Hawk was unusually good, the ailerons remaining crisp and positive right down to the stall. The Spitfire in contrast, tended to lose aileron feel at approach speeds. The Hawk's landing characteristics were also rated as superior as it felt 'stuck to the ground' and heavy braking could be used early in the run.

As well as the trials carried out by Aerodynamics Flight, the Airworthiness and Mechanical Test Departments of the RAE collabo-rated on the problems associated with the Spitfire's lateral control. An assessment was made of the loss of aileron effectiveness due to wing twist on both the Hawk and the Spitfire. Although the Spitfire wing complied with all relevant stiffness requirements of the time, it was found that there was a 41 per cent loss in effectiveness owing to wing twist, compared with only 16 per cent on the Hawk. There was little difference between the two in terms of wing loading, the Spitfire having a loading of 24 lb/sq.ft compared to 25.5 lb/sq.ft on the Hawk.

The Hurricane was superior to the Spitfire in terms of lateral control at high speed and a comparison of aileron response and stick force with the Hawk had the following results (for the corresponding figures relating to the Spitfire and Buffalo, see page 122).

| | | Curtiss Hawk | | Hurricane | |
|---|---|---|---|---|---|
| EAS | ASI | Time to bank 45 degrees (sec) | Max force (lb) | Time to bank 45 degrees (sec) | Max force (lb) |
| 214 | 200 | 2.2 | 8 | 1.3 | 10 |
| 267 | 250 | 2.3 | 14 | 1.4 | 15 |
| 320 | 300 | 2.7 | 20 | 1.5 | 21 |
| 372 | 350 | 4.0 | 27 | 1.6 | 38 |
| 413 | 390 | 5.2 | 33 | 1.9 | 34 |

Further trials were carried out on the Curtiss fighter at Boscombe Down after it had entered service with the RAF as the Mohawk. One criticism was that on entering the cockpit, the control column was positioned too far forward for comfort. It was also found that the operating lever for the sliding canopy did not provide sufficient leverage to open the hood at speeds above 330 mph IAS. As a result, the length of the lever was doubled, allowing the hood to be opened up to the maximum permissible diving speed of 415 mph IAS.

With the flaps and undercarriage up, the stall occurred at 75 mph IAS at forward CG. There was very little warning and at the stall either wing could drop, followed by the nose. The dropped wing could not be raised by aileron alone. If the control column was brought further back, the aircraft tended to spin when on the aft CG limit, usually to the left. With the aircraft on the forward CG limit, there was no tendency to spin. Recovery was immediate when the control column was eased forward, although a change of direction of up to 40 degrees could occur. With the flaps and undercarriage down, the left wing dropped sharply and once again the aircraft was liable to flick into a spin at aft CG loadings. On the forward limit a spin did not occur, the nose simply dropping away until speed was regained. Recovery was straightforward, but the aircraft was liable to come out in a direction 90 degrees removed from its original course.

Performance testing took place in early 1941 using AR645 and AR678, both Mohawk IVs powered by Wright Cyclones. The top speed was measured as 302 mph at 14,000 ft and the best rate of climb was 2600 ft/min at 8000 ft. The rate of climb did not fall below 1000 ft/min until a height of 27,000 ft had been attained. The greatest height reached was 33,000 ft and it was estimated that the absolute ceiling would have been 34,000 ft. When climbing, the change from MS to FS gear generally took place at around 11,000 ft. The speed trials and times to height were as follows:

| Height | 10,000 ft | 14,000 ft | 20,000 ft | 26,000 ft | 28,000 ft |
|---|---|---|---|---|---|
| TAS – mph | 290 | 302 | 292 | 277 | 271 |

| Height | 10,000 ft | 15,000 ft | 20,000 ft | 26,000 ft | 30,000 ft | 32,000 ft |
|---|---|---|---|---|---|---|
| Time from start – min | 3.9 | 6.2 | 8.8 | 13.3 | 18.0 | 23.2 |

Fuel consumption tests were also carried out at 15,000 ft, using AR678. These tests showed that the greatest range was obtained in MS blower, with the propeller controlling at 1500 rpm. At 130 mph IAS, which was the minimum speed for comfortable control, the range was 525 miles with a normal fuel load of 84 gallons, after allowing for 15 minutes at full throttle for take-off and climb. With an overload fuel tank, the range could be extended to 960 miles under the same conditions.

A comparison was also made with a Mohawk III (AR631) powered by a Pratt & Whitney Twin Wasp R-1830-SG3-G. The top speed was slightly lower at 300 mph at 10,000 ft and the maximum rate of climb was only 2260 ft/min at 9600 ft. The climb performance was substantially reduced, the Mohawk III taking 7.3 minutes to reach 15,000 ft and 17.5 minutes to reach 26,000 ft, by which the time rate of climb was only 615 ft/min. The estimated service ceiling was 31,200 ft.

Despite having been rejected for operational flying in the European theatre as a result of the trials carried out at Farnborough and Boscombe Down, the Mohawk was to give long-term service in India and Burma. Against Japanese opposition, a lack of outright speed was not as important a requirement as excellent manoeuvrability, its superbly efficient controls and good all-round view giving pilots great confidence. Roles ranged from air defence to operations in support of the Army, for which a bomb load of up to 400 lb could be carried under the wings. The Mohawk remained in first-line service in small numbers until January 1944, when No. 155 Squadron finally converted to Spitfire VIIIs.

# CHAPTER TWELVE

# Bell Airacobra

I n terms of its design, the Bell Airacobra broke with convention in several respects. It was powered by an Allison V-1710-E4 liquid-cooled engine of 1150 hp, but this was mounted in the centre of the aircraft behind the pilot, the power being transmitted to the nose-mounted propeller via a long extension shaft. It was hoped that positioning the engine over the aircraft's CG would aid manoeuvrability, but a further advantage of this arrangement was that it allowed the fitment of a large-calibre cannon, firing through the propeller spinner. Although it was capable of accommodating a gun of 37 mm, most Airacobras flown by the RAF were fitted with a 20-mm Hispano cannon in addition to two nose-mounted 0.50-in and four wing-mounted 0.303-in machine-guns. The Airacobra also featured a tricycle undercarriage in place of the more normal tailwheel undercarriage fitted to most other fighters of the time.

The prototype Bell XP-39 was flown for the first time on 6 April 1938. Initial flight testing was encouraging and very soon a speed of 390 mph had been recorded, together with a time of five minutes to reach 20,000 ft. However, these figures were achieved before the fitment of guns, protective armour or other operational equipment. Encouraged by the performance figures being quoted in the US, 200 examples of the Airacobra were ordered for the French Air Force in March 1940 and 675 were ordered by the Air Ministry the following month. After the French collapse, interest in the Airacobra (known for a time in Britain as the Caribou) was taken over by the British Direct Purchase Commission and the first 'Caribous' were flown in April 1941. Deliveries to the UK commenced with three P-39Cs, which became DS173, DS174 and DS175, the first two being tested at A&AEE and AFDU respectively, before the delivery of the first batch of Airacobra Is.

One of the first Airacobras to be assessed by Boscombe Down was AH573 in August 1941. Even before the pilot had settled into the cockpit, there was plenty for him to consider for his subsequent report. Entry was extremely difficult, especially with the engine running (ground running of the Allison engine had to be at 1000–1200 rpm to minimise vibration). A handhold had been provided for the pilot to pull himself onto the mainplane, but there was then no further assistance until reaching the cockpit door. A further handhold would have made entry much easier. Getting into the cockpit itself was not an easy task as the roofline was so low and the roof itself did not open. Three hands would also have been useful, two to gain access to the cockpit and one to hold the door open.

Once inside, unlike many other American aircraft, the cockpit was found to be small and only suitable for pilots of small or medium frame, as there was no headroom for taller pilots. However, it was understood at the time that this problem was under investigation with a view to lowering the seat. Exiting the aircraft when on the ground was not particularly difficult, although it was considered that this would be an entirely different matter in the air in an emergency situation, and a much more difficult operation compared with an aircraft with a jetti-sonable hood. There was also a good chance of the pilot hitting the tail as he baled out, as he was forced to exit from the side door. Two sliding windows were provided for ventilation and with both shut, no carbon monoxide fumes were detected and no stuffiness was apparent in flight. The cockpit was rated as being slightly less noisy than that of a Spitfire. The view out of the Airacobra was generally good in all directions except straight ahead, where it was spoilt by the metal top of the bullet-proof windscreen and the metal frame of the cabin top. This was again due to the pilot sitting too high and would have been improved by lowering the seat.

The elevator and rudder controls could be moved without undue friction being felt. However, there was excessive friction in the aileron control, which increased with the angle of movement. The elevator trim wheel was located to the left of the pilot and operated satisfactorily, although the associated indicator was not easily seen as it was positioned too close to the seat. To the rear of this was the rudder bias gear, which was operated by a large knob. This performed in an acceptable manner, but due to lack of space, it was difficult to operate. The aileron bias gear was situated forward of the elevator trim wheel, low down on the left-hand side of the cockpit, where it could not be reached by the pilot when he was strapped in tightly. To operate this control, the pilot was thus forced to slacken his straps and lean forward.

The throttle, mixture and propeller controls were mounted on a quadrant in the conventional manner on the pilot's left and were satis-factory in operation. However, there was no adjustable friction grip for the throttle, which tended to slip a little. The fuel cock was considered to be badly positioned as it was forward and to the right of the aileron bias and was extremely difficult to reach, even when the pilot released his straps. The radiator shutter control was operated by a crank handle on the right-hand side of the pilot's seat and was easy to operate.

The flaps were operated electrically and were controlled by a three-position tumbler switch situated on the front left corner of the cockpit. An indicator was provided, consisting of a pointer moving over a scale graduated in quarters. Although this system worked well enough, A&AEE pilots criticised the lack of any alternative method of lowering the flaps in the event of electrical failure. The undercarriage was operated in similar fashion to the flaps, but in this case there was a manual back-up system. The pilot could select either 'electric' or 'manual' and there was the usual pictorial type of indicator, together with a visual indicator to show when the wheels were locked down, although there was nothing to confirm that they were locked up. The brakes were operated by pedals above the rudder bar and were easy to operate. A locking device was provided for parking. No standard blind flying panel was fitted, but all instruments were clearly visible and the layout was considered to be adequate.

During the assessment of the Airacobra's flying qualities, AH573 was flown at an all-up weight of 7850 lb and with the CG 20.6 in aft of datum (normal setting). Taxying was very easy and even over rough ground was comparatively smooth and comfortable. The undercarriage performed adequately and exhibited good shock-absorbing qualities. It was felt, however, that the aircraft's ground handling was over-dependent on the efficiency of the brakes, and in the event of them failing it was thought that the aircraft might be difficult to control. The take-off was straightforward with a slight tendency to swing to the left as the engine was opened up but this was easily checked by the application of right rudder. The take-off speed was approximately 100 mph IAS, whilst the initial climb was made at around 140 mph IAS. The undercarriage could be raised as soon as the aircraft had left the ground and the retraction sequence took around fifteen seconds. There was no noticeable change of trim as the undercarriage was raised. Owing to the limited amount of time available for the tests on the Airacobra, the optimum flap setting for take-off was not determined, although 15 degrees was used quite successfully. Raising the flaps caused the aircraft to sink slightly.

Once in the air, the rudder and elevators were found to be light, quick in response and effective. The fabric-covered ailerons were light in normal flight, but tended to become much heavier during dives at speeds above 300 mph IAS. Lateral control was considered to be comparable with the early Spitfire Is with fabric-covered ailerons, but by mid 1941 more was required. Much effort had been expended to improve the Spitfire's handling in this respect by developing metal-covered ailerons and these had first appeared on the Spitfire V. Although there was no time for full stability tests, early indications showed the Airacobra to be stable throughout the full speed range. Aerobatics could be flown with ease and there were no undesirable handling qualities.

The stall speed with the flaps and undercarriage up was 105 mph IAS and 88 mph IAS with the flaps and undercarriage down. Compared with most other fighters of the early war period, these speeds were quite high, being approximately 25–30 mph faster than the Spitfire, and consequently led to higher approach speeds. There was no real stall warning, only a slight wallowing, followed by a gentle nose drop at the point of stall. With the flaps and undercarriage down, a gentle drop of the left wing was noted before the nose went down. The best glide speed when coming in to land was about 110 mph IAS with a little power and the approach and landing was simple and easy in execution. It was recommended that the nose be held up as long as possible on landing, to achieve the lowest touchdown speed and shortest run. However, it appeared that old habits were slow to change, as it was noted that the aircraft could also be landed by flying it onto the ground as for a three-point touchdown – a recipe for disaster in a tricycle-undercarriage aircraft if attempted by low-time pilots.

Climb and level speed performance tests were carried out, commencing on 29 July 1941. The aircraft used for climbing tests was AH573 once again, but following a crash, it was replaced by AH589. This machine, however, suffered from constant ignition trouble and the trials were eventually carried out by AH701, which was already at A&AEE for an investigation into gun heating. Both AH573 and AH701 were powered by an Allison V-1710-E4 engine driving a Curtiss Electric constant-speed propeller. The aircraft had similar exhausts, which consisted of two backward-facing open-ended stub pipes per cylinder. Full armament was carried, but all the gun muzzles were sealed. A small bead sight was fitted to both aircraft in front of the windscreen. Aerial masts were fitted (but no aerial) and only AH573 had IFF aerials fitted. AH573 was flown at a take-off weight of 7830 lb and with CG at 20.3 in aft of datum (CG range was established as being between 18.8 in and 22.3 in aft of datum). Climbs were made with the oil cooler and radiator shutters fully open. For the level speed tests using AH701, the shutters were flush with the surface of the fuselage. The limitations of the Allison engine were as follows:

| Take-off (5 min) | 3000 rpm | 44½ in of Hg pressure |
|---|---|---|
| Max on climb (30 min) | 2600 rpm | 37 in |
| Max for rich level flight (5 min) | 3000 rpm | 42 in |
| Max for rich mixture cruise | 2600 rpm | 37 in |
| Max for weak mixture cruise | 2300 rpm | 30½ in |

During the climbing tests, it was established that the maximum rate of climb was 2040 ft/min at 10,300 ft (full throttle height) and the service ceiling was calculated as being 29,000 ft, with an absolute ceiling of 30,200 ft. The time to 10,000 ft was 5.1 minutes and it took 11.7 minutes to reach 20,000 ft. The best climbing speed was found to be 150 mph IAS below full throttle height, decreasing by 3 mph per 2000 ft above this height. The full results were as follows:

| Height | 2000 ft | 4000 ft | 6000 ft | 8000 ft | 10,300 ft |
|---|---|---|---|---|---|
| Time from start – min | 1.1 | 2.05 | 3.0 | 4.0 | 5.15 |
| Rate of climb – ft/min | 2040 | 2040 | 2040 | 2040 | 2040 |

| Height | 14,000 ft | 18,000 ft | 20,000 ft | 24,000 ft | 29,000 ft |
|---|---|---|---|---|---|
| Time from start – min | 7.2 | 9.95 | 11.65 | 17.0 | 34.8 |
| Rate of climb – ft/min | 1585 | 1190 | 985 | 600 | 120 |

The Maximum True Air Speed (TAS) in level flight was 355 mph at 13,000 ft, which represented the aircraft's full throttle height. Measured readings up to 24,000 ft were:

| Height | 6000 ft | 8000 ft | 10,000 ft | 12,000 ft | 13,000 ft |
|---|---|---|---|---|---|
| TAS – mph | 326 | 335 | 343 | 351 | 355 |
| IAS – mph | 293 | 291 | 289 | 287 | 287 |

| Height | 14,000 ft | 16,000 ft | 18,000 ft | 20,000 ft | 24,000 ft |
|---|---|---|---|---|---|
| TAS – mph | 354 | 351 | 347 | 342 | 325 |
| IAS – mph | 281 | 271 | 259 | 247 | 220 |

Trials were later carried out using AH574 fitted with an Allison V-1710-E12 engine in place of the normal -E4. The -E12 had a revised supercharger impeller gear ratio of 9.6 to 1 and a propeller reduction gearbox with a gear ratio of 2 to 1. Corresponding figures for the -E4 engine were 8.8 to 1 and 1.8 to 1 respectively. The aircraft was flown at similar weights and CG to that of the previous tests. It was discovered that the full throttle height on the climb was raised by about 2000 ft, but the maximum rate of climb was rather less. The full throttle height in level flight was also raised by about 2000 ft and the maximum speed increased by 10 mph. In the climb, the full throttle height occurred at 12,500 ft (6.85 minutes from start, rate of climb 1845 ft/min) and during level speed runs, the full throttle height was achieved at 15,600 ft (365 mph TAS, 283 mph IAS).

Although it was the fastest of the early American fighters, the Airacobra I was handicapped by its Allison engine, which had a full throttle height of only 13,000 ft. As a result, the Airacobra was hopelessly out-performed at higher altitudes. The Allison had also developed a reputation of being somewhat fragile and a number of aircraft were lost as a result of engine failure. Difficulties were also experienced with servicing and excessively long rearming times. It was apparent at an early stage that the Airacobra was unlikely to make it as a fighter, nor was it suitable for any other role within the RAF. Despite this, No. 601 Squadron was earmarked as the first Airacobra unit and moved to Duxford in August 1941 to begin its work-up period. By the time that it converted to Spitfire VBs in March 1942 , it had suffered eight accidents with the Airacobra, causing the death of three of its pilots. Three of the crashes were as a result of engine failure, two were due to fuel problems and three to pilot error – all this for a few desultory Rhubarb operations over northern France the previous year when a small detachment operated from Manston. [Rhubarb operations were normally carried out by two aircraft at low level looking for targets of opportunity].

The Airacobra was still to be seen in the skies over Duxford until the end of 1942. Len Thorne of AFDU was tasked with carrying out an air test in one on 29 August. He recalls:

> It was a little strange because it was the first time that I had flown an aeroplane with a tricycle undercarriage, but it was quite nice to fly. It had the engine mounted at the rear of the cockpit and I approached the flight with a certain amount of trepidation as I had an uncomfortable feeling about what was in that high revving propeller shaft between my legs. I had visions of it breaking with lots of sharp ends flying about but, to the best of my knowledge, that never happened. The Russians, of course, used them extensively and rated them quite highly but most of their combats were at low altitude which suited the Airacobra and its Allison engine. I only got to fly it the once, which, I think, was enough!

The aircraft that remained with the RAF were eventually flown to Maintenance Units by ATA pilots, the majority being prepared for packing and delivery to Russia, where they were used in the ground-attack role. Further deliveries heading for Britain were diverted to the USAAF, many being taken on by the 350th Fighter Group, which formed at Bushey Hall in October 1942, before moving to Duxford prior to being transferred to the Twelfth Air Force in the Middle East.

# CHAPTER THIRTEEN

# Curtiss Tomahawk

T he emergence of the new generation of fighters in Europe, epitomised by the Supermarine Spitfire and Messerschmitt Bf 109, caused certain US aircraft manufacturers to re-evaluate some of the more traditional aspects of American pursuit aircraft. The simplicity and ruggedness of the air-cooled radial engine had been major factors in its dominance in the inter-war years, but the apparent advantages of the high-performance, water-cooled inline engines that had been developed on the other side of the Atlantic encouraged some US firms to adopt the same philosophy. Even so, the US Army Air Corps (USAAC) would have to make do with a fighter whose performance was still best suited to ground attack and for aerial combat at low to medium levels.

With its P-36 fighter already in production, Curtiss began to look at developments with an inline engine. After experimenting with a 12-cylinder Allison V-1710 in the XP-37 of 1938, the same type of engine was fitted to the tenth production P-36A, which became the XP-40 prototype. It was flown for the first time on 14 October 1938 and was ordered in quantity for the USAAC the following year under the Curtiss model designation Hawk 81A. An export model (the H-81A-1) was ordered by France but, like the Airacobra, no deliveries had been made before the German occupation. Once again, the contract was taken over by Britain, and the aircraft was given the name Tomahawk. The RAF eventually took delivery of 140 Tomahawk Is (equivalent to the H-81A-1/P-40A), 110 Tomahawk IIAs (H-81A-2/P-40B) and 635 Tomahawk IIBs (H-81A-3/P-40C).

The first Tomahawk Is arrived in the UK in September 1940, devoid of bullet-proof windscreens, protective armour and self-sealing fuel tanks – all items that were specified in subsequent batches, some of which were dispatched to Takoradi in West Africa to be flown to Egypt for service in the Middle East. The armament was eventually standardised at six machine-guns – four 0.303-in Brownings in the wings and two 0.5-in or 0.303-in guns in the forward fuselage synchronised to fire through the propeller arc.

The P-40 was of all-metal construction, the fuselage monocoque being built in two halves and divided horizontally. The wings were multi-spar and the individual sections were formed into a single unit before being joined with the fuselage. The high-speed aerofoil was of NACA 2215 section at the root, becoming NACA 2209 at the tip. Split flaps extended between the ailerons and all control surfaces were fabric-covered with individual trim tabs. Fuel could be carried in two tanks in each inner wing section and an auxiliary tank in the fuselage behind the pilot's seat. The undercarriage was similar to that of the Mohawk, the main oleo-pneumatic legs retracting backwards while turning through 90 degrees to lie flush with the underside of the wing. Although the main wheels were left exposed, the retractable tailwheel was enclosed by two small doors. The radiator was initially located in a ventrally mounted duct aft of the wing trailing edge, but disappointing level-speed performance with the XP-40 prototype in this configuration soon led to it being moved to a position under the nose.

British testing of the Tomahawk soon showed that it would be no match for the Messerschmitt Bf 109E/F in air-to-air combat. This was mainly due to its low-altitude rated Allison engine which performed best at heights up to 15,000 ft. This was at a time when combats between Spitfires and Bf 109s were beginning to take place at heights of around 30,000 ft.

Tomahawk IIB AK176 (Allison V-1710-C15) was one of several machines to pass through Boscombe Down and was reported on in September 1941. Entry to the cockpit was made by climbing onto the port wing root, using a handhold provided on the side of the fuselage. There was no further assistance for the pilot and as the walkway was rather steep; it was felt that a non-slip coating would have been a big improvement. Once in the cockpit, there was insufficient downward travel of the seat, and the pilot's head was well above the top of the bullet-proof windscreen (this point had not been noticed during the testing of earlier Tomahawks). Like the Mohawk before it, the position of the control column was too far forward when in its central position, and the pilot's arm was always at full stretch. The Sutton harness was also attached to the seat too low down, and it was considered that this would not prevent the pilot's shoulders moving forward in the event of a crash-landing. The cockpit had the benefit of heating, but this was not particularly effective as a result of draughts from holes in the hood, which provided access to the fuselage fuel and oil tanks. This problem was eventually remedied by using special covers designed by A&AEE.

Like most fighters of the period, the view forwards when taxying was considerably impaired by the long nose. No clear-view panel was fitted. In flight, the view was good and icing was prevented by the inclusion of a space between the windscreen and the bullet-proof safety glass, through which warm air was passed. Prior to the fitting of the draught covers, misting on the internal face of the bullet-proof glass occurred during rapid descents, but this was completely eliminated with the covers in place. Occasionally, a film of moisture formed between the two screens, but there was always a clear area in the centre where it was swept by the ducted hot air. Sighting through the reflector gunsight was not impeded, but the use of the ring and bead sight was often impossible.

On the ground, all the controls could be operated without undue friction or play. The rudder and ailerons could be moved fully, but full downward movement of the elevators involved a considerable forward stretch. The control column had a solid, vertical handgrip, incorporating a gun-firing trigger and a button that operated the electro-hydraulic motor for the flaps and undercarriage. The rudder pedals were of the pendulum type and were provided with fore-and-aft adjustment. When not in use, the controls had a locking device consisting of wires that ran from the rudder, round the stick and then onto the seat. It was thus impossible for the pilot to sit in the seat without first unlocking the controls.

The elevator trim control was fitted on the left-hand side of the cockpit about level with the pilot's thigh. Although it had a small protruding handle, it was of relatively small diameter and due to its awkward position, it could not be rotated quickly. The rudder trimmer was situated just above the elevator trim wheel and was of similar size, but without the handle. The gearing was rather low, but was otherwise satisfactory. Dials behind the wheels showed the positions of the tabs.

The engine throttle, mixture and propeller controls were mounted in the normal position on the left-hand side of the cockpit. However, the throttle lever was rather close to the cockpit side, making it difficult for the pilot to get his gloved hand around it. As in other American aircraft, there was no automatic boost control. The boost therefore had to be hand-adjusted with the throttle all the time, a considerable disadvantage for a fighter aircraft. A gate was provided to limit boost on take-off, but this was quite ineffective as the gate position did not make itself felt when the throttle was moved forward. There were four positions on the mixture control quadrant – fully rich, auto rich, auto weak and idle cut-off. A spring stop ensured that the lever could not be moved to the idle cut-off position accidentally. The electric propeller was controlled both by the lever on the engine controls quadrant and by toggle switches on a panel just below the quadrant. The petrol cock was situated low down on the left of the cockpit, but was too far forward for convenience, as the pilot had to release his harness to reach it.

In contrast, the flap selector lever was on the left side of the cockpit, but too far aft to use conveniently. After moving the selector, the button on top of the control column was depressed to set the electro-hydraulic motor working to move the flaps. Full flap movement could be obtained in 1–2 seconds and the flaps could be stopped in any position. When subject to air loads, the flaps closed automatically when the 'up' position was selected. The undercarriage selector lever was situated slightly forward of the flap lever. On AK176 and later aircraft, a latch bolt had to be pulled forward before the lever could be moved. The undercarriage was operated in a similar fashion to the flaps, i.e. movement of the selector followed by activation of the control column button until the movement was complete. In the case of the undercarriage, the selector lever then had to be returned to the neutral position. The wheels retracted backwards, turning through 90 degrees as they did so. Indicators for both flap and undercarriage operation were located on the lower left-hand side of the instrument panel. When the throttle was closed with the undercarriage not locked down, a red warning light appeared and a klaxon sounded. The latter could be switched off, but it re-engaged automatically when the throttle was opened again. A hand-operated hydraulic pump was fitted on the cockpit floor to the right of the pilot, for use in an emergency situation following failure of the electrical system.

The control knob for the hot and cold air intake was situated on the top right of the panel, but was disliked as it was impossible to select hot air above 140 mph IAS. The lever to control the radiator flaps was to the right of the pilot and, again, too low for convenient operation. The brakes were hydraulic and were toe-operated. They could be locked by depressing both pedals, engaging the parking brake beneath the panel and releasing the pedals. The lock could be deactivated by depressing both pedals again. As for instruments, the lack of a gyro horizon caused adverse comment and it was also noted that some instruments were obscured by the reflector gunsight. The opening handle for the hood was of the longer design recommended by A&AEE for the Mohawk, and it was now possible to open the hood at all speeds up to 400 mph IAS. There was also a jettison handle to release the hood, located on the cockpit roof just above the pilot's head.

For ground handling, the tailwheel was made steerable via the rudder controls about 35 degrees each side of central. Beyond this range it became fully castoring. Because of this arrangement, the rudder loads when taxying were rather heavy, and there was considerable kickback on rough ground. The brakes were efficient, if rather fierce in operation, but were not particularly smooth, nor progressive in action. With CG forward, the tail tended to lift easily, so harsh brake application was to be avoided.

Flaps were not required for take-off (though a successful take-off was made with full flap) and during the run there was a slight tendency to swing to the left, which could easily be corrected with rudder. With forward CG the tail was reluctant to rise, but even when it was in the correct attitude the view over the nose was poor. The aircraft became airborne at around 80 mph IAS, and the undercarriage could be raised as soon as it was clear of the ground. The retraction time was a very long 40–45 seconds and as the pilot's thumb had to remain on the button on the control column all this time, he was prevented from doing anything else with his right hand, such as closing the hood. As the wheels retracted the aircraft became slightly tail heavy, but this could be held easily with the stick and it could be trimmed to fly 'hands and feet off' when the recommended climb speed of 140 mph IAS had been attained. The Tomahawk was longi-tudinally stable with normal CG (22.7 in aft of datum), but with the aircraft at an extended aft CG (25.2 in aft of datum) it was generally unstable, and in this condition it also tended to tighten up during turns. The only exception to this instability occurred during glides with the flaps and undercarriage down.

The Tomahawk's stalling characteristics were explored with CG at the extended aft position to simulate the worst case scenario. With the flaps and undercarriage up, the aircraft tended to become unstable and tail-heavy as it approached the stall, which occurred without any control force at around 85 mph IAS. Below 90 mph IAS the aircraft exhibited strong self-stalling characteristics, and the pressure on the control column had to be relaxed to check the fall in speed. There was little or no warning of the stall, but just before it came there was a tendency to yaw to the right and for the port wing to drop. The position of the control column at the point of stall was approximately central.

With the flaps and undercarriage down, the tail heaviness as the stall was approached was still apparent, but not as much as previously and the actual stall occurred at 77 mph IAS. The aircraft again showed self-stalling characteristics, but on this occasion below 80 mph IAS. There was little warning of the stall, except for a slight tendency for the port wing to drop, which became more severe at the stall itself. Use of aileron to try to pick up the left wing only caused the machine to flick sharply over to the right. Closing the radiator shutter reduced the stall speed by 1–2 mph and the self-stalling characteristic was slightly more pronounced.

All aerobatic manoeuvres could be performed with ease. As the Allison was fitted with a Stromberg Bendix carburettor, the pilot was able to apply as much negative-g as he could withstand, without fear of the engine cutting out. Loops could be flown normally and upward rolls and rolls off the top of loops were also straightforward. Diving trials were carried out up to a limiting speed of 450 mph IAS and 3120 rpm, with an all-up weight of 7370 lb and with CG at the normal setting. The aircraft proved to be steady in the dive and could be kept on a target, provided that left rudder bias had been applied. As speed increased, the rudder tended to become very heavy and there was a pronounced tendency to swing to the right. The ailerons also became heavy and the left wing was prone to dropping. In contrast, the elevators remained light and effective and there was only a slight decrease in lightness with increase in speed. No vibration or instability of the control surfaces was experienced and recovery from the dive was easy.

The best glide speed on the approach to land was 100 mph IAS. The landing was easy, but it was important to ensure that the nose was brought up to achieve a three-point landing. Flap was adequate and the landing run was a little longer than most fighter types of the time. If the landing was baulked, the effect of opening up the engine with the flaps and undercarriage down was to make the aircraft tail-heavy, but this could be easily held with forward stick. There was also a slight tendency to yaw to the left. The climb out was accomplished with ease, although when the flaps were raised this tended to increase the aircraft's tail heaviness and there was some sink, but at no point did this become a cause for concern.

Performance trials were carried out on AK176, which was fitted with guns but was devoid of blast tubes. No flame dampers or air cleaners were fitted, but a wireless mast was carried forward of the fin. The take-off weight was 7300 lb. The maximum rate of climb was 1960 ft/min from ground level up to 13,500 ft (full throttle height) and the service ceiling was calculated as being 31,400 ft. The results of the climbing trials were as follows:

| Height | 1000 ft | 5000 ft | 10,000 ft | 13,500 ft | 18,000 ft |
|---|---|---|---|---|---|
| Time from start – min | 0.5 | 2.0 | 5.1 | 6.9 | 9.4 |
| Rate of climb – ft/min | 1960 | 1960 | 1960 | 1960 | 1590 |

| Height | 20,000 ft | 23,000 ft | 26,000 ft | 28,000 ft | 30,000 ft |
|---|---|---|---|---|---|
| Time from start – min | 10.8 | 13.3 | 16.8 | 20.2 | 25.9 |
| Rate of climb – ft/min | 1360 | 1030 | 700 | 480 | 140 |

Level speed trials showed a maximum of 331 mph TAS at 15,500 ft (full throttle height).

| Height | 10,000 ft | 13,000 ft | 15,000 ft | 15,500 ft | 18,000 ft |
|---|---|---|---|---|---|
| Speed – TAS | 314 | 323 | 329 | 331 | 328 |
| Speed – IAS | 261 | 256 | 253 | 252 | 240 |

| Height | 20,000 ft | 23,000 ft | 26,000 ft | 28,000 ft |
|---|---|---|---|---|
| Speed – TAS | 326 | 321 | 315 | 310 |
| Speed – IAS | 231 | 216 | 202 | 192 |

Take-off and landing tests were performed on BK853 at a weight of 6366 lb. With zero wind and in ISA conditions, the take-off run was measured at 215 yards, with 440 yards being required to clear 50 ft. The landing run was 350 yards.

Although it was a more effective warplane than the Airacobra, the Tomahawk was powered by the same Allison engine and as a result was wholly unsuited to fighter operations in the European theatre. Consequently, its service with home-based squadrons was mainly in the low-level tactical reconnaissance role, with the first deliveries being made to No. 2 Squadron at Sawbridgeworth in August 1941. The Tomahawk was also operated by the Desert Air Force in the Middle East, mainly for ground attack, from June 1941. Despite the fact that it had been rejected as a fighter, the Tomahawk was to give a good account of itself in aerial combat and several pilots ran up quite large scores. The highest-scoring Tomahawk 'ace' was Australian Flight Lieutenant Clive 'Killer' Caldwell of No. 250 Squadron, whose claims amounted to seventeen, including eight Bf 109E/Fs. The Tomahawk continued to give valuable service in the Middle East until early 1942, when it was gradually replaced by the Kittyhawk.

# CHAPTER FOURTEEN

# Curtiss Kittyhawk

The later variants of the P-40 were given the company designation Curtiss Model 87 and were named Kittyhawk by the RAF and Commonwealth Air Forces. They saw widespread action in the Middle East and Pacific theatres. Although the Kittyhawk looked generally similar to the earlier Tomahawk, it had a revised engine cowling housing an up-rated Allison and a remodelled canopy. The armament comprised wing-mounted guns only (the nose guns having been deleted). The first twenty-two aircraft delivered to the RAF were fitted with four 0.50-in machine-guns, but all subsequent aircraft were fitted with six 0.50-in guns. The Kittyhawk I was the equivalent of the American P-40D and this was followed by the Kittyhawk IA (P-40E), Kittyhawk III (P-40K and M) and the Kittyhawk IV (P-40N). The aircraft entered USAAF service in July 1941 and deliveries to the RAF commenced later the same year.

The Kittyhawk introduced the 'F' model Allison engine, in place of the 'C' model as used in the Tomahawk. Although the take-off rating of the 'F' was little different at 1150 hp, it could deliver 1470 hp for combat, albeit limited to a maximum of five minutes. The spur reduction gear for the propeller was mounted externally on all P-40s powered by the 'F' model Allison (instead of internally as on the Tomahawk). This reduced the length of the aircraft by 6 in and raised the thrust line, allowing the undercarriage to be shortened slightly. The radiator was moved further forward under the nose and the fuselage cross-section was reduced, reprofiling of the rear fuselage allowing better lookout to the rear and below. Provision was also made for a ventral tank to be carried under the fuselage or a 500-lb bomb. Although it offered more power and slightly better altitude performance, this was offset by an increase of approximately 1000 lb in gross weight, with a combat-ready Kittyhawk IA tipping the scales at 8400 lb. As a result its take-off and climb performance was actually worse than that of the Tomahawk, and its manoeuvrability (never a strong point with the P-40) was also inferior.

Boscombe Down received its first Kittyhawks in February 1942 and trials were carried out over the next six months using AK572 and AL229. In contrast with the Tomahawk tested previously, there was much more room in the cockpit, with ample seat adjustment for height. Once again, however, the control column was set too far away from the pilot, which made it difficult to obtain full forward movement. The Sutton harness was satisfactory and a release lever was provided on the left of the seat to permit the pilot to lean forward. The view forward was similar to the Tomahawk and to the rear was good through transparent side panels, but the rear view mirror mounted above the windscreen was of little use.

The Kittyhawk was fitted with trimming controls to the elevator, rudder and ailerons, the trim tab controls for the elevator and rudder being similar to the Tomahawk. The aileron trim tab was fitted to the port wing and was actuated by an electric motor controlled by a switch on the electric control panel. This switch was not particularly easy to operate, but as the changes in lateral trim were so small in flight, it was used very infrequently. Operation of the trimmer was satisfactory with no tendency to slip. However, overall, it was felt that the provision of aileron trim was an unnecessary complication and a fixed trim tab that could be set on the ground would have been sufficient. Engine throttle, mixture and propeller controls were in a box on the pilot's left. However, with no friction damper, the throttle lever tended to slip back. If adjustments were made on the ground to stop the throttle from slipping when in the air, the propeller control was then almost immovable.

The electric propeller control was that normally fitted on Curtiss aircrews. A master safety switch, with ON and OFF positions, was fitted on the electric control panel. This switch was normally kept in the ON position, except in an emergency. On the right of this switch was a three-position selector for selecting either manual or automatic operation of the propeller. When this switch was moved up to 'auto', engine rpm was controlled through a governor unit and a change of rpm was obtained by moving the propeller control lever located beside the throttle lever. When the switch was moved to either of the two down positions, then 'manual' operation was obtained. When the switch was moved to the bottom left position, propeller pitch decreased and rpm increased, whilst if it was moved to bottom right there was an increase in pitch and decrease in rpm. The circuits for the 'auto' and 'manual' positions were independent, and in the event of failure of the governor, the pitch of the propeller could be changed by the 'manual' switch.

The fuel cock and flap selector lever were in the same positions as on the Tomahawk. They elicited the same adverse comments as regards their inconvenient location on the left-hand side of the cockpit. In the event of failure of the electric pump the flaps could be raised or lowered by a hand-operated hydraulic pump to the right of the pilot. The undercarriage selector lever was the same as that used on the Tomahawk and the operating procedure was identical. Once again, the emergency hand pump could be used should the electric system fail, the pilot first having to select the required direction of motion of the undercarriage. Should the main hydraulics fail, an emergency system was provided. This consisted of a further hydraulic pump with two changeover cocks on the floor of the cabin. The emergency system operated via a different set of pipelines to those of the main hydraulic system, and would therefore operate when the latter had been punctured. It could only be used for lowering the main wheels; the tailwheel could not be lowered.

The layout of the instruments was generally satisfactory and no undue vibration was noted. The compass was fitted in the centre of the panel and was clearly visible. All the flying instruments were located above and to the left, there being no standard blind flying panel. The Directional Gyro and Artificial Horizon were on opposite sides of the gunsight mounting, which from the pilot's point of view was not ideal. Engine instruments were located on the right of the panel and were conveniently grouped.

Handling trials were carried out with the aircraft at an all-up weight of 8480 lb at CG 26.5 in aft of datum (the CG range due to dissipation of load was from 20.9 in to 26.5 in aft of datum). The ailerons were discovered to be light and quick in response at all speeds up to maximum level speed. They were effective in level flight, and during climbs and glides, but there was deterioration at speeds close to the stall, although control remained satisfactory. Aileron control tended to become heavier with increase in speed, but it was only when diving at speeds above 400 mph IAS that any serious difficulty was encountered. By the time that the limiting dive speed of 460 mph IAS was reached, the ailerons were virtually immovable. At slow speeds there was a slight tendency for the ailerons to snatch. There was little change of lateral trim with speed, engine on or off, and as a result the aileron trimmer was little used.

Elevator control was moderately light and effective throughout the speed range, becoming heavier with increase in speed. Response was quick, although the aircraft's positive stability at the CG position tested made movement in pitch appear a little heavy and sluggish. The elevator trimmer was effective and gave adequate trim for all conditions of flight.

The rudder was the heaviest of the three controls, particularly with engine on and with increase in speed. With engine off, it was still moderately heavy, but became light at landing speeds and near the stall. Despite this, the rudder was effective under all conditions of flight and the response was quick. Even though the rudder was rather heavy, there was no adverse effect on overall manoeuvrability, owing to the aircraft's excellent aileron control. One aspect that did cause concern was a fairly large change of directional trim between engine on and off. This was important in view of the rudder's heaviness because, although the rudder trimmer was effective, the gearing was rather too low and it was not possible to re-trim rapidly to cater for this change of trim.

Directional control of the Kittyhawk was looked at in some detail because of reports received from the USA that the rudder was liable to lock when displaced through more than two-thirds of its range of movement to the left (through about 20 degrees) with the engine on. It was found that rudder locking could occur, but only under abnormal conditions of flight. Most of the tests were made by doing a quarter slow roll to the right and then applying top rudder. When the rudder had been moved through two-thirds of its range, the extreme control heaviness was replaced by extreme lightness, although it did not flick over to the full position but could be moved between the two-thirds and full rudder positions in either direction with very little foot load. Although full rudder was held for a considerable time, there was no tendency for the aircraft to spin, but it tended to go into a sideslip before the nose would drop.

Other methods of inducing rudder lock were tried, and it was noted that it would occur whenever more than two-thirds left rudder was applied with engine on, irrespective of the position of the ailerons and elevator, or of the attitude of the aircraft. The rudder did not lock when the engine was throttled right back, or when the rudder was moved to the right. When locking had occurred, the rudder could be moved back to the two-thirds position quite easily. However, a very large foot load was required to move it beyond this point with engine on. If the engine was throttled back, centralisation was easy and recovery immediate. Although it was proved that rudder locking could occur, it was felt that it would not be encountered often and, even then, was not dangerous provided the method of recovery was known.

At the loadings tested, the Kittyhawk was directionally and long-itudinally stable under all flight conditions. With the flaps and undercarriage up, there was little warning of an approaching stall, except for the high position of the nose and a tendency for the aircraft to yaw to the right. At the stall, which occurred with the control column central at a speed of 90 mph IAS, a shuddering was felt and this was followed by a drop of the nose. When the stick was pulled further aft, the left wing dropped sharply, as would occur before entry into a spin. Recovery was effected by moving the control column forward. With the flaps and undercarriage down, there was a tendency for the right wing to go down as speed was decreased below 83 mph IAS, but the aircraft could be kept level by coarse use of aileron at speeds as low as 80 mph IAS. Control forces to stall the aircraft were light. If the control column was pulled back at the stall, there was slight fore-and-aft pitching and the aircraft flicked to the right. Recovery once again was immediate when the elevator force was removed.

High-speed dives were carried out up to the limiting dive speed of 460 mph IAS and the maximum permitted engine speed of 3200 rpm as follows:

| Dive | Throttle | Height 'in' | Max rpm | Max IAS | Height 'out' | Trim setting |
|---|---|---|---|---|---|---|
| 1 | Fully open | 18000 ft | 2600 | 450 | 9000 ft | Full throttle, level flight |
| 2 | One third | 15000 ft | 2600 | 430 | 7000 ft | Full throttle, level flight |
| 3 | Fully open | 15000 ft | 2600 | 460 | 5000 ft | Trimmed to reduce elevator and rudder loads in dive |

In dives 1 and 2, above 400 mph IAS the elevator and rudder forces needed to hold the aircraft in the dive were very heavy. At about 440–450 mph IAS, the pilot was unable to exert enough force on the controls to prevent it from coming out of the dive and yawing to the right. Prior to this, the aircraft was steady in the dive and could be held onto a target. The dives were continued into bumpy air at lower levels, but there was no instability or control surface vibration. Recovery was made by decreasing the forward pressure on the control column, although this had to be maintained to some extent to prevent the recovery becoming too rapid, which may have led to overstressing.

In the third dive, the elevator and rudder trimmers were used to reduce the force needed on the relevant controls as the limiting speed was reached. A small adjustment of the elevator trimmer was sufficient to reduce the force on the control column to a reasonable value, but the rudder had to be trimmed 4 divisions left (of the available 6¾ divisions) at the limiting speed of 460 mph IAS. Even so, a large foot load was required to hold the aircraft straight in the dive. Recovery was accomplished easily, and there was less chance of the aircraft coming out of the dive too quickly.

The optimum approach speed with the flaps and undercarriage down was the same as the Tomahawk – 100 mph IAS. The aircraft could be sideslipped but pilots found it difficult to maintain a steady rate of slip, as the nose tended to drop and speed increase. The landing was straightforward, with touchdown occurring at around 75 mph IAS. The handling characteristics in the case of a baulked landing were the same as for the Tomahawk.

Tests were also made with an overload tank fitted, which increased the weight to 8840 lb, but there was little difference in the way the aircraft handled. On take-off there was slightly more bucketing on rough ground and in the climb there was a slight tendency to wander in yaw, although directional stability was maintained. Stalling speeds with the tank were marginally higher at 92 mph IAS with the flaps and undercarriage up, and 82 mph IAS with the flaps and undercarriage down. Loops, slow rolls, climbing rolls and rolls off the top of loops in each direction were performed, the behaviour being similar to the clean configuration. The aircraft was dived to its limiting speed with the tank fitted (280 mph IAS) with trim set for full throttle level flight. The behaviour on recovery was similar to that at the lighter load at the same speed. The best approach speed with the tank fitted was higher at 110 mph IAS, the rate of sink becoming too rapid if a slower speed was attempted. Apart from this, the landing characteristics were the same as those at the lower weight.

Climb tests were made using AK572, the second aircraft in the first batch of Kittyhawk Is. As a very early four-gun model, it was not representative of aircraft that would be used operationally. It did not have an aerial mast or aerials fitted, nor did it have a rack for a bomb or overload tank. Its exhausts were individual stubs as distinct from the multi-fishtail ejectors that were fitted subsequently. The propeller was a Curtiss Electric of 11 ft diameter. Climbs were made using an initial speed of 145 mph IAS, which was the recommended best climb speed from testing carried out in the USA. The trials showed that there had been deterioration in climb performance compared with tests carried out on the earlier Tomahawk, due to the higher all-up weight, which was recorded at 8480 lb (1180 lb more than the Tomahawk).

| Height | 2000 ft | 6000 ft | 8000 ft | 10,000 ft | 11,400 ft |
|---|---|---|---|---|---|
| Time from start – min | 1.3 | 3.8 | 5.05 | 6.25 | 7.15 |
| Rate of climb – ft/min | 1570 | 1600 | 1610 | 1630 | 1640 |

| Height | 12,000 ft | 16,000 ft | 20,000 ft | 24,000 ft | 28,000 ft |
|---|---|---|---|---|---|
| Time from start – min | 7.5 | 10.4 | 14.25 | 20.1 | 33.15 |
| Rate of climb – ft/min | 1580 | 1220 | 870 | 520 | 160 |

The full throttle height was thus 11,400 ft (compared with 13,500 ft for the Tomahawk) and the greatest height recorded during the trials was 28,500 ft. It was estimated that the absolute ceiling would have been 29,900 ft.

Level-speed performance was measured from trials with several machines, including Kittyhawk IA ET573 in May 1943. By now, the take-off weight had crept up to 8650 lb, but compared with the Tomahawk, the maximum speed was improved slightly to 344 mph TAS at a full throttle height of 13,800 ft. All speed runs were made with the radiator cooling gills in the neutral position. The full test results were as follows:

| Height | 2000 ft | 4000 ft | 6000 ft | 8000 ft | 10,000 ft |
|---|---|---|---|---|---|
| Speed – TAS | 298 | 305 | 313 | 321 | 329 |
| Speed – IAS | 280 | 278 | 277 | 276 | 275 |

| Height | 12,000 ft | 13,800 ft | 16,000 ft | 18,000 ft | 20,000 ft |
|---|---|---|---|---|---|
| Speed – TAS | 337 | 344 | 341 | 337 | 330 |
| Speed – IAS | 273 | 271 | 260 | 249 | 236 |

The inadequacies of the Allison engine at altitude were recognised by Curtiss at an early stage in the development of the P-40. Shortly before the end of 1940, a Rolls-Royce Merlin 28 was fitted to the second production P-40D, which became known as the XP-40F. This led to the production of 1311 P-40Fs powered by a Packard-built Merlin V-1650-1 rated at 1300 hp for take-off and 1120 hp at 18,000 ft. In comparison with Allison-powered P-40s, the 'F' model could be easily recognised by the lack of a carburettor air intake on top of the engine cowling. A number of P-40Fs were supplied to the UK under the Lend-Lease scheme and were designated Kittyhawk II. One of these was FL220, which was tested at A&AEE in August 1942. The aircraft was armed with six 0.5-in machine-guns, the muzzles of which protruded about 3 in from the leading edge and were tape-bound during the course of the trials. Aerials were stretched from the fin to the wing tips and to the rear of the cockpit, but there was no aerial mast. IFF aerials were fitted, as was an external rear-view mirror and fittings for an over-load tank. The take-off weight was 8910 lb.

Climbs were made at 160 mph IAS to 20,000 ft, reducing the speed by 2 mph per 1000 ft thereafter. The change from MS to FS supercharger gear was made at 13,000 ft and the engine speed was increased from 2850 rpm to 3000 rpm at 20,000 ft. The cooling gills were left fully open during all climbs. Testing showed a considerable improvement as the following results show (* denotes full throttle height in MS gear and ** in FS gear).

| Height | 2000 ft | 6000 ft | 10,200 ft* | 16,000 ft | 17,000 ft** |
|---|---|---|---|---|---|
| Time from start – min | 1.0 | 3.0 | 5.0 | 8.3 | 9.0 |
| Rate of climb – ft/min | 2020 | 2020 | 2020 | 1620 | 1620 |

| Height | 20,000 ft | 24,000 ft | 28,000 ft | 32,000 ft | 34,000 ft |
|---|---|---|---|---|---|
| Time from start – min | 10.9 | 14.2 | 18.5 | 26.7 | 35.8 |
| Rate of climb – ft/min | 1500 | 1100 | 720 | 320 | 130 |

The service ceiling was considered to be 34,300 ft and the absolute ceiling 35,400 ft. Further trials showed a more moderate advance in level top speed.

| Height | 8000 ft | 10,000 ft | 12,000 ft | 14,700 ft* | 18,000 ft |
|---|---|---|---|---|---|
| TAS – mph | 320 | 328.5 | 336 | 347 | 344 |
| IAS – mph | 277 | 276 | 274 | 271 | 255.5 |

| Height | 20,000 ft | 20,400 ft** | 22,000 ft | 24,000 ft | 26,000 ft |
|---|---|---|---|---|---|
| TAS – mph | 352.5 | 354 | 352 | 349 | 344.5 |
| IAS – mph | 254 | 253.5 | 245.5 | 235.5 | 224.5 |

Although the Kittyhawk II possessed superior performance to the Allison-powered variants, it did not see widespread use with the RAF and only 330 examples of the P-40F were delivered. This was largely due to the fact that the Kittyhawk was employed principally as a fighter-bomber and, as the difference in performance between the Allison and Merlin below 10,000 ft was only marginal, from an operational point of view there was little to be gained by any major changeover. To further reinforce this situation, the Kittyhawk III, deliveries of which commenced in mid 1942, was powered by the uprated Allison V-1710–81, which offered 1200 hp on take-off and 1125 hp at 17,300 ft.

Having given valiant service as a close air support fighter, the Kittyhawk was largely obsolescent by mid 1944, and former Desert Air Force aircraft operating in Italy were gradually replaced by the North American Mustang. It was to remain in first-line service with the Royal

Australian Air Force until the end of the war. Indeed, the last aircraft to be lost by the RAAF in the Second World War was Kittyhawk A29-1161 of No. 80 Squadron, which was shot down by ground fire on 9 August 1945 at Samarinda in Borneo.

CHAPTER FIFTEEN

# North American Mustang

One of the finest fighter aircraft of all time, the P-51 Mustang was designed to a British requirement in 1940 by a relatively new company, North American Aviation Inc (NAA) of Mines Field, Southern California. Desperate for fighter aircraft of any sort, members of the British Purchasing Mission had been touring US manufacturers placing orders, but it was obvious that most of the products on offer would be of limited use and would soon become obsolescent. However, James H. 'Dutch' Kindelberger, President of North American, whose company was about to commence production of the Tomahawk under licence, managed to persuade the British that this would be a waste of time and that his designers could come up with something much better. As a young organisation, North American was forward thinking. Although committed to using the Allison engine like many of its competitors, the company's creation of a low-drag airframe, employing a radical laminar flow wing, raised performance expectations. The clean lines of the aircraft were also enhanced by the particularly neat design of the radiator, which was set well back under the fuselage centre section.

With many aspects of the design already established, contracts were finalised on 23 May 1940. The prototype NA-73X was flown for the first time on 26 October 1940 by Vance Breese. The performance was way ahead of any other contemporary American fighter, and large contracts for production aircraft, to be named Mustang I, were soon placed. The first machine for the RAF (AG345) was flown on 1 May 1941 and the initial examples arrived by sea at Liverpool docks in November 1941. After re-assembly, the aircraft were test flown at nearby Speke before delivery to the RAF.

Pilots at A&AEE were soon able to get their hands on the new machine, as AG351 and AG383 were delivered for trials in early 1942. Entry to the cockpit involved the usual climb up the port wing with the help of a recessed handhold in the fuselage. Once on the wing, however, access was relatively easy, as the hood and side panel folded up and down respectively, leaving a large area for entry and a low ledge to step over. In the cockpit, the first thing the pilot noticed was a distinct lack of headroom, even with the seat fully down. The view ahead was better than in a Spitfire, due to the narrowness of the nose, and although there was no clear view panel, the side panels were fitted with sliding windows. A rear-view mirror was mounted on the inside of the hood, but this proved to be of limited use.

The control column was of the plain stick type, but it was considered to be too long and would have benefited from being 3–4 in shorter. The rudder pedals were individual pendulum types with toe-operated brakes and could be adjusted fore-and-aft through five different positions. The control for the elevator trim tab consisted of a 6 in diameter plain rimmed wheel with a large cut in the rim, which indicated the neutral position when at the top. It was positioned near the pilot's left knee and fell readily to hand. The rudder and aileron trim controls were conveniently located on a ledge on the left-hand side of the cockpit.

To operate the flaps, undercarriage and radiator, a hydraulic pressure control knob on the left of the panel was pushed in, and when the appropriate selector lever was moved to the required position, the operation commenced. The undercarriage selector lever was located on the left side of the cockpit floor and was not easy to reach. Three positions, 'UP', 'DOWN' and 'EMERGENCY' were provided, the latter only being used when the undercarriage had not locked correctly in the down position. When the lever was placed in this position, the locking pins were mechanically forced into place. In the event of the engine-driven hydraulic pump failing, a hand pump was located to the right of the seat. Should there be a complete failure of the hydraulic system, the undercarriage could be lowered by pulling an emergency knob on the left-hand side of the panel, which allowed the wheels to come down under their own weight.

The wing flaps were controlled by a yellow-handled lever on the left of the cockpit, and the amount of air entering or exiting the radiator was controlled by another lever just forward of that for the flaps. The undercarriage, wing flap and radiator shutter positions were shown by mechanical indicators sliding in calibrated grooves on the left-hand side of the cockpit. The usual red and green indicator lights and a warning horn were fitted for the undercarriage system. The tailwheel was steerable to the extent of rudder pedal movement and could be locked for take-off and landing. Throttle and mixture controls were positioned on the top left-hand side of the cockpit panelling, the propeller pitch control being just below.

Take-offs were easy, although to obtain the shortest run the tail had to be raised early by positive use of the elevators and the aircraft pulled off the ground. The best flap setting for take-off was recommended as 15 degrees. At flap settings greater than this, there was a strong tendency to drop the left wing, full aileron being needed to check this when using 30 degrees of flap. The aircraft became airborne at 80 mph IAS and flap could be raised when a height of 500 ft had been reached, by which time the IAS was in excess of 120 mph. Slight tail heaviness was noted when the flaps were raised, but there was no tendency to sink. With the undercarriage and flaps up, the best initial climb speed was 160–170 mph IAS.

The controls were tested at speeds up to 500 mph IAS, and although the forces were large for small movements, all were usable. Special attention was paid to the effectiveness of the ailerons and rate of roll tests were carried out up to 400 mph IAS. Although no stick force indicator was fitted, the force on the control column was light enough for full aileron to be applied without undue effort. At 200 mph IAS, aileron control was very light, but the time to roll through 90 degrees was not too fast, due to the aircraft lagging behind control application. The times for a 90-degree roll at this speed were consistently in the region of 1.8 to 2 seconds. The force on the control column was still light at 300 mph IAS, and the times to roll through 90 degrees were virtually identical. By the time that 400 mph IAS had been reached, stick force had increased, but only to around 20 lb and it was still possible to apply full aileron. Rate of roll tests were carried out at normal loadings by rolling from 45 degrees port to 45 degrees to starboard using the left hand to push the control column. All pilots were unanimous that the aileron control of the Mustang was superior to any aircraft previously tested at Boscombe Down.

Generally, the Mustang was stable laterally and directionally at all CG positions, with the flaps and undercarriage up or down. At aft CG it was stable longitudinally at normal flying speeds, engine on, decreasing to neutrally stable at climbing speeds. This was quite acceptable and allowed pleasant manoeuvring qualities. With forward movement of CG the stability was, naturally, increased and the aircraft felt rather heavy longitudinally. Aerobatics were straightforward and there was an improvement in manoeuvrability with a rearward shift of CG. At the aft CG limit the force on the control column in a tight turn was reduced almost to zero, but there was no tendency to tighten up.

Stalling tests were carried out at the extended aft CG limit, as this was the worst condition in which the aircraft could be flown in this respect. At this loading (8600 lb all-up weight and CG 2.7 in aft of datum) the stall speeds were 92 mph IAS with the flaps and undercarriage up and 80 mph IAS with the flaps and undercarriage down.

In the clean configuration there was little warning of the stall, except for the high position of the nose. As speed fell below 100 mph IAS, the aircraft became increasingly left wing low, until at the stall about half aileron had to be applied to keep the wings level. Immediately before the stall, a shudder was felt throughout the airframe and the aircraft started to pitch and rock laterally. The controls were still effective and the aircraft could be controlled by coarse movements, but as the speed continued to drop, the left wing down tendency could not be held and it fell away. There was no tendency to spin. The same sharp shudder before the stall occurred with the flaps and undercarriage down, but in this condition the right wing went down accompanied by the nose. The right wing could not be picked up by using aileron and the aircraft then fell away in a steep spiral, which could, on occasion, lead to a spin.

Dives were made with AL973 at normal CG loadings up to 500 mph IAS and at extended aft CG up to 480 mph IAS, the lower speed being as a result of problems with the hood, which showed distinct signs of breaking away. In full throttle dives at both CG settings, the aircraft was stable. The dives were smooth and steady except for intermittent engine cutting, which had not been experienced with other aircraft. The push force required to hold the aircraft in the dive was very light, and relaxation of this brought about instant recovery. All controls were effective in the dive and although the ailerons became heavier with increase in speed, they were still usable. With one third throttle set, the dives were as smooth as at full throttle, but a much stronger push force was needed to hold the aircraft in the dive. The aircraft also tended to drop its right wing and turn in that direction, requiring aileron and rudder to keep straight. In all dives, hood locking was very unreliable and at high speed a ½-in gap appeared between the hood and the frame. This was most disconcerting for the pilots involved, as the hood showed signs of being sucked out completely .

The best approach speed with the flaps and undercarriage down was 95 mph IAS, in which condition the aircraft was slightly nose-heavy. There was sufficient elevator control to make a tail down landing at all loadings, but at forward CG the limit was just about reached in this respect. The touchdown speed when using full flap was about 80 mph IAS, and there was no tendency to nose over when the brakes were applied, even at the forward CG limit. The climb away from a baulked landing was good. The flaps and undercarriage could be raised at 120 mph IAS without any appreciable sink, and the tail heaviness that became apparent when the engine was opened up could easily be held.

Performance tests were carried out using AG351 and AP222 and showed that at the highest boost setting (56 in Hg) the Mustang could attain 392 mph TAS at a full throttle height of 7900 ft. The full results were as follows:

| Height | 1000 ft | 2000 ft | 4000 ft | 6000 ft | 7900 ft |
|---|---|---|---|---|---|
| TAS – mph | 360.5 | 365 | 374.5 | 384 | 392.5 |
| IAS – mph | 370.5 | 370 | 369 | 368 | 366 |

| Height | 10,000 ft | 12,000 ft | 14,000 ft | 16,000 ft | 18,000 ft |
|---|---|---|---|---|---|
| TAS – mph | 390 | 387 | 384 | 380 | 376 |
| IAS – mph | 352 | 338.5 | 325 | 311.5 | 297.5 |

The maximum rate of climb was 1890 ft/min at 11,500 ft. The rates of climb and times to height were as follows:

| Height | 2000 ft | 4000 ft | 6000 ft | 8000 ft | 11,500 ft |
|---|---|---|---|---|---|
| Time from start – min | 1.05 | 2.15 | 3.20 | 4.30 | 6.15 |
| Rate of climb – ft/min | 1865 | 1870 | 1875 | 1880 | 1890 |

| Height | 14,000 ft | 16,000 ft | 18,000 ft | 20,000 ft | 28,000 ft |
|---|---|---|---|---|---|
| Time from start – min | 7.55 | 8.85 | 10.35 | 12.05 | 25.50 |
| Rate of climb – ft/min | 1640 | 1445 | 1250 | 1060 | 290 |

One uncomfortable aspect of flying the early Mustangs was excessive heat in the cockpit. Hot and cold air could be admitted to the cockpit area and two louvres were situated behind the pilot to remove ventilated air. The hot air supply proved to be totally unnecessary, however, due to heat coming from the radiator unit, as the top of the radiator shell was exposed to the interior of the fuselage. Air that leaked through the fairing joint and various holes for the coolant pipes, combined with convection currents from the radiator, tended to sweep upwards, striking the pilot on the back of the neck before passing out through the louvres. It was recommended that a false fuselage floor be fitted, which would also protect the pilot from coolant fumes should the radiator be damaged in combat.

At the same time as Mustang I testing was taking place at Boscombe Down, AFDU were carrying out tactical trials and armament tests using AG360 and AG365, which had been delivered to Duxford on 28 January 1942. During stop butt trials on AG365, however, a wing gun jumped off its mounting and fired through the wing, which led to this aircraft being replaced by AG422.

The Mustang I was compared with a Spitfire VB and was found to be 30–35 mph faster up to 15,000 ft, reducing to 1–2 mph faster at 25,000 ft. Its rate of climb at all heights was not as good as the Spitfire.

At low altitudes the difference was only slight, but was more marked with height. From 20,000 ft, the Mustang took one minute longer than the Spitfire to reach 25,000 ft. This was considered to be the aircraft's operational ceiling, as at this point the rate of climb had fallen below 1000 ft/min. The Mustang was climbed, rather laboriously, to 30,000 ft, at which height the controls were relatively sloppy and accurate flying was necessary to avoid losing height in turns. In contrast, it was very fast in the dive, the initial acceleration being particularly good, and it was easily able to leave the Spitfire behind. Recovery was straightforward, even at an indicated speed of 500 mph. During prolonged dives, it was necessary to lower a deflector plate in front of the radiator to maintain the correct glycol temperature. This tended to affect trim slightly and cause some minor vibration.

The Mustang was compared to a Spitfire VB as regards turning circles and dogfighting at all heights up to 25,000 ft. At that height, there was little to choose between the two, but at lower altitudes the Spitfire held the advantage, being able to turn marginally tighter. One tactic tried on the Mustang was to lower partial flap to improve the rate of turn. Although it was quite effective, the Spitfire was still able to outmanoeuvre its rival. Up to 15 degrees of flap could be used in this situation, but lowering flap could prove to be an embarrassment for any Mustang pilot should he suddenly be required to break away in a fast dive. The clean design of the Mustang, together with its weight, led to high speeds being generated in the dive, and this speed could be retained for a long time after levelling out. This characteristic, together with its superior speed below 25,000 ft and the ability to dive with full power from straight and level flight by applying negative 'g', allowed the Mustang to break off combat or re-engage at any time. One aspect that emerged during this part of the trial was that it was much more difficult to bring about a high-speed stall in a Mustang than it was in a Spitfire, mainly because of the latter's light elevator control.

With an inferior rate of climb to that of the Spitfire, the Mustang could not make use of climbing turns to obtain a tactical advantage, unless it had already dived from a higher level. The best tactic for the Mustang was to engage from above and to use the speed gained in the dive to zoom up out of range for another attack. One difficulty encountered during dogfights was the lack of an automatic boost control, which meant that the pilot had to constantly check his boost gauge, especially during dives below 15,000 ft. In such circumstances, the boost limitations of the engine could easily be exceeded during combat. With a total fuel capacity of 140 gallons, the endurance of the Mustang was considerably better than the Spitfire and at economical cruise (1800 rpm, 25 in Hg) it was around four hours. Even at maximum continuous cruise (2600 rpm, 37 in Hg), the endurance was 1 hour 40 minutes.

The Mustang was also flown at night, but glare from the open exhausts severely affected the pilot's night vision. Flame dampers, similar to those used on the Airacobra, were then fitted and these resulted in a big improvement. The aircraft's stability was a particular asset at night, as was its controllability. On the downside, the lack of a sliding hood hindered the pilot's ability to search the surrounding area. The opening side panels that were provided were not really large enough and the canopy frames tended to restrict the view. If the aircraft was landing with the aid of an airfield floodlight, it was found that the perspex of the canopy tended to produce bright reflections, which were rather distracting. Cockpit lighting was seldom required due to the luminosity of the instruments.

When flying in cloud on instruments, the aircraft could be trimmed to fly 'hands and feet off' in level flight, or when climbing or diving. As the view forwards and downwards was better than a Spitfire, low flying was considered easier, except in conditions of bad visibility, when the lack of a clear vision panel was badly missed. Brief trials were also carried out against a Typhoon from 10–15,000 ft. The Mustang proved to be more manoeuvrable, although it tended to be out-climbed. During dives, it was found that the Mustang held the initial advantage due to its excellent acceleration. However, the Typhoon quickly caught up, and if the dive was prolonged, it would begin to draw away.

The Mustang I was quite heavily armed, with two 0.5-in machine-guns mounted in the lower front fuselage, together with two 0.5-in and four 0.303-in machine-guns in the wings. The guns were fired by electric solenoids operated by a trigger on the front of the control column. A switch mounted on the left-hand side of the panel allowed the pilot to select 'Wings', 'Fuselage' and 'All'. A comprehensive series of air and ground firing trials were carried out. It was during one of these trials that one of the 0.303-in guns jumped free from its mounting. Shots went through the blast tube and the leading edge of the wing. On examination, it was found that the locking clips were at fault; as a result, revised clips were designed and fitted by AFDU, with no further problems being experienced. In the air, the guns were fired at low altitude under positive and negative 'g', with only occasional stoppages of the 0.303-in guns due to a misfed round under negative 'g'. The guns were tested up to 26,000 ft (OAT −26 degrees C), the only stoppage being caused by a damaged round in the starboard wing 0.50-in gun. No problems were encountered as a result of the guns icing up at high altitude. Pilots were aware of fumes in the cockpit when the fuselage guns were fired, but these quickly dispersed. All who flew the Mustang remarked on the lack of vibration when the guns were fired.

It was noted during the trials that the Allison engine, although easy to start even under the severest winter conditions, took several minutes to warm up after a cold start, as the minimum oil temperature re-commended for take-off was far higher than that quoted for the Merlin. If a quick take-off was required, the engine needed to be kept warm, in which case the time from the order being given to the aircraft becoming airborne was around six minutes.

Due to the limitations of its Allison engine, the Mustang I was used to replace the Tomahawk in Army Co-operation Command squadrons, and proved its worth during low-level armed tactical reconnaissance operations. However, the impression made by the Mustang at AFDU was such that the CO, Wing Commander Campbell-Orde, invited Rolls-Royce test pilot Ronnie Harker to fly the aircraft. Harker was astounded by the Mustang's speed and immediately wondered what the performance would be like if it was re-engined with the latest two-stage supercharged Merlin. Enlisting the assistance of Air Marshal Sir Wilfrid Freeman, the Vice-Chief of the Air Staff, an Allison Mustang was quickly delivered to Rolls-Royce at Hucknall to be converted to Merlin 61 power. Performance predictions were made by Witold Challier, an exiled Polish engineer, who calculated a top speed of 441 mph at 25,600 ft, faster than any other fighter in service at the time.

The first Merlin-engined Mustang (AL975/G) was flown by Rolls-Royce Chief Test Pilot Captain R.T. Shepherd on 13 October 1942 and was unique in featuring a large air intake under the nose. It was referred to as the Mustang X and went on to confound the cynics and prove that Challier's figures had been correct. The results of initial testing were made available to North American via the US Air Attaché in London and NAA soon designed their own set of modifications to mate the Merlin to the Mustang airframe. An agreement was quickly made whereby the Packard motor company would supply licence-built versions of the Merlin, the subsequent V-1650-3 being rated at 1520 hp. Merlin-powered Mustangs as flown by the RAF were designated the Mustang III (equivalent to the USAAF P-51B and P-51C) and the Mustang IV (P-51D).

The first examples of the new Mustang were made available to the testing establishments as soon as they were delivered and AFDU received FZ107 on 26 December 1943 for a tactical evaluation. Apart from the Merlin engine, the Mustang III differed from the Mustang I in having only four wing-mounted 0.50-in guns, a four-blade propeller, an air intake immediately under the propeller hub (instead of over it), a deeper rear fuselage housing radiators and oil coolers, and a slightly larger fin and rudder. The Mustang III was very similar to fly to the Allison-powered variant, but its increased performance meant that compressibility speeds were much more likely to be encountered during dives. Pilots were warned not to use the elevator trim wheel in an attempt to prevent the nose from dropping, as there was every likelihood of a sudden nose-up change of trim occurring as the aircraft came out of the compressibility range, which could lead to high accelerations and possible structural failure.

One of the most interesting aspects of the trial was a tactical comparison with a Spitfire IX (BS552), as both aircraft were powered by basically the same type of engine. Although it was slightly heavier, the Mustang III was cleaner aerodynamically and had a higher wing loading at 43.8 lb/sq.ft compared with 31 lb/sq.ft for the Spitfire. The Mustang III's normal fuel capacity was 154 gallons, which gave it endurance up to 175 per cent greater than the Spitfire. It could also carry two 62½ gallon overload tanks under the wings. The Spitfire could carry a 'slipper' tank under the centre section of 45- or 90- gallon capacity. The fuel consumption was approximately the same at similar boost and engine rpm settings.

The best performance heights were similar, being between 10–15,000 ft and 25–32,000 ft but for the same engine setting the Mustang was 20–30 mph faster in level flight at all heights. It was also significantly superior in the dive, the Spitfire IX requiring 4–6 lb/sq.in more boost to remain in formation at the same engine rpm. The Mustang could also use its excellent dive performance to good effect in a zoom climb, but the Spitfire held the upper hand during full power climbs, needing 5 lb/sq.in less boost to stay in formation. The Spitfire could also roll more quickly than the Mustang at normal speeds (the aircraft used in the trial had clipped wings) and its lighter wing loading meant that it could turn inside its adversary, even if the Mustang lowered partial flap.

The opportunity was also taken to compare the Mustang III with several other aircraft including a Spitfire XIV (RB141). The results were similar to those obtained with the Spitfire IX, except that there was virtually no difference in maximum speed between the two aircraft and the margin in terms of dive performance was not as great. Against a Tempest V (JN737), the Mustang was slower by 15–20 mph up to 15,000 ft. After this height there was little to choose until 24,000 ft was reached, when the Mustang began to pull ahead, being 30 mph faster at 30,000 ft. Maximum rates of climb compared directly with the results of the speed tests, except that the Tempest had a better zoom climb at all heights. The Tempest was able to leave the Mustang during prolonged dives, but its rate of roll and turn performance were not as good.

Brief comparisons were made between the Mustang III and captured examples of the Focke-Wulf Fw 190A (PM679) and Messerschmitt Bf 109G (RN228). When flown against the Fw 190A, the Mustang was nearly 50 mph faster at all heights, increasing to 70 mph faster above 28,000 ft. It also had a decisive advantage in the dive, but the Fw 190 was able to match the Mustang in climb performance and turning circles. Not surprisingly, the Fw 190 could initiate rolling manoeuvres much quicker than its rival, thanks to its large ailerons and excellent response. This agility meant that it was not a good idea for Mustang pilots to attempt to dogfight with Fw 190s, rather to maintain high speed and regain height after each attack. A good defensive tactic for a Mustang was to carry out a steep turn (an attacking Fw 190 would be carrying more speed and would be unable to turn as quickly) and to follow this with a full power dive, which would rapidly increase range.

The Mustang III also had a speed advantage over the Bf 109G, although of slightly more modest proportions. It was 30 mph faster below 16,000 ft and above 25,000 ft, becoming 50 mph faster at 30,000 ft. There was little to choose between the two during maximum rate climbs, the Mustang being very slightly better above 25,000 ft but worse below 20,000 ft, and zoom climb performance was also evenly matched. The rate of roll was similar, but the Mustang did hold sway when it came to turning circles and dive performance. The recommended tactics against the Bf 109G were the same as for the Fw 190A.

The combat performance of the Mustang III was also assessed when carrying long-range tanks. There was a serious loss of speed in the order of 40–50 mph at all engine settings and heights. However, it was still faster than the Fw 190A above 25,000 ft, although slower than the Bf 109G. The rate of climb was greatly reduced, and the Mustang could be out-climbed by both the Fw 190A and Bf 109G. However, if the tanks were reasonably full the Mustang was still superior in the dive. The tanks did not make as much difference as might have been expected as regards turning circles, and the Mustang could still turn as tightly as the Fw 190A, and more tightly than the Bf 109G. The general handling and rate of roll were also very little affected. With a greatly reduced performance when carrying drop tanks, AFDU concluded that a half-hearted attack could be evaded by a steep turn, but it would be difficult to avoid a determined attack without losing height.

If there was anyone who still did not believe the transformation that had taken place with the Mustang, the results of performance testing carried out at Boscombe Down left absolutely no doubt that the adoption of the two-speed, two-stage supercharged Merlin in place of the Allison engine had turned an aircraft of limited value into a world beater. Mustang III FX953 was put through its paces in May 1944 at a take-off weight of 9200 lb, without bombs or drop tanks. At a normal engine rating of 2700 rpm and 46 in Hg manifold pressure, the maximum rate of climb in MS gear was 2060 ft/min at 16,700 ft and 1555 ft/min at 30,200 ft in FS gear. At the full combat rating of 3000 rpm and 67 in Hg manifold pressure, the best rate of climb was 3610 ft/min at 10,600 ft in MS gear and 2690 ft/min at 23,400 ft in FS gear. The service ceiling was 42,800 ft (approximately 12,000 ft higher than the Mustang I), with an absolute ceiling of 43,600 ft.

Level speed trials showed the Mustang III to be faster at cruise settings than the Mustang I at full combat power. With 2700 rpm and 46 in Hg manifold pressure set, the Mustang III achieved 406 mph at 20,600 ft in MS gear and 438 mph at 33,000 ft in FS gear. However, at 3000 rpm and 67 in Hg manifold pressure, the maximum speed in MS gear was 424 mph at 15,500 ft, and in FS gear it was 450 mph at 28,000 ft.

Although the early-type hood as fitted to the Mustang I had not been received with much enthusiasm, the later Mustangs were fitted with sliding canopies. These considerably improved lookout, as Len Thorne recalls.

> On 8 December 1942 I tested a Mustang at AFDU with a sliding canopy instead of the up-and-over hood and it certainly impressed me. The Americans were very loath to change their design as they thought that the bubble hood would upset the airflow and spoil the aircraft but, in fact, it worked the other way as it made the tail surfaces more effective. The bubble hood (and the later teardrop canopy) were both very pleasant to fly because the all-round visibility was very much better than it was with the slab-sided design, and for me it was something of a revelation because you could actually stick your head over the side and look straight down behind the wing which was a peculiar sensation.

In addition to performance testing at A&AEE and tactical trials at AFDU, the Mustang was also used for aerodynamic trials work at RAE Farnborough, including a comparison of its ailerons with those of the Spitfire. Lateral control problems at high speed on the Spitfire were still causing concern and the excellent aileron effectiveness of the Mustang generated considerable interest. The Mustang's ailerons were of the plain type with geared tabs, while the Spitfire was fitted with Frise ailerons with a sharp leading edge. An unusual feature of the Mustang's ailerons was their relatively small range of movement ($+/-10$ degrees) compared with that of the Spitfire ($+24$, $-20$ degrees).

Tests showed there to be little difference in aileron effectiveness (rate of roll per degree aileron) at speeds up to 150 mph, but above this speed the Mustang's aileron became much more effective. This was mainly due to the greater stiffness of the Mustang wing, which gave much less twisting, the aileron reversal speed (the theoretical speed at which wing twist due to lack of torsional rigidity overrides the effect of the ailerons) for the Mustang being 820 mph, compared with 580 mph for the Spitfire. The aileron angles and stick forces required to generate a steady rate of roll of 45 degrees per second were measured in both aircraft. At 400 mph IAS, the Mustang had an aileron deflection of 4.5 degrees and needed a stick force of 23 lb, whereas figures for the Spitfire were 10.3 degrees and 71 lb respectively.

Although the Mustang I had been used for terminal velocity dives at RAE Farnborough to test its behaviour at compressibility speeds (see Chapter 2), these trials had been severely limited by the aircraft's lack of altitude performance. As the dives could only be commenced at around 28,000 ft, the maximum Mach number achieved before safety height was reached was 0.80, compared with 0.89 for the Spitfire XI, which was able to dive from a height of 40,000 ft. As the later Mustangs were able to match the Spitfire in terms of service ceiling, this allowed the opportunity to find out more about its handling characteristics at the highest speeds that could be attained. A series of thirty-one dives were carried out at the USAAF test establishment at Wright Field, Dayton, Ohio, commencing on 3 August 1944 using P-51D 44-14134, equivalent to the RAF's Mustang IV.

The dives were entered by a variety of means, including nosing over from level flight and from a diving turn. A half roll and pull through was also tried, but extreme care had to be taken during this manoeuvre as high Mach numbers could be reached within a few seconds. If this was tried at rated power above 36,000 ft, it could well lead to a structural failure. As speed built up, longitudinal instability or 'porpoising' set in. This condition could be induced at Mach 0.70 and above, but it was not unknown for it to be encountered at lower Mach numbers at low altitude. The motion was often pilot-induced, and although not severe, any effort to counteract it was likely to result in the motion increasing in amplitude. The most effective solution was to hold the stick firmly in one position or to trim forward to nearly zero stick force as the dive was entered, thus reducing the amount of forward stick force necessary to maintain the angle of dive.

As the speed increased to Mach 0.75, a slight rolling motion became apparent with simultaneous reduction in aileron sensitivity. This did not become severe and could be easily controlled. At Mach 0.76, however, a steady vibration set in due to compressibility effects on the wing and tailplane, and this became worse with increase in speed, becoming heavy by the time that Mach 0.80 had been reached. Several dives were made to Mach 0.84 (and one to Mach 0.85), and on each occasion the vibration caused some structural damage. This included a buckled leading edge skin of the wing flap, a cracked coolant radiator and a broken hydraulic line. During the period the aircraft was in heavy buffet, even a relatively low acceleration could lead to a primary structural failure.

Recovery had to be gradual and executed with extreme caution, as relatively light stick forces or rapid application of trim could easily result in excessive load factors. At the beginning of the pull-out an increase in vibration could occur, but this would gradually decrease as the recovery was completed. At no time was it necessary to select elevator trim to aid the recovery. The P-51D also showed no tendency to 'tuck-under' when power was increased or decreased in the dive. From these dives it was recommended that the Mustang be restricted to a Mach number of 0.80, as difficulties caused by compressibility above this point made it increasingly dangerous for the pilot.

In addition to its duties evaluating and comparing the Allied single-engined fighters and their German counterparts, AFDU was also responsible for testing a wide range of weapons for use against ground targets. In September 1944, the unit was required to carry out tests to determine whether standard aircraft drop tanks could be used offensively as so-called fire bombs. Two types of incendiary mixture were considered, perspex in benzole, and aluminium laurate and creosote in 'pool' petrol. The aircraft used for the trials were Typhoon IB MN974 and Mustang III FZ107. Initial tests were carried out with water-filled 'dead' bombs. The first 'live' drops were made over the Holbeach ranges, the benzole mix proving to have the better qualities. To be able to observe the trials more closely, several trenches and a gun emplacement were dug at Collyweston airfield, complete with straw dummies. By this stage only the Mustang was being used and the tactics recommended by AFDU were to make an approach at 5–8,000 ft, according to cloud conditions, and then to turn through 90 degrees on sighting the target. A descent would be made to a height of 1500 ft about 1500 yards from the target. The attack would be carried out in a shallow dive at limiting speed, which, for the Mustang, was set at 350 mph IAS due to the risk of the tanks hitting the aircraft when released. In the final stages the attack was delivered down to a minimum height of 50 ft, which also allowed full use of the aircraft's guns.

Len Thorne was heavily involved in these trials, but dropping live ordnance was always liable to cause some anxious moments. He recalls one particular occasion when things did not quite go according to plan.

As the war progressed we hung all sorts of things on those lovely fighters: bombs, rockets and drop tanks for longer range. In 1944 thought was given to the problem of winkling the Japanese out of fox holes and slit trenches and the idea of 'napalm' was born [from two constituent components naphthalenic and palmitic acids]. One Sunday I had the very doubtful honour of demonstrating this weapon to a group of Army top brass, both American and British. Dummy trenches had been dug at Collyweston, and two 62½-gallon drop tanks filled with jellyfied benzole were hung on my P-51. The idea was to release the tanks in a shallow dive about 100 yards short of the target, the tanks would burst on impact throwing the napalm forward to run down into the trenches. Strapped to the outside of each tank was a white phosphorus grenade attached by a wire to the bomb rack so that when the tank was released it pulled on the wire and made the grenade live. If it was done at the right altitude, when it hit the ground it exploded and ignited the napalm which travelled forward for a distance of about 350 yards.

On the day in question the weather was atrocious as it was blowing half a gale. I said it was ridiculous to try to do a test in such weather but, as everybody was in position, I had no choice. I released the drop tanks at the appropriate moment but one of them hung up. I then pulled round in a fairly steep climbing turn and in the middle of the turn the remaining tank came off and hit an American Army camp a couple of miles to the south of the airfield, falling right in the middle of the parade ground. As I landed I had visions of having killed countless American soldiers but because it was a Sunday afternoon they were all off camp so the napalm didn't do any serious damage. They insisted I repeat the run and the same thing happened the second time but on this occasion I flew straight on and managed to get to the Wash before it came off.

The Mustang III entered service with the RAF in February 1944 when No. 19 Squadron took delivery of the first aircraft at Ford. The old-type hood was fitted to early production aircraft but this was quickly replaced by the bulged Malcolm hood. As previously stated, this improved the pilot's search view, but it was not until the arrival of the Mustang IV with its moulded one-piece canopy that the problem of rearward vision in particular was fully addressed. As the profile of the rear fuselage had been reduced slightly by the adoption of the new hood design, a dorsal fin was incorporated to restore directional stability. The armament on the Mustang IV comprised six 0.50-in wing-mounted machine-guns.

The role of the Mustang in the final months of the war ranged from high-level bomber escort to ground attack in support of the Allied armies. From the beginning of 1944 Mustangs began to replace obsolescent Kittyhawks and Hurricanes in Italy, and with the withdrawal of German forces in northern Europe, Mustangs of the 2nd Tactical Air Force ranged far and wide seeking to destroy targets with their 500-lb bombs.

Even UK-based Mustang squadrons could play a big part in the fighting over Europe. On 16 April 1945, No. 611 Squadron became the first RAF unit to encounter Russian aircraft over Berlin, when

Shturmovik ground-attack aircraft, escorted by Yak fighters, were seen. Shortly afterwards No. 611 Squadron ran into a gaggle of Fw 190s. Six were shot down, including one that fell to the guns of Pilot Officer Ian Walker flying Mustang IV KH743. At the time No. 611 Squadron was based at Hunsdon in Hertfordshire and their duties that day involved escorting medium bombers to Swinemunde, followed by a sweep of the area around Berlin. Ian Walker's logbook shows a total flight time for the mission of 5 hours 55 minutes. Such a stark fact may seem of little interest, but it highlights just one aspect of the Mustang's success, its remarkably long range. When this is added to extremely high performance, excellent handling characteristics and an impressive load-carrying capability, the combination becomes overwhelming, and puts the Mustang not only at the pinnacle of all Second World War fighters, but in a select group of weapons that helped to shorten the course of the war.

CHAPTER SIXTEEN

# Republic Thunderbolt

By mid 1940, it had become obvious to the US Army Air Corps that the current crop of American fighters were no match for corresponding types being developed by the warring nations in Europe. The USAAC therefore set about formulating a series of requirements that would close the gap. One of the firms contacted was the Republic Aviation Corporation of Farmingdale, Long Island, which had recently changed its name from the Seversky Aircraft Corporation.

Seversky had been formed in 1922 and had produced the stubby P-35 fighter of 1935. Designed by Alexander Kartveli, the P-35 was moderately successful (120 being ordered by the Swedish Air Force). However, the USAAC favoured the Curtiss P-36, which had better performance, although the Seversky design had superior manoeuvrability and range. In order to be able to compete with rival manufacturers more effectively, Kartveli's thoughts turned to turbo-supercharging as a means of extracting greater speed at higher altitudes. This led to the YP-43, which had a top speed of 350 mph at 20,000 ft.

Although a turbo-supercharged radial engine offered great potential, the design trend in Europe was very much towards use of inline, water-cooled engines, which offered low frontal area and reduced drag. This theme had been perpetuated in the US with the Allison V-12, and Kartveli realised that to ignore this powerplant might prejudice the chance of Republic receiving orders. He thus proposed the Model AP-10 (ordered in prototype form as the XP-47 in November 1939), but by the following summer the Air Corps hierarchy had begun to recognise the limitations of the Allison engine and designers were being encouraged to look elsewhere. The most powerful engine available was the new Pratt & Whitney XR-2800 Double Wasp air-cooled radial offering around 2000 hp but the original XP-47 was too small to accept it. Following a complete redesign, the XP-47B Thunderbolt eventually emerged in early 1941, bearing a strong resemblance to the earlier P-43. It was first flown on 6 May 1941 by Lowery L. Brabham and had a gross weight of 11,600 lb, more than twice that of the XP-47.

By the standards of the day, the P-47 Thunderbolt was truly colossal for a fighter, its capacious body housing the ducting for the R-2800's turbo-supercharger. The fuselage was of semi-monocoque, all-metal, stressed-skin construction and employed transverse bulkheads and longitudinal stringers. A General Electric turbo-supercharger was located in the lower rear fuselage and exhaust gases were passed through insulated pipes to the turbine, before being expelled through a waste gate on the aircraft's underside. Air for the supercharger, in the meantime, was passed from an intake at the bottom of the NACA cowling. After passing through the supercharger, the air was fed to the engine via an intercooler.

To harness the power of the engine a four-blade Curtiss Electric propeller of 12 ft 2 in diameter had to be used, but this caused problems with ground clearance. As each wing was to house a battery of four 0.50-in machine-guns with 500 rounds per gun, the amount of space for the undercarriage was limited. Republic therefore came up with the novel solution of a telescopic landing gear that was 9 in shorter when retracted than when extended. The tailwheel was fully retractable and had its own doors.

The P-47B Thunderbolt entered USAAF service with the 4th, 78th and 56th Fighter Groups at Debden, Goxhill and Kings Cliffe respectively in early 1943, and was to be a stalwart of Eighth Air Force operations over northern Europe. Used mainly in the escort role, the Thunderbolt offered fighter protection over part of Germany, although even when fitted with overload fuel tanks it could still not provide cover for American B-17 and B-24 bombers on deep-penetration raids. The Thunderbolt was also flown in the Mediterranean theatre. It was here that a comparative trial was conducted by the USAAF involving a P-47D-4 and a captured Focke-Wulf Fw 190A. As one of the early variants, the D-4 had the original 'high-back' fuselage and hood, but its performance was enhanced by the inclusion of water-injection equipment, which increased the top speed for short periods.

The Thunderbolt was flown with a full war load and the Fw 190 also carried full ammunition for its two wing cannon and fuselage-mounted machine-guns. The Focke-Wulf was considered to be in exceptionally good condition for a captured aircraft and it easily developed 42 in Hg manifold pressure on take-off. Four flights were made, each of one-hour duration. The aircraft were compared in terms of acceleration, climb and dive performance and turning capability. During low-level acceleration tests up to 5000 ft, the Fw 190 was initially able to pull ahead of the Thunderbolt and gain about 200 yards, but this could not be sustained. If full power was maintained, the P-47 (using its water-injection) quickly caught up again and assumed the lead. A similar trial was carried out at 15,000 ft, with almost identical results.

Climbs were attempted from 2000 ft commencing at 250 mph IAS, both aircraft being pulled up rapidly to the angle of maximum climb and held until an altitude of 8500 ft had been reached. The Fw 190 climbed faster than the Thunderbolt through the first 1500 ft, but, once again, it was quickly overtaken and was then out-climbed by around 500 ft per minute. When similar climbs were made from 10,000 ft the Fw 190 again had the initial advantage, but by the time that 15,000 ft had been reached, the Thunderbolt was 500 ft above its rival. Dives were carried out from 10,000 ft with an entry speed of 250 mph IAS, the dive being flown at a constant throttle setting and an angle of around 65 degrees. The Fw 190 pulled away rapidly in the early stages of the dive but the Thunderbolt passed it, flying at much greater speed as the two aircraft passed through 3000 ft. It also appeared to have a much better angle of pull-out than the Focke-Wulf.

At speeds in excess of 250 mph IAS, the two aircraft were turned on each other's tail as tight as possible, alternating the turns to the left and right. The Thunderbolt easily out-turned the Fw 190 at 10,000 ft and had to throttle back to keep from overshooting, a level of superiority that increased with altitude. During turning manoeuvres, it was found that the Fw 190 had a nasty habit of blacking out its pilot. Below 250 mph IAS, however, the situation was rather different as the Fw 190 could be made to hang on its propeller. This made life extremely difficult for the pilot of the Thunderbolt and the Focke-Wulf's ability to turn inside its opponent was very evident. The Fw 190's superb rate of roll also allowed it to change direction very quickly. When this was used in conjunction with its excellent initial acceleration, the Thunderbolt was unable to follow and the Fw 190 was able to rapidly move to a more advantageous position.

As Britain did not have a requirement for another high-altitude fighter, the Thunderbolt was used for ground attack, carrying up to three 500-lb bombs. The RAF received a total of 830 P-47s, which were put to good use in the Far East against Japanese forces. Of these, 240 were Thunderbolt Is (equivalent to the P-47B) and 590 were Thunderbolt IIs with 'low back' fuselage and clear-view canopy, equivalent to the USAAF P-47D-25.

Handling trials were carried out at A&AEE Boscombe Down in August 1944 to clear the Thunderbolt for operations in the fighter-bomber role. Most of the test work was performed by FL849, although 274699 was also used when the former aircraft became unserviceable towards the end of the trial. Both aircraft were powered by an R-2800-59 of 2300 hp with water-injection (limited to a maximum of 51½ in Hg manifold pressure and 2700 rpm for take-off) and carried the normal armament of eight 0.50-in machine-guns. Trim tabs were fitted to each elevator and the port aileron, and a combined balance/trim tab was fitted to the rudder. The normal take-off weight (as a fighter) was 14,170 lb, but with two 500-lb bombs under the wings and one 500-lb bomb under the fuselage, this figure increased to 15,715 lb, or slightly more than twice that of a fully loaded Spitfire IX.

The test flying that was carried out involved take-offs, stalls, dives and landings at all loadings. The effect on handling characteristics of releasing bombs singly in the dive was tested, but due to its limited operational role with the RAF, the dives were restricted to low altitude. When carrying a single 500-lb bomb under the fuselage, a flap setting of 20 degrees was used for take-off, but even so the run was long. This was no great surprise, as a clean aircraft required around 600 yards to get airborne, which was longer than most other fighters of the period. The aircraft took off at around 110 mph IAS and although carrying the bomb did not affect handling, the climb away was noted as being poor.

The stall speed with the flaps and undercarriage up was 112 mph IAS. As speed was decreased, the aircraft became nose-heavy, about half elevator trim being required to keep the stick force down to a reasonable level. A decrease in lateral control became apparent as speed dropped below 120 mph IAS, and there was snatching of the ailerons. As speed was reduced further, lateral control deteriorated rapidly until at the stall the port wing dropped, followed by the nose. There was no stall warning apart from the aileron snatch mentioned above. With the flaps and undercarriage down, the stall came at 98 mph IAS. The nose-heaviness experienced in the 'all-up' case was even more marked, to the extent that full elevator trim was needed. Aileron snatching was again present, but in addition there was vibration of the whole aircraft before the port wing dropped and the nose went down. At the point of stall, the control column was about two-thirds back from its central position. In each of the above cases, the rate of sink prior to the stall was high and control forces were heavy, but recovery on centralising the controls was normal and there was no tendency to spin.

Trimmed dives were made between 16,000 ft and 7000 ft with the engine set to 40 in Hg manifold pressure and 2550 rpm. The rate of increase of speed was low, unless the dive was entered very steeply. A general 'roughness' of the whole airframe was noted as speed increased to 400 mph IAS, but this did not get any worse with further increases in speed. Changes in directional trim with increases in speed were marked, a heavy left foot load being required to keep the aircraft straight. When this was trimmed out, the aircraft became left wing low and lateral re-trimming was necessary. Only a slight change in longitudinal trim occurred, the aircraft becoming slightly tail-heavy above 400 mph IAS. Recoveries from trimmed dives were made at 400 and 450 mph IAS. In each case, the recovery felt sluggish and a fairly heavy backward pressure was needed to initiate the pull-out and to maintain it.

Landings were carried out with the bomb still in place. No difficulties were encountered, provided that about 70 gallons of fuel had been used to reduce the landing weight to permissible limits. The rate of sink on the approach was high and the best speed was found to be 115 mph IAS.

With two bombs in place under the wings, the take-off run was noticeably longer and the stall speeds with the flaps and undercarriage up and down were 120 and 102 mph IAS respectively. The handling characteristics were similar to the previous test, except that in each case the effect was slightly worse and in some cases significantly worse. The loss of lateral control was almost complete, and the aircraft entered a right- or left-hand spiral, the direction depending on wing drop. Recovery was normal, but the height loss was considerable. In dives from 13,000 ft, the left wing low tendency was more marked and a considerable amount of aileron was required to keep the wings level at speeds above 420 mph IAS. This had to be counteracted by use of the controls, as there was insufficient time to re-trim laterally.

A further loss in take-off performance occurred when carrying bombs on all three stations, with lift-off taking place at 115 mph IAS. Acceleration and initial climb also showed a further slight deterioration. Some differences were apparent at the stall, and with the flaps and undercarriage up, vibration could be felt at 135 mph IAS, with aileron snatching from 125 mph IAS. If no attempt was made to control this, and the control column was left about one-third back from neutral, an indefinite stall occurred at 120 mph IAS, the aircraft becoming right wing heavy and the nose dropping very gradually. The snatching could, however, be controlled and by applying a considerable force to pull the control column hard back, the aircraft stalled properly at 110 mph IAS. In this case, there was no tendency for a wing to drop and the nose dropped quite sharply at the full stall. The characteristics were similar with the flaps and undercarriage down, occurring at 10–15 mph IAS less in each case.

The wing-mounted bombs were also dropped asymmetrically to check for any handling problems. The left wing bomb was released in a dive at 450 mph IAS and there was a very quick lateral rocking motion, which damped out immediately. Releasing the right wing bomb had no noticeable effect on handling; there was no 'kick' as it departed.

Trials were also carried out at Boscombe Down from November 1944 to clear various sizes and combinations of overload fuel tanks for carriage by the Thunderbolt. The aircraft used was FL844 and the tanks ranged in size from 108 to 165 US gallons. Handling was confirmed in all cases, the 165 US gallon tanks being cleared to 320 mph IAS and the smaller 150 US gallon tanks to 400 mph IAS. Jettison tests were satisfactory, except for the 165-US gallon tank, which caused damage to the wing flaps when dropped at 200 mph IAS

Although the Thunderbolt was never used as anything other than a fighter-bomber in RAF service, a comparative assessment was carried out by AFDS in early 1945 to determine its capabilities against the latest offering from Hawker, the Centaurus-powered Tempest II. As the Tempest had been designed as a short-range, low-medium altitude fighter, it naturally lost out in terms of endurance and the Thunderbolt had a greater radius of action at all engine settings and heights. The Thunderbolt allotted for the trial was not fitted with water-injection and so allowance had to be made for this in the calculation of its maximum speed. Even so, it was found that the Tempest II was some 80 mph faster at low levels up to 2000 ft, this advantage reducing to 40 mph by the time that 20,000 ft had been reached. Parity occurred at around 28,000 ft, and the Thunderbolt began to come into its own above this height, being 20 mph faster at 31,000 ft. The Tempest II had the advantage in acceleration in straight and level flight at all heights. Even at high altitude, where the Thunderbolt was faster, the Tempest was able to pull away initially.

There were also significant variations in climb performance, which reflected the widely differing roles for which the aircraft had been designed. At sea level the Tempest II was totally dominant, having a climb rate 2000 ft/min better then the Thunderbolt, but this advantage gradually diminished until the two aircraft were equal at 21,000 ft. Thereafter, the Thunderbolt was superior and by the time that 28,000 ft had been reached, it had a climb rate 500 ft/min better than the Tempest II. At low altitude and with equal power settings, the Thunderbolt was slightly superior during zoom climbs, but at full power and at high altitude the Tempest II was the better. The Tempest II could always out-dive the Thunderbolt. This advantage was particularly noticeable at full throttle.

In the lateral plane, at speeds up to 300 mph IAS there was little advantage either way as regards rate of roll. The Tempest II had a slight advantage to the right and the Thunderbolt to the left, due to the different direction of propeller rotation, the former being a left-hand and the latter a right-hand tractor. Above 300 mph IAS, however, the Tempest II became increasingly superior. The Tempest II could also out-turn the Thunderbolt at any height, due to its considerably lower wing loading of 38 lb/sq.ft, compared with 49 lb/sq.ft for the American fighter.

In many ways, the AFDS trial was rather meaningless as the Tempest II had been designed as a relatively low-altitude fighter-bomber, whereas the Thunderbolt had been conceived with a very different role in mind, that of a high-altitude, air superiority fighter. There was also little likelihood of the two aircraft ever having to confront each other in combat. As a tactical exercise, however, it was of considerable interest. It showed that the Tempest II was definitely superior up to 21,000 ft (except in range and endurance), but that the Thunderbolt began to assert ever greater authority above this height.

The RAF was the second largest operator of the P-47 Thunderbolt. Nearly all were despatched directly from the USA to India, where they were reassembled for use by sixteen squadrons operating in Burma with South-East Asia Command. Duties included operations in support of the Army, often involving 'Cab-Rank' patrols and dive-bombing attacks when requested by a forward controller, escort to C-46 and C-47 transports and medium and heavy bombers, and long-range interdiction sorties attacking Japanese airfields and communications.

The Thunderbolt was popular in RAF service. Pilots were appreciative of the roomy well laid out cockpit and wide-track undercarriage, which was of particular benefit when operating from hastily improvised airstrips. Less well liked was the poor view when taxying (due to the P-47's massive nose), its poor take-off performance and a somewhat less than sprightly climb rate when airborne. Because of its weight, it also had a much higher landing speed than the Spitfires that most pilots had been used to. Once in the air, however, it came into its own. Unlike a number of other fighters of the period, its handling characteristics were largely unaltered at altitude, and its stability in the dive was one of the prime reasons for it achieving levels of accuracy previously unseen during dive-bombing sorties. The Thunderbolt also possessed excellent range; sorties of up to three hours were commonplace, with some trips extending to five hours when carrying drop tanks and flying at economical power settings. A poor rate of turn was not too much of an embarrassment, as by this stage of the war, contacts with Japanese fighters were fairly infrequent.

The rugged nature of the P-47 was also ideally suited to the tropical environment, in particular its Pratt & Whitney engine, which gave far less trouble than the water-cooled Merlins of the Spitfires that the Thunderbolt replaced. Problems occured with the later Mark IIs, however, when Curtiss Electric paddle-blade propellers replaced the Hamilton Hydromatic propellers used on earlier aircraft. The humid conditions played havoc with the various electrical connections. Both the airframe and engine were able to take considerable battle damage and still get home, and Thunderbolt units were able to claim a very low fatality rate among pilots. Sadly, some aircraft were lost, including a number that blew up when recovering from dive-bombing attacks. It transpired that excessive 'g' during the pull-out from dives was causing the internal fuel tanks to rupture, and spilt fuel was coming into contact with the hot supercharger ducting to produce an explosion. Tactics were amended when the cause of the accidents was known, and dive-bombing attacks were subsequently flown at a shallower angle of about 30 degrees.

The Thunderbolt did not remain in RAF service for very long after VJ-Day, with many fighter-bomber squadrons being disbanded. Those that did form part of the post-war RAF were quick to re-equip with British-built aircraft, Nos 5 and 30 Squadrons at Bhopal receiving Tempest IIs and No. 60 Squadron at Surabaya the Spitfire FR.XVIII.

# CHAPTER SEVENTEEN

# Grumman
# Martlet/Wildcat

The Grumman F4F Wildcat was conceived around the same time as the Brewster Buffalo, and was a direct competitor for a US Naval order for shipboard fighters. Its short, rotund fuselage was reminiscent of the biplane fighters that preceded it, and it was powered by a fourteen-cylinder two-row Pratt & Whitney R-1830-66 Twin Wasp of 1050 hp. The F4F was of all-metal construction with fabric-covered control surfaces and featured a mid-set wing of NACA 230 series section. The undercarriage retracted into wells in the fuselage to the rear of the engine. The armament initially comprised two fuselage-mounted 0.5-in Browning machine-guns firing through the propeller arc, although provision was also made for two further Browning guns in the wings.

The prototype XF4F-2 was flown for the first time by Robert L. Hall at Bethpage on 2 September 1937. It was delivered to the Anacostia Naval Air Station for trials work and a comparative assessment with the Brewster XF2A-1 and the Seversky HF-1 (a naval adaptation of the P-35). As the maximum speed of the latter was only 250 mph, it was quickly dropped from the competition, leaving the contenders from Grumman and Brewster to fight it out. Although a production contract was awarded to the XF2A-1, the promise shown by the Grumman fighter was sufficient for the drafting of a development contract for a more advanced version. This was the XF4F-3, which was powered by an XR-1830-76 Twin Wasp with a two-stage supercharger offering 1200 hp for take-off and 1000 hp at 19,000 ft. Other modifications included a wing of increased span and area, squared off wing tips and a taller fin. Although the weight had gone up by 600 lb to 5986 lb, the maximum speed was now 334 mph at 20,500 ft.

The first production F4F-3 took to the air in February 1940, and the type was selected by France for use as a shipboard fighter, but with a 1200 hp Wright Cyclone R-1820-G205A-2 with a single-stage, two-speed supercharger. No deliveries had been made by the time of the French collapse and the order was transferred to Britain for the Fleet Air Arm, where the aircraft became known as the Martlet I. The first examples did not feature wing-folding and were armed with four 0.50-in guns in the wings. Subsequent variants were the Martlet II and III, (both powered by a Twin Wasp), the Martlet IV and V (which from January 1944 became known as the Wildcat IV and V) and the Wildcat VI.

Handling trials were carried out at A&AEE Boscombe Down using Martlet I AX826. The cockpit could be entered from either side of the aircraft, as a foothold and handhold were provided on each side of the fuselage, together with a 'non-slip' coating on the wing root. Having climbed up the wing, access to the cockpit was rather awkward, and another handhold at the top of the windscreen would have been a big improvement. The pilot's seat was relatively comfortable and could be adjusted for height by releasing a catch on the right-hand side of the seat. However the counter balance arrangement proved to be insufficiently strong, and to raise the seat the pilot had to take his feet off the rudder pedals and press on the floor. Even so, a further 1–2 in of upward movement was really needed to provide the best possible view around the nose for landing.

At cruising rpm the cockpit was quieter than most other fighters of the period, and the noise did not become excessive at any time. Although no heating was provided, the cockpit did not get particularly cold, but after flying for a considerable period with the hood closed, pilots became aware of a distinct smell of engine fumes. This posed something of a dilemma, as on opening the hood to disperse the fumes, the pilot was hit by almost unbearable draught, which buffeted the head quite violently, except when flying at very low rpm. The hood was not particularly easy to move and both hands were required to slide it backwards or forwards. More marks were lost by the American-type oxygen equipment, which was considered unsatisfactory as there was no indication of the rate of flow or any warning should the supply fail. As a result of the severe draughts experienced at high power settings, most pilots elected to take-off with the hood closed.

The view from the cockpit was good at all times, especially to the rear. There was no clear view panel fitted, but this was not missed during the approach, as the hood could be opened without too much discomfort when the engine was throttled back. A clear view panel would have been of use, however, during longer flights in bad weather. On a number of occasions, the windscreen iced up badly when descending from high altitude. As there was no cockpit heating, this took some time to clear at low level, an aspect of the Martlet that would be of obvious concern to pilots returning low on fuel.

On the ground, all the control surfaces could be moved without excessive friction or play. The control column had a solid vertical hand-grip incorporating a gun-firing trigger and bomb release. For ease of use, it was felt that it needed to be slightly longer and a little nearer the pilot. The rudder pedals were of the pendulum type and could be adjusted fore-and-aft. Trim tabs were provided for the elevator, rudder and port aileron, and the controls were mounted on the left-hand side of the cockpit near the pilot's forearm. Indicators were provided for all three. The controls were easy and smooth to operate, and showed no tendency to slip. In flight, however, the trimmer controls iced up on several occasions, and attempts to free them resulted in failures.

The throttle and mixture controls were located in a quadrant on the left-hand side of the cockpit, and fell nicely to hand. Once again, there was no automatic boost, the throttle having to be readjusted after every change in height or speed, particularly in a dive when boost would quickly rise above limiting values if not constantly watched. A gate was provided on the throttle at the position for maximum take-off boost. The mixture control lever could be moved to any one of four positions – fully rich, automatic rich, automatic weak or idle cut-out – and the control for the constant-speed propeller consisted of a 'push-pull' knob at the bottom left-hand side of the panel. The fuel cock was positioned behind the throttle and elevator trimmer.

Other major controls included the supercharger gear change, consisting of a 'push-pull' handle on the bottom right-hand side of the panel, and the emergency hand-operated fuel pump and ignition switches on the opposite side. The flap control was also on the left of the cockpit behind the rudder trimmer. As it was of similar shape to the fuel cock handle located nearby, there was a distinct possibility that a pilot would operate the wrong one if distracted, or when flying at night. The undercarriage was retracted by a manual crank handle near the pilot's right knee and a safety catch had to be moved before it could be turned. For a manual system the operation was relatively easy, and the wheels could be retracted in 25–30 seconds. If the engine was throttled back with the undercarriage up: a red light appeared on the left of the panel and a horn sounded. A lever to lock the tailwheel was located just forward of the throttle quadrant.

The brakes were operated via toe pedals and were not particularly efficient, being too stiff and insensitive in operation. Each wheel had its own independent system and so it was difficult to apply equal pressure to each side when pulling up from a straight run. The instruments were generally well positioned, except for the engine speed indicator, which was positioned at the extreme right-hand side of the panel. No heating was provided for the pitot head.

Taxying was relatively straightforward and the view on the ground was good. Owing to the narrowness of the undercarriage, however, there was a tendency for one leg to compress more than the other, and the aircraft tended to list considerably in a strong crosswind. It was also difficult to turn against a strong wind. Before attempting to takeoff, the tailwheel lock had to be engaged and the aircraft taxied a short distance to ensure that the lock had taken effect. Take-offs were normally made with the flaps up, but with full right rudder trim (three divisions) and about half a division of nose-down elevator trim. Despite the application of full right rudder trim, there was still a tendency to swing to the left and further right rudder was required. The tailwheel did not come up particularly quickly during the early part of the take-off, but the aircraft left the ground at 82 mph IAS after a relatively short run. It was recommended that the undercarriage be raised immediately the aircraft became airborne, and some trimming was required to remove the slight tail heaviness produced.

Once in the climb, the aircraft could be trimmed to fly 'hands and feet off'. In all manoeuvres, the controls were light and effective, particularly the ailerons. The lightness of the aileron control was consistent throughout the speed range, but the rudder and elevators tended to become heavier with increases in speed. Response to all controls was excellent and aileron trim was regarded as superfluous.

Stability checks were made using Martlet I AX828 with a normal CG loading. Although it was stable in level flight, it showed signs of instability on the climb with the flaps and undercarriage up. As CG was moved further back, the aircraft became increasingly unstable longitudinally in the climb, when cruising, in full throttle level flight and in the glide (flaps and undercarriage up). Any displacement of the control column produced a divergence, which at extended aft CG would normally have been regarded as unacceptable. As the initial stages of the divergence were not vicious, however, and in view of the generally good flying qualities of the aircraft and its operational duties, it was felt that the aircraft could be cleared at this CG position. When CG was moved forward, the aircraft's longitudinal stability became practically neutral. Following any disturbance from a trimmed condition, it tended to remain in its disturbed position, the speed only changing very slowly back to its original value.

Stall speeds were found to be 83 mph IAS with the flaps and undercarriage up and 70 mph IAS with the flaps and undercarriage down. When gliding at 1.2 × stall speed in the clean configuration, the aircraft was pleasantly stable, the control column having to be brought back about one-third of its total travel in order to produce a stall. Very little stick force was needed to do this, and the only warning of the approaching stall was a slight shake of the control column and the high position of the nose. With the flaps and undercarriage down, it was impossible to trim the aircraft to glide at 1.2 × stall speed, unless the airscrew was fully coarse. The control column had to be brought back four-fifths of its travel and the nose was very high at the stall.

A comfortable approach could be made using full flap at about 90 mph IAS with 1600 rpm set. Most pilots elected to open the hood prior to landing to obtain a good view of the landing area, but it was imperative to wear goggles when leaning over the side because of the violence of the slipstream. To minimise the risk of swinging on landing, it was best to adopt a three-point attitude on touchdown and to apply the brakes carefully and evenly. Any tendency to swing in the latter stages of the landing run had to be checked immediately. There was no tendency to nose-over on braking, even with CG in the extended forward position.

The first Martlet Is entered service with No. 804 Squadron at Hatston on 8 September 1940 and a total of ninety-one ex-French aircraft were delivered. The next in line was the Martlet II, which differed from its predecessor in having a Twin Wasp S4C4-G engine, folding wings and six 0.5-in wing-mounted machine-guns instead of four. Handling trials were carried out at Boscombe Down in early 1942 using AM969. Many of the unsatisfactory aspects of the Martlet I cockpit were still present, although a control was now provided to supply heated air to the wind-screen and a rear-view mirror had been positioned in the roof above the pilot. The view over the nose, both on the ground and in the air, was an improvement on the previous aircraft due to the revised shape of the engine cowling. However, problems were still experienced when flying with the hood open. On this occasion a shrill screaming noise that was painful to the ears was experienced when the hood was moved to the two-thirds open position.

Unlike the Martlet I, the controls could be locked on the ground by a cap, which fitted over the control column with wires extending to the rudder pedals and to each side of the bulkhead behind the pilot's seat. The trimming controls were as before, except that one more division of right rudder trim was available to counter the swing on take-off. The controls for the Curtiss Electric propeller, consisting of a master switch, four-position selector switch and push-pull control knob, were grouped together at the bottom left-hand side of the panel. When the selector switch was set to 'automatic', the control knob increased propeller speed when it was pushed and vice versa. When set to 'manual', the control knob became inoperative and the propeller speed could be changed by moving the switch to the left or right, and holding it there until the desired rpm was reached. The supercharger gear change control was located on the lower left-hand side of the panel (instead of the right as on the Martlet I). The flap control lever had been moved forward of the aileron trimmer to avoid any con-fusion with the fuel cock handle. The instruments were the same as on the Martlet I, except that there was now provision for heating the pitot head.

In case of emergency, the hood could be jettisoned by pulling on two red rings at the forward end of the hood on each side. It was considered that it would be extremely difficult to open the hood if the aircraft was inverted on the ground, even from the outside. However, as it was relatively fragile, it should have been easy to break to allow a pilot to escape. The bulkhead behind the pilot appeared to be substantial enough to take the weight of the aircraft when inverted.

On take-off, the tendency to swing to the left was even more pronounced, but this could be anticipated with the extra rudder trim that was available. The controls were not quite as good, the ailerons in particular being noticeably heavier, but they were still pleasant to operate. The landing characteristics were the same as on the Martlet I.

Performance testing took place at A&AEE in April 1942 using AM991 at a take-off weight of 7790 lb. The testing showed a maximum rate of climb of 1940 ft/min at 7600 ft in MS gear and 1570 ft/min at 13,700 ft in FS gear. Compared with most land-based fighters, the climb performance of the Martlet II was relatively sedate, taking 5.3 minutes to reach 10,000 ft and 12.5 minutes to reach 20,000 ft. For its naval role this was considered acceptable, but its climb rate deteriorated rather dramatically above this height, the aircraft taking a full 30.6 minutes to get to 30,000 ft. Its service ceiling (100 ft/min climb rate) was estimated at 31,000 ft. Level speed tests showed a maximum of 293 mph TAS at 5400 ft in MS gear, with an identical speed at 13,800 ft in FS gear. The recommended height to change supercharger gear was around 11,500 ft.

Only ninety Martlet IIs were delivered, although some of these ended up at the bottom of the sea *en route* to the Far East. The Martlet III was also powered by a Twin Wasp, but was delivered in even smaller numbers, ten arriving under British contract and thirty from a defunct Greek order. The first variant to be flown by the FAA in any great number was the Martlet IV, which reverted to the Wright Cyclone engine (unlike its US Navy equivalent which retained a Twin Wasp). A total of 220 were delivered.

In September 1942 handling trials at aft CG took place at Boscombe Down using Martlet IV FN111 at an all-up weight of 7750 lb. Unlike the previous variants, exhaust fumes did not appear to seep into the cockpit, and the aircraft could be flown with the hood closed when required without danger of contamination. The cockpit controls were virtually identical to the Martlet I, except that cowling gills were fitted. These were adjusted by a small cranked handle on the right of the panel (as in the Martlet II).

The flying controls were tested in a series of high-speed dives.

Although they became progressively heavier with increases in speed, they remained relatively light and pleasant to use up to about 350 mph IAS. Above 400 mph IAS, however, the ailerons were almost immovable and the rudder was extremely heavy. Three dives were made to a speed of 410 mph IAS, with the aircraft trimmed for all-out level flight. During these dives the aircraft became uncomfortably nose-heavy. As a result, a considerable pull force had to be exerted on the control column and much height was needed to effect recovery. It also showed a tendency to yaw to the right, but this could be held with rudder, even though it was not possible to yaw the aircraft more than three degrees

A fourth dive was made to 460 mph IAS. However, in view of the large pull force previously required, the dive was entered with the elevator trimmer set to zero, a slightly more nose-up setting from that previously used. With this setting, tail heaviness was maintained throughout the dive. As soon as recovery was initiated, with not more than 4 g being imposed, the top surface of the inboard end of the starboard folding wing lifted approximately half an inch clear of the upper surface of the centre section. This was not considered serious and was because the top surface of the folding wing was spring-loaded at the inboard end.

With CG in the rearmost position, the aircraft was markedly unstable longitudinally on the climb and slightly less so during level flight. With the flaps and undercarriage up, it was unstable on the glide to the extent that if it was disturbed from its trimmed state and the control column left free, the amplitude of the resultant oscillation would increase to the point where the aircraft stalled. On the glide with the flaps and under-carriage down, longitudinal stability became neutral. Directionally and laterally, the Martlet IV was stable under all conditions of flight.

Trials to assess the climb rate and maximum level speed were also made using FN111, which although capable of carrying two 100-lb bombs under the wings, did not have racks fitted. Take-off weight was 7740 lb. Its performance proved to be somewhat worse than the Martlet II, with a maximum rate of climb of 1580 ft/min at 6200 ft in MS gear and 1440 ft/min at 14,600 ft in FS gear. The times to height were: 10,000 ft – 6.6 minutes; 20,000 ft – 14.6 minutes; 28,000 ft – 29.1 minutes. The estimated service ceiling was 30,100 ft. The maximum speed in MS gear was 278 mph TAS at 3400 ft and 298 mph TAS at 21,000 ft in FS gear.

The Martlet IV was followed by the Martlet V, which was the British equivalent of the US Navy's FM-1. The new designation denoted that the aircraft was built by the Eastern Aircraft Division of General Motors instead of Grumman. Total deliveries amounted to 312 aircraft. The final variant was known from the outset as the Wildcat VI (US Navy FM-2). It was aerodynamically similar to the previous machines, except

for increased fin and rudder area to counteract take-off swing accentuated by the use of a more powerful Cyclone R-1820-56 engine of
1350 hp. The Wildcat VI was the most numerous of the Martlet/Wildcat
variants in FAA service, with 340 being delivered.

Handling and performance trials involving JV642 took place at
Boscombe Down in April 1944. The taller fin and rudder proved to be
a big improvement and provided sufficient directional control to
enable full flap take-offs to be made with ease. Directional stability on
glides was also much better. The latest version of the Cyclone engine
not only produced more power, but also weighed less as forged
cylinder heads were used. JV642 weighed in at 7100 lb. As a result,
performance was improved, with a maximum level speed of 307 mph
TAS at 3400 ft in MS gear and 322 mph TAS at 16,800 ft in FS gear. The
performance on some late production examples of the Wildcat VI was
improved still further by the use of Cyclone engines with water-
injection, designated R-1820-56W. Trials with JV782 showed an
increase in the top speed of 13 mph TAS at all heights up to 9300 ft, as
a result of the increased manifold pressure available when using water-
injection.

The Martlet/Wildcat had the distinction of serving with the FAA
from the beginning of the war to the very end. An early success was
achieved by two Martlet Is of No. 804 Squadron when a Junkers Ju 88
attacking the Home Fleet at Scapa Flow was forced down on 25
December 1940. This was the first German aircraft to be lost to
American aircraft in British service. With the arrival of the Martlet II
with folding wings, the type was taken to the seas, mainly on light
escort carriers. Its duties included protecting convoys from attacks by
long-range Focke-Wulf Fw 200 maritime reconnaissance bombers, and
acting as fighter cover for strikes by Swordfish torpedo-bombers.
Martlets also took part in cover operations during the Allied invasion
of North Africa in November 1942 and the Salerno landings in the
Mediterranean in September 1943. With the delivery of the Wildcat VI,
commencing in July 1944, the FAA maintained its connection with the
Grumman fighter and this variant was used mainly in the Far East. The
culmination of a remarkably long career in FAA service was the
shooting down of four Bf 109s on 26 March 1945 by Wildcats of No. 882
Squadron during a fighter sweep over Norway.

# CHAPTER EIGHTEEN

# Grumman
# Hellcat

Although the Wildcat remained in first-line service throughout the Second World War, its performance in comparison with its principal rival, the Mitsubishi Zero, was deficient in several respects, most notably in terms of speed, climb rate and manoeuvrability. The Hellcat came from the same Grumman stable and, together with the Vought Corsair, was to secure a level of superiority in the air war over the Pacific that proved vital in pushing Japanese forces back towards their homeland.

Grumman's long association with the US Navy led to close links with those at the sharp end of naval aviation. Pilots' experiences with the Wildcat were instrumental in the design philosophy that produced the Hellcat. Compared with its predecessor, the top speed was increased by 50 mph, its climb rate was significantly better and its service ceiling and range were much improved. The pilot had more armour protection and the use of a low-set wing allowed the undercarriage to be retracted into the centre section instead of the fuselage, thereby allowing a wider track for better ground handling. The cockpit was also placed as high as possible to aid lookout. This was also helped by a three degrees downwards inclination of the engine thrust line, which produced a tail-down attitude in flight.

A contract was awarded to Grumman on 30 June 1941 for two prototype XF6F-1s and the first flight took place on 26 June 1942. The engine to power the Hellcat was to have been the Wright Cyclone R-2600 14-cylinder radial of 1600 hp. However, this was dropped in favour of the 2000 hp Pratt & Whitney R-2800 Double Wasp 18-cylinder radial, which was installed in the second prototype, becoming the XF6F-3. The Hellcat entered service with US Navy Squadron VF-9 aboard the USS *Essex* in January 1943, and saw action for the first time in August 1943 with VF-5 during strikes on Marcus Island in the Pacific.

Shortly before its operational debut with the US Navy, the Hellcat was made available to Britain under Lend-Lease. It was known initially as the Gannet I. This name was soon dropped and aircraft in FAA service were known as the Hellcat I (equivalent to the US Navy F6F-3 with R-2800-10 engine) and Hellcat II, which was equivalent to the F6F-5 with the R-2800-10W engine featuring water-injection that increased emergency power to 2200 hp. A total of 1182 had been delivered to the FAA by the end of the war.

One of the first Hellcat Is to arrive in the UK was delivered in July 1943 to the Carrier Trials Unit at Crail in Fife. Although the family resemblance was obvious, the Wildcat appeared almost toy-like in comparison with its big brother which, with a loaded weight of 12,727 lb, was over twice that of its forebear. Unlike the cramped conditions to be found in most British cockpits, the Hellcat offered the commodious proportions to be expected of an American fighter. The positioning of the cockpit at the high point of the fuselage, together with the shorter nose afforded by the use of a radial engine, meant that the view forwards was better than many aircraft tested previously.

Taxying was straightforward thanks to the wide-track undercarriage, although it was necessary to lock the tailwheel in a crosswind to prevent the aircraft weather-cocking. The huge mass of the R-2800 Double Wasp meant that a nose-over was also a distinct possibility if the pilot did not hold the elevator full up, especially on soft ground. Engine torque produced a moderate swing to the left on take-off, but this could easily be corrected by rudder. The initial climb rate was 3000 ft/min, performance being adequate up to 20,000 ft. However, above this height it began to deteriorate. Although the service ceiling was quoted as being 37,800 ft, the Hellcat struggled much above 30,000 ft.

When flown in the clean configuration, there was very little warning of the stall, which could be accompanied by wing drop, although recovery was straightforward. The stalling speed with the gear and flaps down was a very low 67 mph IAS. One slightly disconcerting aspect of the Hellcat's performance was a tendency towards auxiliary supercharger surging in high gear when weak cruise had been set. This caused rough running and a deep rumbling noise, but it could be quickly stopped by selecting low gear, or advancing the throttle and reducing rpm.

At higher speeds, the controls tended to become heavy on early aircraft, although this problem was addressed on the Hellcat II with the introduction of spring-tab ailerons. These produced a dramatic improvement in lateral control. The aircraft was stable about all three axes, but exhibited quite large changes of trim with changes of speed and throttle setting, which had to be carefully monitored.

For deck landings, the speed was reduced to 125 mph IAS before the landing gear and arrester hook were lowered. The other pre-landing checks to be made were: tailwheel unlocked, mixture to AUTO RICH, supercharger to NEUTRAL, propeller to fine pitch, booster pump ON, cowl gills CLOSED and flaps fully down. On final approach to land, the aircraft was flown at around 90 mph IAS, depending on the weight. It was important to leave the power on until the last second, to achieve the correct touchdown attitude. Throttling back slightly too early was likely to lead to a nose-down pitch. This could lead to problems as the mainwheels hit the deck, although in general the undercarriage was substantially built and was not as prone to bouncing as the Vought Corsair.

Intensive flying trials were carried out at Boscombe Down between July and August 1943 using FN331 and FN333. Both aircraft carried the standard armament of six 0.50-in machine-guns, three in each wing. The gun barrel fairings and muzzles, but not the ejector chutes, were sealed with fabric. An aerial mast was situated immediately behind the pilot's hood, with an aerial running to a short mast on top of the fin, the aerial lead entering the fuselage on the starboard side. IFF aerials ran from the tailplane tips to the fuselage. The elevators were fabric-covered and balanced only by a set-back hinge with trim tabs fitted to both surfaces. The horn-balanced rudder and Frise-type ailerons were also fabric-covered. The rudder had a tab for trimming purposes and the ailerons (on the Hellcat I) had a ground-adjustable tab on the starboard surface and a movable tab on the port surface.

The supercharging system of the R-2800-10 Double Wasp was rather unusual. A normal mechanically-driven blower supercharged the mixture between the carburettor and the engine. When required, however, the air supply to the carburettor could be boosted by an auxiliary two-speed blower. Before reaching the carburettor, the air passed through an intercooler to lower the temperature and reduce the risk of detonation. The pilot was thus left with three supercharger options: a) main blower, b) main blower plus auxiliary low and c) main blower plus auxiliary high. When using the main stage, the intake air passed through an air cleaner, but that for the auxiliary stage was not cleaned. The pilot could, however, select air from the forward facing cold air intake or from warmed air taken from the engine bay. The exhaust system consisted of ten individual pipes of approximately 2-in diameter, eight of which carried the exhaust from two cylinders, the remaining two pipes being each connected to a single cylinder. The propeller was a metal Hamilton Standard Hydromatic of 13 ft 1 in diameter, with a pitch range of 26–65 degrees.

The cockpit could be entered from either side of the aircraft, but the hood could only be opened from the starboard side. The size of the cockpit was appreciated, but the seat was found to be rather uncomfortable after flying for some time and was liable to cause cramp in the pilot's back. An American-type harness was fitted. Although it held the pilot down better than a Sutton harness, it was difficult to adjust and irritating across the shoulders. The Hellcat proved to be very noisy at about 2200 rpm, and it was necessary to keep the hood firmly shut. A tightly fitting helmet was also a priority or the radio became inaudible. There was also considerable vibration when the engine was operated in the range 1500–1900 rpm.

Like a number of other American aircraft, the control column of the Hellcat was too far away from the pilot and also too short. As a result, it could not be pushed right forward, even by a tall pilot, without undoing the harness. Difficulty was therefore experienced in keeping the nose up when inverted. The other controls were generally well positioned, except that several pilots commented adversely on the position of the aileron trimmer, which was too near the pilot's side. The usual American blind flying panel was fitted and all the flying and engine instruments were clearly visible.

The view was reasonably good, except directly forward, where it was obscured by the engine cowling and gunsight. The windscreen pillars were very thick and there was annoying distortion at the curved parts of the screen. When the gills were opened, the forward field of vision was reduced further. This situation was made even worse when cruising in conditions of bad visibility at the recommended speed of 115 mph IAS, as the nose attitude was somewhat higher. There was no clear-view panel, which meant that the hood had to be opened when flying in conditions of bad visibility.

Taxying was relatively easy and could be assisted considerably in crosswinds by locking the tailwheel. The brakes were toe-operated and performed well. Take-offs were often performed with the flaps up and the tendency to swing to the left could be overcome by selecting one division of right rudder trim. Ideally, it was best not to lower full flap for take-off, due to deterioration in lateral control. The slotted flaps operated by means of an electro-hydraulic system, with manual control being available in an emergency. Any intermediate position of the flaps (up to the maximum of 50 degrees) could be selected as desired, the flap position being shown by an indicator connected to the port wing flap. There was no mechanical inter-link between the port and starboard wing flaps and it was possible for the flap on one side to be at a different angle to that on the other side, particularly when an intermediate position had been selected. The flaps were spring-loaded so that speed had to be reduced to about 195 mph IAS before partial flap could be used, and they could not be lowered fully until speed had been reduced to around 107 mph IAS.

At a take-off weight of 11,420 lb (CG 27.3 in aft of datum – normal forward) the Hellcat was very stable in the climb. The best climb speed was about 150 mph IAS, and at this speed full right rudder trim was necessary. At lower speeds, there was not enough rudder trim to give zero foot load. There was no tendency for the engine to overheat at 150 mph IAS with the gills closed, and the oil temperature was easily kept within limits by opening the oil cooler shutters, which produced a slight nose-down change of trim. Generally, it was necessary to use the fuel booster pump at heights above 15,000 ft to maintain fuel pressure, and to throttle back slightly when changing supercharger gear to avoid over-boosting. Some trouble was experienced with the trim tabs freezing up during sustained flight above 20,000 ft. The aircraft was stable in level flight and could be trimmed to fly 'hands and feet off' at all speeds above 130 mph IAS. Right rudder trim was required up to about 215 mph IAS, with left rudder trim being needed above this speed.

The Hellcat was found to be very manoeuvrable, although the controls, in particular the ailerons, became heavy at high speed. This defect was accentuated by the awkward position of the control column. During a quick turn it was necessary to wind the elevator trimmer back to reduce the load on the stick, and coarse rudder was needed to come out of a turn quickly. In the dive, the aircraft became tail-heavy, and it was necessary to trim into the dive and apply some left rudder to keep straight. There was also considerable vibration, which was felt mainly through the rudder pedals and was most marked at high power settings. At lower engine speeds, the amount of vibration was reduced, but not entirely eliminated.

The approach was made at about 150 mph IAS, which was the recommended speed for lowering the flaps. The speed could be reduced very quickly by throttling back gradually and easing the control column back. With full flap set, lateral control was much less precise and the undercarriage could be lowered at speeds below 125 mph IAS. The final approach was made at 105 mph IAS. If baulked, no difficulty was experienced in going around, the undercarriage coming up quickly and the change of trim being easily held on the control column. On the whole, the Hellcat was well liked and it was thought that it would make a good fighter for naval operations.

Handling trials were carried out using FN322 and FN323, with FN360 joining the programme later. This aircraft featured a strengthened tailplane with extra internal stiffening, but this did not appear to reduce the amount of vibration experienced at high speed. It also had modified trimmer control circuits, but these proved as difficult to operate at high altitudes as the previous design, and it was not until a special lubricating oil was used (DTD.539) that the tabs were not subject to 'freezing up'.

The handling trials were carried out at a take-off weight of 12,140 lb.

Take-offs could be made with 15 degrees of flap without upsetting lateral control too much, and the normal technique was to keep the tail low. This method was found to be more comfortable and also had the benefit of protecting the propeller, which had very little ground clearance in the take-off attitude. Acceleration was high and the lift-off speed was around 80–85 mph IAS.

With the flaps and undercarriage up; the aircraft was trimmed to glide at 140 mph IAS, the speed gradually being reduced until a 'hooting' noise commenced at about 110 mph IAS, the note changing as speed was reduced further. At about 90 mph IAS there was slight shuddering, rudder buffet and instrument vibration. The stall occurred at 86 mph IAS and was characterised by either wing dropping gently, followed by the nose. With the flaps and undercarriage down, there was a tendency for the port wing to drop during glides below 100 mph IAS, but this could easily be corrected by aileron. The stall warning was similar to the previous case and the stall came at 72 mph IAS, the nose dropping about 30 degrees and the port wing about 20 degrees.

The force to hold the aircraft in a tight turn at 5 g was rather large for a fighter, but there was no tendency to tighten up. Over the speed range 150–300 mph IAS the elevators were light and effective, but the ailerons became heavy above 240 mph IAS, and full aileron could only be applied below 290 mph IAS to the left and 260 mph IAS to the right. The ailerons of FN323 tended to overbalance slightly when full deflection was applied at 180–200 mph IAS. Very brief handling checks were made on FN322 at 32,000 ft, the aircraft being put into a gradually tightening turn at 200 mph IAS (Mach 0.52). When the acceleration had increased to an estimated 2½ g a violent vibration commenced, which appeared to originate in the tailplane. This vibration ceased immediately the force on the control column was released.

A number of out-of-trim dives were made at full and one-third throttle, up to the limiting speed of 460 mph IAS. The longitudinal control characteristics were satisfactory, although the push force to hold the aircraft in the dive was large, and the pull on recovery was of a similar magnitude. At speeds above 300 mph IAS, the ailerons were considered to be too heavy for a fighter; and by the time that 350 mph IAS was reached, they were almost immovable. The rudder was fairly heavy, but was effective in producing yaw up to the limiting speed.

The Hellcat was looped with the engine operating at climbing power (2550 rpm, 44 in Hg), starting at an initial speed of 350 mph IAS and applying an estimated 4 g. At the top of the loop, the speed had reduced to around 120 mph IAS, before it increased again to 240 mph IAS in the recovery. The stick forces involved were not excessive. Rolling performance was best at speeds between 180–230 mph IAS, being approximately 60 degrees per second. At higher speeds, the ailerons were too heavy for good manoeuvrability. The initial force required to apply full aileron was large, but once the roll had been started the force needed to maintain full deflection reduced.

Owing to engine unserviceability with FN323, the handling trials had to be continued with FN322 and JV224. The latter was a Hellcat II that differed from the earlier aircraft principally in having a Double Wasp R-2800-10W engine with water-injection and spring-tab ailerons. Tests with JV224 showed there was no noticeable difference between the longitudinal handling characteristics at the recommended aft and normal forward CG positions. The stick forces in out-of-trim dives changed from a 4 lb push to a 3 lb pull at 460 mph IAS, and the stick force per 'g' was around 14 lb at accelerometer readings of 4-5 g. The effect of fitting spring tabs to the ailerons was to lighten the control considerably at high speeds, although this tended to affect harmonisation, with the elevator becoming the heaviest control.

Compressibility dives were carried out from 25,000 ft, and a speed of 460 mph IAS was reached by the time that the aircraft passed through 17,000 ft. At this speed, the nose became very heavy and speed increased rapidly. This sudden change of trim was attributed to compressibility effects, commencing at a Mach number of 0.77. The pull force to recover at 480 mph IAS was initially around 70 lb, but when speed had reduced to 460 mph IAS, the stick force reduced rapidly. During high-speed recoveries, pilots noticed sheets of vapour forming over the wing roots.

Performance trials were carried out at the same time as the handling assessment and involved FN322. Readings could only be made up to 28,000 ft, due to internal sparking in the magnetos when the aircraft was flown at higher altitudes. The maximum rate of climb in main supercharger gear was 2260 ft/min at 5400 ft and 20,000 ft was reached in ten minutes. The recommended height to change supercharger gear was 9200 ft. The full results were as follows (* and ** denote full throttle heights).

| Height | 2000 ft | 4000 ft | 5400 ft* | 8000 ft | 10,000 ft |
|---|---|---|---|---|---|
| Rate of climb – ft/min | 2260 | 2260 | 2260 | 2000 | 1880 |
| Time from start – min | 0.9 | 1.8 | 2.4 | 3.6 | 4.65 |

| Height | 14,000 ft | 18,000 ft | 20,500 ft** | 24,000 ft | 28,000 ft |
|---|---|---|---|---|---|
| Rate of climb – ft/min | 1880 | 1880 | 1880 | 1400 | 840 |
| Time from start – min | 6.75 | 8.9 | 10.25 | 13.35 | 16.1 |

Level-speed performance was measured for 'main blower', which was maintained up to 6000 ft, and for 'main blower plus auxiliary low', the setting used above this height. All the speed runs were made with the cooling gills and flaps closed and the maximum achieved was 371 mph TAS at 18,700 ft.

| Height | 2000 ft * | 4000 ft | 6000 ft | 8000 ft | 10,000 ft |
|---|---|---|---|---|---|
| TAS – mph | 315 | 314 | 314 | 323 | 332 |
| IAS – mph | 292 | 284 | 275 | 274 | 273 |

| Height | 14,000 ft | 18,700 ft | 20,000 ft | 22,000 ft | 24,000 ft |
|---|---|---|---|---|---|
| TAS – mph | 350 | 371 | 370 | 369 | 367 |
| IAS – mph | 270 | 264 | 258 | 248 | 239 |

Several aircraft were tested with a variety of under-wing and fuselage stores, including FN344, which was fitted with four rocket projectiles under each wing, just outboard of the undercarriage. With RP in place, there was little effect on handling characteristics, although considerable vibration was experienced in the dive. It was found that this emanated from the front of the blast plate. By careful modification of the nose fairing, the intensity of the vibration could be much reduced. During the tests, it was also established that end fairings fitted to the rocket installation had no noticeable effect on handling or the level of vibration. The Hellcat was eventually cleared for service use at all typical loadings with the revised nose fairings and no end fairings. FN360 was tested with a 125-US gallon drop tank on a rack under the fuselage. Once again, there was no noticeable effect on handling in any condition of flight. The ground clearance was minimal however, so care had to be taken when taxying on rough ground.

In August 1944 JV127, a Hellcat I, was used for brief handling trials with a 1000-lb bomb. This was an ANM.65 with a British tail, which was 48 in long and had a diameter of 15 in. Compressibility effects came into play during dives, as the blunt shape of the bomb caused excessive airframe shuddering at speeds in excess of 400 mph IAS. The maximum speed attained was 440 mph IAS, which at the height tested was equivalent to Mach 0.675. In view of its characteristics at high speed, it was recommended that the Hellcat be limited to a maximum dive speed of 400 mph IAS when carrying a 1000-lb bomb.

JV127 was also used to test the Hellcat's suitability as a dive-bomber. However, problems were experienced with insufficient braking effect with the undercarriage retracted. Dives were then attempted with the undercarriage locked down, but owing to excessive shuddering at moderate to high speeds, these was not particularly successful. As a compromise, the aircraft was flown with the undercarriage trailing (down, but not locked), with the engine operating at one-third throttle, at speeds up to 350 mph IAS. Even with the undercarriage trailing, there was hardly sufficient braking effect, and there was also considerable airframe disturbance. The stick forces in out-of-trim dives, as well as the stick force per 'g' on recovery, were considered to be excessive, although the sight could easily be held on the target and releasing the bomb had no unusual effects on handling. Although the previous 400 mph IAS limit was retained, it was recommended that the maximum speed in the dive in this condition be kept below 350 mph IAS wherever possible, as the push force to hold the aircraft at higher speeds became too large and the ailerons were excessively heavy to the detriment of lateral manoeuvrability. At lower speeds, the recovery could also be commenced at a lower altitude, with better accuracy, and the disturbance due to the trailing undercarriage was not so severe.

In December 1944, JV109 was tested with a balloon hood, which considerably improved the vision to the rear as a result of the elimination of the vertical and horizontal stiffening members of the original hood. Handling was not affected, so the modified canopy was a worthwhile improvement. At the same time JX822, a Hellcat II, was being flown with two 1000-lb bombs at a take-off weight of 14,600 lb. No particular problems were experienced and the aircraft was considered acceptable for service use at the same limiting speed as the Hellcat I. In early 1945, JX901 was tested with six 60-lb RP on zero-length launchers with little effect on handling. It later flew with the US Mk. 5 rocket launcher.

The arrival of the Hellcat II with its R-2800-10W water-injected engine led to further performance testing with JV224. The rate of climb was assessed in auxiliary low gear, with level-speed performance being measured in auxiliary high gear. The use of water-injection allowed a higher manifold pressure of 60 in Hg to be used, instead of the previous take-off and combat limit of 54 in Hg. The rate of climb was increased by 650 ft/min (from 2570 to 3160 ft/min) at all heights up to 11,200 ft, which was the full throttle height. The top speed was also increased by about 20 mph TAS, up to the full throttle height of 18,600 ft. At this height, the speed was measured at 377 mph TAS, which compared with 367 mph TAS at 21,800 ft, the full throttle height for the maximum manifold pressure without water-injection.

The Hellcat provided a welcome boost to the operational capability of the FAA. It was introduced to service by No. 800 Squadron, which converted from Sea Hurricanes in July 1943. The Hellcat's operational debut came in December 1943 during anti-shipping strikes off the Norwegian coast from the escort-carrier HMS *Emperor*. Its major work, however, was carried out in the Far East and Hellcats of Nos. 1839 and 1844 Squadrons flying from HMS *Indomitable* comprised the escort for strikes against oil refineries in Sumatra in January 1945. By March, operations had moved on to the Sakashima Islands and two months later Hellcats were involved in the fighting around Formosa. The Hellcat was also used by the FAA as a night-fighter with 892 Squadron forming at Eglinton in April 1945, followed by No. 891 Squadron in June 1945. Like all Lend-Lease aircraft, the Hellcat was quickly withdrawn from active service at the end of the war. The last operational aircraft were retired when No. 888 Squadron was disbanded in August 1946. One Hellcat (KE209) continued to fly at RNAS Lossiemouth until 1953 and this aircraft is now preserved at the Fleet Air Arm Museum at Yeovilton.

# CHAPTER NINETEEN

# Vought Corsair

T he Chance Vought Corporation was formed in 1917 and in the inter-war years designed a number of general-purpose biplanes for the US Navy and Marine Corps. By the late 1930s, however, the company was keen to make a name for itself as a builder of fighter aircraft. Chief Engineer Rex B. Beisel and his team came up with two designs, the Model V-166A to be powered by a Pratt & Whitney R-1830 Twin Wasp, and the V-166B with the same manufacturer's XR-2800 Double Wasp, which was still in the experimental category. Of the two proposals, the US Navy preferred the latter and a contract for the proto-type XF4U-1 was issued on 10 February 1939.

To absorb the power of the R-2800 engine, which even in its development stages was producing 1850 hp, a three-blade Hamilton Standard propeller was chosen with a massive 13 ft 4 in diameter. Beisel's solution to the obvious ground clearance problem that came with such a large propeller, was to adopt an inverted gull-wing, with the undercarriage legs located at the wing's lowest point. This allowed the undercarriage leg to be shorter and lighter, and by incor-porating a 90-degree twist, it could be retracted rearwards to lie within the wing. Further advantages when compared with a more conventional straight wing, were better pilot lookout, reduced drag at the fuselage/wing junction and reduced height with the wings folded.

The XF4U-1 was first flown on 29 May 1940 by Lyman A. Bullard. It was forced to return without its elevator trim tabs, which had departed due to flutter, the first of a number of teething troubles that were to plague the Corsair. The initial armament comprised one 0.303-in gun and one 0.50-in gun in the forward fuselage, together with a single 0.50-in gun in each wing. Combat experience filtering back to the US from Europe led to the Corsair losing its nose-mounted guns and having its outer wings modified to take a total of six 0.5-in guns. The fuel system was radically altered to reduce the possibility of damage from enemy fire, with a large self-sealing tank of 237 US gallons being mounted in the fuselage behind the engine firewall to replace the four tanks previously mounted in the wings. This necessitated the pilot's cockpit being moved back by 2 ft 8 in.

Early experience with the Corsair was not encouraging, as the aircraft showed a habit of dropping a wing just before the stall. This tendency did not endear it to low-time pilots confronted with the prospect of putting the aircraft down at slow speed on a pitching deck. In the case of an aborted landing, if the throttle was opened too quickly the massive torque from the engine was liable to flick the aircraft out of control. A further problem was that the undercarriage oleos, instead of absorbing the shock, tended to rebound after a firm arrival. This led to a bounce, which could spell disaster with aircraft ranged on the forward deck of a carrier. It would be many months before the US Navy took its Corsairs to sea. As a result, it was left to VMF-124 of the US Marine Corps to introduce the F4U to action at Guadalcanal on 14 February 1943.

In contrast to the US Navy, the FAA showed rather less concern as regards the Corsair's deck-landing characteristics. The first FAA Corsair squadron was No. 1830, which was formed at the US Navy base at Quonset Point, Rhode Island on 1 June 1943, and seven more squadrons had been equipped by the end of the year. After working up in the USA, the units boarded escort carriers to be shipped to the UK. Corsairs of No. 1834 Squadron aboard HMS *Victorious* were the first to be used operationally when they took part in attacks on the *Tirpitz*, which was under repair at Kaafiord in Norway, on 3 April 1944.

The initial batch of 95 Corsair Is (equivalent to the F4U-1) were soon followed by 510 Corsair IIs, a mixed batch of F4U-1A/Ds. These were supplemented by 430 Brewster-built F3A-1As designated Corsair III and 942 Goodyear-built FG-1A/Ds designated Corsair IV. A major modification from the Corsair II onwards, was the clipping of the wing tips so that aircraft could be accommodated in the below-deck hangars of British aircraft carriers with their wings folded. Approximately 5 in was removed from the wing tips, but a further 2½ in had to be taken off due to the use of a longer tailwheel yoke, which was introduced to improve deck handling. Compared with a standard Corsair, the stall speed of the British version with clipped wings was 4–5 kt higher.

On its arrival in the UK, the Corsair was put through its paces at a number of testing establishments, including RAE Farnborough. It was here that Eric Brown flew JT118, an early production Corsair I, in January 1944. He recalled his experiences with the aircraft in his book *Wings of the Navy* (Airlife, 1987).

The Corsair's inordinately large proboscis was its most outstanding feature – in the USA it was referred to as 'Old Hog Nose'. Coupled with its fairly acute and most distinctive ground stance, it imparted an impression of rugged strength rather than aerodynamic refinement. The cockpit was inordinately spacious and tailored for an extremely tall pilot – I subsequently learned that the principal Corsair project pilot was 6 ft 4 in, and one of more modest stature, such as myself, inevitably experienced some discomfort keeping one's feet on the rudder with the seat adjusted to a height from which what little forward view that existed could be gained. The layout of the cockpit was poor and on the ground the only reasonable view was upward!

The immense R-2800-8 Double Wasp was turned over by hand four or five times, the fuel booster pump was switched ON, the priming switch was flicked several times, the ignition switch activated and the starter cartridge fired. The Double Wasp usually burst into life immediately and with the firing switch depressed and the mixture control moved slowly to AUTO RICH was soon purring with all the smoothness so characteristic of this family of engines. The Double Wasp was opened up to 1,000 rpm to warm up, pressure and magneto checks performed, the flaps lowered and raised, and the revs increased to 1,400, the operation of the two-speed supercharger being checked by moving the control from NEUTRAL to LOW and, after a pause of a few seconds, to HIGH. With the propeller control fully down, the throttle was opened and take-off boost and static rpm checked, the stick being held hard back to contain a strong tendency for the tail to lift.

During taxying the totally inadequate forward view necessitated swinging the nose from side to side, but the tailwheel had to be unlocked which made the Corsair very unstable directionally, necessitating constant use of brakes with the danger of nosing over in the event of too harsh application. For take-off, if trim was correct, the Corsair demonstrated no tendency to swing and unstick was rapid. With 30 degrees flap, such as would be employed for a carrier take-off, and about two-thirds normal fuel at a take-off weight of about 11,150 lb, the Corsair would take-off within 185 yards without wind and about 120 yards into a 15 knot wind.

The speed for maximum climb rate was 125 kts from sea level up to 21,000 ft and the intercooler shutters had to be opened fully, but the cowl gills were only half opened otherwise there was some buffet. Climb was impressive, 10,000 ft being passed in 4 minutes 40 seconds and 20,000 ft in 9 minutes 40 seconds. Above 21,000 ft climb speed was reduced by 3 kts per 2,000 ft, but the two-stage, two-speed supercharger ensured good climbing capability well over 30,000 ft. Once in level flight, the Corsair could be trimmed to a very stable hands-off flying condition. The harmony of control was poor, the elevators being heavy but the ailerons moderately light, enabling the Corsair to be rolled to its maximum rate even at fairly high diving speeds, valuable in the South Pacific as the opposing Zero had poor aileron control at high speeds.

Acceleration was dramatic, and a clean aeroplane with about two-thirds fuel in the main tank only and 200 rounds for each of its six 0.50 in guns could reach a maximum of 342 kts at the critical altitude of 24,000 ft on normal maximum power. At combat power of 1,650 hp at 2,700 rpm (limited to 5 minutes), maximum speed was 343 kts. Stalling characteristics were very poor, with little warning other than the stall warning light on the instrument panel operated by the breakdown of airflow over the centre section. At the stall, the right wing dropped sharply and an incipient spin developed if the control column was not moved smartly forward. If the Corsair stalled in a steep turn it would normally flick out, but recovery was rapid if control column pressure was relaxed quickly. At about 11,500 lb with engine off and all up, the Corsair would stall at 90 kts, and with flaps and undercarriage down at 76 kts, the warning light coming on at 80 kts.

In the deck landing configuration with approach power, the Corsair could demonstrate a very nasty incipient torque stall with dangerously little warning and a simulated deck landing at 80 kts gave very poor view and sluggish aileron and elevator control. A curved approach was necessary if the pilot was to have any chance of seeing the carrier, let alone, the batsman! When the throttle was cut, the nose dropped so that the aircraft bounced on its mainwheels, and once the tailwheel made contact, it proved very unstable directionally, despite the tailwheel lock, swinging either to port or starboard, which had to be checked immediately with the brakes. I tried a baulked landing and discovered that the sudden opening of the throttle at 80 kts also produced the torque stall, but this time the port wing dropped. I needed no more convincing of the US Navy's wisdom in withholding the Corsair from shipboard operations!

In addition to trials work carried out in the UK, the Corsair was also assessed in the USA by pilots attached to the British Air Commission in Washington. The cockpit layout was considered adequate. The most serious criticism affecting all Corsair Is and early Corsair IIs (in which the fault was made worse by raising the pilot's seat) was the location of the undercarriage operating lever, which was too far forward and too low down. This meant that the pilot had to bend forwards and down when retracting the wheels, a dangerous procedure when near the ground. In all Corsairs after JT270 (the 171st production aircraft) the lever was moved to a more convenient position. The control column was a little on the short side and, like many other American aircraft, it was positioned too far away from the pilot.

The view forwards when taxying was extremely poor, and was made even worse by opening the gills. With its raised seating position the Corsair II showed a slight improvement, but the view was still far from good. This meant that it was even more important to weave when taxying, but this was made difficult by the aircraft's directional instability when the tailwheel was free. The Corsair's ground-handling characteristics could be vicious and selective brake was constantly required to prevent a ground loop developing. This caused the brakes to overheat and fade, and since the pedals were not particularly easy to operate, taxying for some distance could be rather exhausting and was something to be avoided. In practice, the tailwheel had to be locked as much as possible, as in this condition the aircraft ran straight, but this could not be done for any length of time without risk of collision.

Provided that the aircraft had been correctly trimmed, the Corsair showed little tendency to swing on take-off, the run being blind until the tail was up. For a carrier take-off with full flap, however, the tail came up directly the brakes were released. Once airborne, the undercarriage could be raised very quickly, producing a slight nose-up change of trim. The cowling gills were best left at no more than two-thirds open, as considerable buffeting could result. Handling in the climb at 130 kt IAS was quite good, with all three controls being light and responsive. During sustained high-power climbs, there were indications of overheating both of carburettor air and cylinder head temperatures.

The Corsair was very pleasant to fly at cruising speeds, with such low noise levels that some pilots were liable to overboost the engine. Stability was adequate for long-range flights without undue pilot fatigue. In order to avoid excessive fuel consumption and to minimise the danger of CO contamination, the aircraft was normally flown in auto lean whenever possible, or with oxygen in use. The seepage of exhaust gases into the cockpit was one of the major troubles with the Corsair. The main point of entry was around the tailwheel and arrester hook openings, from where the gas was drawn forward by relatively low cockpit pressure. Despite the introduction of a fabric bulkhead behind the radio compartment, excessive CO in the cockpit continued to occur and constituted a considerable danger, to the extent that FAA pilots were instructed to use oxygen at all times.

The flying controls were tested at various speeds. At 200 kt IAS the ailerons and elevators were light and effective, although the rudder was somewhat heavier. When flying at 300 kt IAS the rudder was too heavy to operate without assistance by the trimmer, but the ailerons and elevators, although much heavier to operate than before, still gave good response. At 360 kt IAS the ailerons were just about acceptable, but elevator trim was needed to hold the aircraft in the dive. At this speed the rudder was almost immovable.

When trimmed for the approach with the flaps and undercarriage down, the Corsair was unstable, but a forward pulling spring (tensioned to assist elevator control when the undercarriage was lowered and applicable to nearly all Corsair Is and all Corsair IIs) was brought into action to maintain stick force in the correct sense. There was, however, little change of stick force with reduction in speed, which tended to give a lack of feel to the elevators, and care had to be taken to monitor airspeed when on slow approach. The range of elevator trim provided was adequate for all conditions of flight. The trim changes were as follows:

| Increase speed – tail heavy | Increase power – tail heavy | Lower wheels – nose heavy |
|---|---|---|
| Lower flaps – slightly nose heavy | Open gills – nose heavy | Open shutters – tail heavy |

Directional stability in the air was positive insofar that the aircraft turned correctly on ailerons and elevators alone. However, when a sudden yaw was applied and the rudder released, many oscillations took place before straight flight was eventually resumed. In bumpy air there was a tendency to hunt directionally. An increase in power tended to produce a swing to the left and an increase in speed a swing to the right. At high speeds the rudder trimmer had to be used, owing to the extreme heaviness of the rudder.

The pilot of a Corsair had to be at his sharpest when flying slowly, owing to its sluggish lateral control and lack of feel on the elevators, together with the poor forward view. Adequate control could, however, be maintained when flying in bumpy conditions at around 110 kt IAS, with 30 degrees of flap. At speeds approaching the stall the characteristics of the aircraft were greatly affected by the position of the gills. With the gills even slightly open, considerable warning of the stall was given in the form of buffeting, longitudinal pitching and kicking of the rudder. With the gills closed, there was no warning at all. Observation of wool tufts fitted to the aircraft indicated that the initial breakdown of airflow occurred just outboard of the wing stub, together with disturbance around the cockpit area. The streamlines at the wing tips did not appear to be affected.

The aircraft was comparatively easy to stall with moderate stick force, and it occurred with the control column just aft of central. In all cases, when stalling speed was reached from a steady glide, a wing was liable to drop rather suddenly, followed by the nose, and considerable height could be lost before control was regained. Either wing could go down in a gliding stall, but it was more usually the starboard wing that dropped. This could also occur when landing if the aircraft was held off too high. At a take-off weight of 11,700 lb, the stall speed with the flaps and undercarriage up was 90–92 kt IAS, and 76 kt IAS with the flaps and undercarriage down.

In accelerated stalls a pronounced tendency to flick to the left was noted, although this had been reduced to some extent by fitting a spoiler on the starboard wing. In a 4 g turn, the stall occurred at 140–150 kt IAS and was accompanied by violent buffeting around the cockpit, especially on the left-hand side. Although the Corsair tended to drop a wing at the stall, a spin did not develop unless the control column was held fully back. Should an incipient spin develop, recovery was quick assuming that the pilot took the correct action promptly. If a spin was allowed to progress further, control forces became very high, to the point that the pilot had difficulty in carrying out the necessary recovery procedure.

Aerobatics were performed without difficulty, except that the forward position of the stick meant that the pilot had to reach a long way forward to maintain the correct nose attitude during slow rolls or when flying inverted. Loops were commenced at around 260 kt IAS with an initial acceleration of 4 g, the speed over the top of the loop being approximately 120 kt IAS with the aircraft showing no sign of flicking. There was no abnormal lateral behaviour, although a large change in directional trim with speed, together with the heaviness of the rudder, made accurate manoeuvres difficult and tended to spoil the feel of the aircraft. Rolls off the top of loops could be flown by adding 20–30 kt to that for a normal loop.

The Corsair was dived up to 360 kt IAS, at which speed the ailerons were very heavy and the rudder almost solid. Acceleration was rapid and considerable nose-down and left rudder trim was needed to hold the aircraft straight in the dive. To provide a dive brake, the main wheels could be extended without lowering the tailwheel. This caused some nose-heaviness but the aircraft could be manoeuvred satisfactorily in this condition.

Like many other of its contemporaries, the Corsair ran into problems with compressibility during high-speed dives. A US report seen by the British Air Commission told of a vertical dive being carried out from 37,500 ft. At a speed of 240 kt IAS an incessant pounding commenced and the elevators became immovable. The trimmer was then moved to the full nose-up position and the subsequent recovery from the dive at 13,000 ft was described as 'very rapid', which was probably an under-statement. At one point prior to recovery, the pilot noticed an indicated airspeed of 430 kt. Considerable damage was caused to the horizontal stabiliser with the horn balance, all of the elevator aft of the spar and outboard of the tab, having broken away. In view of the likelihood of pilots getting into trouble due to compressibility, the US Navy produced a series of limitations for the Corsair in relation to speed and acceleration at various altitudes.

The angle of approach, both with the engine on and off, was adequate and generally the aircraft handled well at 90 kt IAS with the flaps and undercarriage down. The ailerons, although positive, appeared to have a 'dead area' covering some 2–3 in of stick move-ment. During the latter part of the approach, the view ahead deteriorated, but it was possible to see fairly well out of the side. The aircraft had to be held close to the ground at the stall due to the tendency of the right wing to drop suddenly, but apart from this the touchdown was straightforward. Although safely on the ground, the landing was far from over. As soon as the tailwheel was lowered, the aircraft would almost certainly try to swing to either left or right. This required the immediate application of full rudder and brake to correct it. If landing on a runway, this characteristic could be alleviated to some extent by using 30 degrees of flap, by keeping the tail slightly above the three-point attitude and by being gentle at the flare. Once on the ground, any amount of braking could be used and the aircraft stopped quickly. On later machines with the raised cockpit, the air loads on the hood were found to be very high, which made it difficult to open before landing. Care had to be taken when the hood was open to ensure that it was securely locked, otherwise it would slam shut when the aircraft landed.

Flight trials on a Corsair with clipped wings by the US Navy Flight Test Section at Patuxent River showed that there was little difference when compared with the standard wing machine. The take-off run was slightly longer and the lift-off speed was a little higher. It was also noted that the aircraft could be flown off from the three-point attitude without loss of control, unlike the USN/USMC version. It was thought that this might be because of a slight alteration in the angle of attack due to the change in wing tip shape. There was an improvement in the amount of stall warning and the stall was also slightly more symmetrical. The control forces and effectiveness, stability and general flying character-istics were virtually unchanged.

Performance tests could not be carried out by BAC pilots, as the only aircraft available at the time had unpressurised magnetos, which precluded operation at the altitudes needed for an assessment. Figures obtained from Patuxent River were therefore relied on. The aircraft used was F4U-1 No. 02155 at a take-off weight of 11,194 lb. When using its best climb speed at military rated power and with minimum cowl flap, the sea level rate of climb was 2890 ft/min. At the critical altitude of 21,200 ft, the rate of climb in auxiliary high blower was 1840 ft/min and the service ceiling (rate of climb 100 ft/min) was 38,200 ft. The maximum speed at military rated power at sea level was 348 mph TAS, rising to 395 mph TAS in auxiliary high blower at 22,800 ft.

Although intentional spinning was prohibited, the recommended recovery procedures were based on a comprehensive series of spin trials, which showed that the Corsair had slightly different characteristics depending on the direction of spin. Spins to the right were normal, whereas those to the left showed signs of oscillation, with the angle of the nose to the horizon varying from 50 degrees below to level during rotation. As the nose approached the horizon, a tendency for the right wing to drop was noted, but the spin continued to the left. Recovery was possible at any time during the spin, but more time was needed when the nose was near the horizon. The IAS during the spin varied from 0–40/50 kt. In the landing configuration, no difference was noted between spins to the left and right.

Successful recoveries were made after four turns in the clean configuration and one turn with the flaps and undercarriage down. It was essential to apply full opposite control, although the control forces in the spin were extremely high, the rudder requiring about 125–135 lb force before it could be moved to its fullest extent. An improvement in recovery was noted if the ailerons were held against the spin and if necessary the trim tabs could be used to lighten stick loads. The speed of rotation tended to increase just before recovery started, but the controls had to be held in the recovery position until the spin had actually stopped. Care had to be taken to avoid high accelerations during the pull out, and approximately 2000–2500 ft was needed to achieve level flight. If a pilot found himself still in a spin by the time that 3000 ft was passed, it was recommended that he abandon the aircraft.

Patuxent River also carried out a combat evaluation of the F4U-1 Corsair against an F6F-3 Hellcat and a Focke-Wulf Fw 190A-4 in early 1944. The take-off weight for the three aircraft ranged from 8690 lb for the Fw 190 to 12,406 lb for the Hellcat. The Corsair was flown at 11,988 lb. The rate of climb was compared in the speed range 140–200 kt IAS and at altitudes from 200–25,000 ft. The Corsair and the Fw 190 were superior to the Hellcat in the climb at all speeds and altitudes except at 140 kt below 15,000 ft, when the Fw 190 and the Hellcat were about equal. The best climbing speeds of the three aircraft were: Hellcat – 130 kt; Corsair – 135 kt; Fw 190 – 160 kt so it was no great surprise when the Fw 190 began to show marked superiority over the Corsair when it was climbed at higher speeds. This superiority was maintained up to 25,000 ft, by which time the advantage had been gradually reduced so that the two aircraft were virtually equal at that height.

Level speed checks were carried out from 200–25,000 ft, with each aircraft maintaining full power for two minutes in the course of two runs at each height. The Hellcat proved to be the slowest of the three, the advantage between the Corsair and the Fw 190 depending on height. The full results were as follows:

| Height | Fw 190A-4 kt IAS | F4U-1 Corsair kt IAS | F6F-3 Hellcat kt IAS |
|---|---|---|---|
| 200 ft | 290 | 315 | 290 |
| 5000 ft | 310 | 314 | 305 |
| 10,000 ft | 310 | 320 | 302 |
| 15,000 ft | 335 | 335 | 320 |
| 20,000 ft | 348 | 343 | 331 |
| 25,000 ft | 356 | 350 | 339 |

Level accelerations were made at the same heights and initial speeds as in previous tests, and were determined by flying the aircraft in line abreast and applying full power simultaneously. It was found that it was much easier to apply full power in the Fw 190, due to its much simpler throttle operation. Once again, the results were mixed. The Corsair and Fw 190 were superior to the Hellcat at speeds over 160 kt, the Corsair having a slight advantage over the Fw 190 up to 15,000 ft. However, above this height the positions were reversed. At speeds below 160 kt the Hellcat and Fw 190 were about equal.

Rate of roll tests showed that both the Corsair and the Fw 190 were superior to the Hellcat. The Fw 190 rolled with extreme ease, without excessive stick force and showing no tendency to drop its nose. Surprisingly, the rates of roll of the Corsair and Fw 190 were considered to be very similar. This caused a few eyebrows to be raised at the British Air Commission who were well aware of the Fw 190's capabilities from the trials results that had been made available from the UK. A direct request was made to Vought who supplied their own figures obtained from tests carried out on a standard F4U-1. When compared with British tests, they showed that the Fw 190 had a considerable advantage over the Corsair at all speeds, although this superiority did tend to diminish at the top end of the speed range. The rates of roll (degrees per second, stick force not exceeding 50 lb) were as follows:

| IAS – kt at 10,000 ft | F4U-1 Corsair | Focke-Wulf Fw 190A |
| --- | --- | --- |
| 150 | 61 | 108 |
| 200 | 77 | 137 |
| 250 | 88 | 160 |
| 300 | 94 | 128 |
| 350 | 95 | 98 |
| 400 | 64* | 75 |

* Control deflection on the Corsair was limited by structural limitations at this speed.

There was no doubt as to which aircraft came out on top when it came to turning circles, as both the Corsair and the Hellcat were far superior to the Fw 190 and could follow it in turns with ease at any speed. When the situation was reversed, the German aircraft was unable to follow. The Fw 190 when in a tight turn to the left and near to its stall speed, exhibited a tendency to reverse aileron control and stall without warning. Similarly, when turning to the right, it tended to drop its right wing and nose and end up in a spiral dive. From a head-on meeting, both the Corsair and the Hellcat could be directly behind the Fw 190 in one turn. From a position directly behind, it was possible to turn inside the Fw 190 and be directly behind it once again in about three turns.

The Corsair and Hellcat were also much more manoeuvrable and could follow any manoeuvre attempted by the Fw 190. The Focke-Wulf required a much greater radius in which to loop than either of the American aircraft and tended to stall sharply if it attempted to follow them. In zoom climbs after dives, all three aircraft were about equal.

The American assessment of the Fw 190 was that it was a very simple aircraft to fly in combat and seemed to have been designed for pilot convenience. Not surprisingly, US pilots found the Fw 190 cockpit to be a little cramped after the more luxurious accommodation provided in the Corsair and Hellcat. However, they did appreciate the semi-reclining seat position and high-set rudder pedals, which were excellent for resisting blackout during high 'g' manoeuvres. Its lack of stall warning was a major deficiency, particularly if it was pitted against an aircraft that could force it to fly near its stall speed, but overall it was considered to be an excellent interceptor-type aircraft. Given the choice, however, the American pilots would have preferred to fly the Corsair or Hellcat in combat.

In all, 1977 Corsairs were delivered to the FAA and the Royal New Zealand Air Force, forming a total of nineteen and seventeen squadrons respectively. FAA operations continued off the Norwegian coast, but the Corsair was mainly used in the Far East against the Japanese in the Pacific. From April 1944, it was used for fleet air defence during attacks by Barracuda and Avenger aircraft in the island-hopping campaign. The aircraft had its greatest success in FAA service during the attack on oil refineries at Palembang on 24 January 1945, when thirteen Nakajima Ki-44 Tojo fighters were shot down by the Corsairs of Nos 1830 and 1833 Squadrons.

Shortly before the end of the war in the Pacific, strikes were carried out on the main Japanese island of Honshu, during which Lieutenant R.H Gray DSC of the Royal Canadian Naval Volunteer Reserve was awarded the Victoria Cross. Gray was leading No. 1841 Squadron on 9 August 1945 when he sighted several Japanese destroyers near Shiogama and dived to attack. He scored a direct hit with one of his 1000-lb bombs, causing one of the destroyers to blow up and sink. However, his aircraft had already been hit by fire from shore batteries and he was killed when it crashed into the Bay of Onagawa Wan. After VJ-Day the Corsair was rapidly withdrawn from FAA service so that by the end of 1945 only four squadrons remained. The last two squadrons (Nos 1831 and 1851) were disbanded on 13 August 1946.

The Corsair continued to be developed and more advanced versions saw widespread use in the Korean War and in the conflicts in Indo-China. After the F4U-1, the next main variant was the F4U-4, which was powered by an R-2800-18W engine of 2450 hp with water-methanol injection and achieved a top speed of 446 mph. The F4U-5 featured an R-2800-32W engine that developed 2500 hp from a two-stage super-charger, endowing much better performance at altitude with a maximum speed of 462 mph at 31,400 ft. Spring tabs were fitted to the elevators and rudder to ease control loads during high-speed flight. Final variants were the F4U-6 (later known as the AU-1), a specialised ground attack machine with a single-stage supercharged R-2800-83W, and the F4U-7 developed for the French *Aeronavale*, which utilised the airframe of the AU-1 with the R-2800–18W engine of the F4U-4. The so-called F2G Super Corsair produced by Goodyear was powered by the massive Pratt & Whitney R-4360 Wasp Major (also known as the 'Corncob'), but poor lateral control and disappointing performance compared with standard production Corsairs led to the project being abandoned after only five aircraft had been built.

# Glossary

| | |
|---|---|
| A&AEE | Aeroplane and Armament Experimental Establishment |
| AFDS | Air Fighting Development Squadron |
| AFDU | Air Fighting Development Unit |
| AI | Airborne Interception |
| ATA | Air Transport Auxiliary |
| BAC | British Air Commission |
| BAFO | British Air Forces of Occupation |
| CG | centre of gravity |
| CO | carbon monoxide |
| EAS | Equivalent Airspeed |
| ETPS | Empire Test Pilots' School |
| FAA | Fleet Air Arm |
| FS | fully supercharged |
| IAS | indicated airspeed |
| IFF | Identification Friend or Foe |
| ISA | International Standard Atmosphere |
| MAEE | Marine Aircraft Experimental Establishment |
| MS | moderately supercharged |
| OAT | outside air temperature |
| PRU | Photographic Reconnaissance Unit |
| RAAF | Royal Australian Air Force |
| RAE | Royal Aircraft Establishment |
| RATOG | Rocket Assisted Take-off Gear |
| RP | rocket projectiles |
| R/T | radio transmitter |
| TAS | true airspeed |
| TBO | time between overhauls |
| USAAC | US Army Air Corps |
| USAAF | US Army Air Force |
| USMC | US Marine Corps |
| USN | US Navy |

# Boost Pressure Conversion Table

| Inches of Hg | Lb per sq.in |
|:---:|:---:|
| 22 | −4 |
| 26 | −2 |
| 30 | 0 |
| 34 | +2 |
| 38 | +4 |
| 44 | +7 |
| 48 | +9 |
| 54 | +12 |
| 60 | +15 |
| 67 | +18 |

# Index